BY SUSAN CAHILL

NONFICTION

For the Love of Ireland:
A Literary Companion for Readers and Travelers

Desiring Italy:
Women Writers Celebrate the Passions
of a Country and Culture

A Literary Guide to Ireland
WITH THOMAS CAHILL

FICTION

Earth Angels

ANTHOLOGIES

Women Write:
A Mosaic of Women's Voices in Fiction, Poetry,
Memoir, and Essay

QPB Anthology of Women's Writing
From the 14th Century to the Present

Wise Women:
2,000 Years of Spiritual Writing by Women

Women and Fiction:
Short Stories by and about Women

The Urban Reader
WITH MICHELE F. COOPER

THE
SMILES *of* ROME

Susan Cahill

THE ──

SMILES *of* ROME

A Literary Companion for
Readers and Travelers

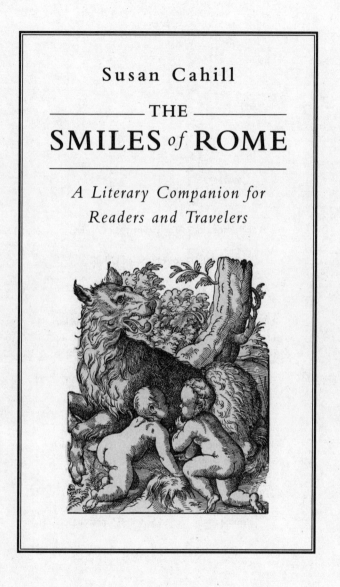

BALLANTINE BOOKS   *New York*

A Ballantine Books Trade Paperback Original

Copyright © 2005 by Susan Cahill

Published in the United States by Ballantine Books,
an imprint of The Random House Publishing Group,
a division of Random House, Inc., New York.

Ballantine and colophon are trademarks
of Random House, Inc.

Owing to limitations of space, permission
acknowledgments can be found on pp. 313–14, which
constitutes an extension of this copyright page.

ISBN 0-345-43420-X

Printed in the United States of America

Ballantine Books website address: www.ballantinebooks.com

2 4 6 8 9 7 5 3 1

Text design by Laurie Jewell

For
Devlin and Lucia
❧

bambini carissimi

CONTENTS

EARLY CHRISTIAN ROME

RENAISSANCE AND BAROQUE ROME

ROME OF THE GRAND TOUR(ISTS)

Eighteenth Century to the Present

ROMANS ON ROME
Since World War II

INTRODUCTION

Rome is Italy's First Beauty. And like any grand diva, she must be seen to be believed. But whether you meet her face-to-face or through the words of this book, you'll find her multiple personalities as fantastical as they play in the movies of Fellini.

Making friends, especially with a diva, takes time. Though if you don't have much to spend, a surface acquaintance is possible. You can observe Rome's most histrionic scenes on the heels of a tour guide, ride a bus past her ruins, go home satisfied you've seen the highlights. Every summer visitors on a tight schedule go through such motions, ignoring the sour aftertaste that Rome-on-the-run can leave. *Rome is crowded, Rome is dirty, it's all churches and pickpockets.*

Hurrying through Rome is travel from hell. Lost in a fog of general impressions, you have a hard time believing there's more to this city than exhaustion. For beauty happens only in the particular, and like friendship, it requires that attention be paid. The particularities of Rome reveal themselves generously, stirring a deep happiness, but her rhythm is more *sostenuto* than *presto*.

Travel and tourism, it must be said, follow different rhythms. Travel means finding yourself through a journey, and letting it change you. Tourism means making a journey with enough cushioning and filtering and microscheduling to assure that it *won't* change you. Richard Eder made this distinction in a review of a travel book about Calabria, *Stolen Figs.*

Rome has the power to blow your mind and heart, delivering man, woman, and child from small-mindedness, bestowing a much larger capacity for the beauty of the world than you started out

with. The pleasure of that new capaciousness is a matter of the particulars people come to love here. Nighttime in the piazzas. Sunset
in Parco Savello on the Aventine. *Carciofi alla guidia.* San Clemente.
Pierluigi, teaching you how to make a perfect espresso. Palazzo Altemps. The fountains.

Delights to take home? Certainly. (*Certo!* exclaims Pierluigi, with
a very Roman seriousness that's not serious at all.) Moments of
the journey to relish forever? Definitely. But moments that could
change your heart? How on earth!

It's the accumulation of sensual particulars that stops us in our
manic tracks. For each phenomenon manifests a past, a story, and,
as André Aciman writes in "Roman Hours," it's the accumulation
of pasts in Rome and one's consciousness of those layers—in the
city and within one's self—that can make Rome a life-changing
experience. Once Rome enters your consciousness, your perspective on human time may change, deepen, mellow. The layers of
history buried under every building you enter, every hill or dome
you climb—the caves, tombs, baths, temples!—they complicate the
territory. Everywhere, something invisible makes itself felt in the
visible, making the whole city seem to pulsate with hidden pres-
ences, a register of the human psyche and of twenty-eight centuries
of history striated by horror, by thrilling legends, and anonymous
kindness. Getting to know Rome, we come home to ourselves, our
labyrinthine and surreal undergrounds of memories and desires and
failures, the partiality of our abstract and absolute convictions. Such
reckoning can turn a tourist into a traveler, especially when accompanied by the rhythmic sensuality of sun and shade, and the faces
of Roman people, their voices like music.

The affectionate intuition of a city's idiosyncratic energies is
certainly the perspective of good travel writing. The writers in *The
Smiles of Rome* consider the city—or some cultural expression of
it—as a friend or intimate, and they put into words the contours
of their attachment. American, British, German, French, Italian,
their impressions are a mix of intimacy and mystification. Most of
them—or their fictional personas—come to cherish the gradations
of time you see everywhere. The peeling of ocher surfaces from a

Renaissance palazzo. The ruins seen from the hills. The brick and mortar strength of the Pantheon. The contradictions of empires and their religions. Rome enacts a dynamic and stunning theater of time's imperfections: what we have done and what we've failed to do. Close up, under her blinding sunlight, they seem more precious than not. This is Rome's secret, which this book unfolds for engaged travelers and for readers who imagine the journey from home.

In fiction, travel essay, journalism, and poetry, *The Smiles of Rome* reflects on a particular of the city's past and present: a historical event; an architectural gem; a great public space; a sculpture; individual human characters; the streets, broad and leafy, narrow and cobble-stoned—whatever it was that first stopped the writer in her or his tracks. First-time novelist Jane Alison, intrigued by Ovid's heartbreaking exile from Rome: she who taught him the art of love. The scholar Simon Schama, thrilled by the genius of Bernini's Fountain of the Four Rivers in Piazza Navona. The famous "Grand Tourists," among them Goethe and Henry James and Edith Wharton, all charged by the beauty they saw everywhere, each of these very private people confessing to feeling happy in Rome, a common theme of Roman travel.

In brief introductions, I've sketched the writers' backgrounds, and their connection with Rome. Sigmund Freud might be described as the Most Reluctant Traveler the city has ever known. Nathaniel Hawthorne began his sojourn with a Puritan sneer, then, like Saul of Tarsus, fell off his high horse as Rome hit him like a new idea. Muriel Spark arrived and never left (like other women who settled in to work in other parts of Italy: Ann Cornelisen in Basilicata, Mary Taylor Simeti in Sicily, Elizabeth Barrett Browning in Florence). André Aciman, an exile from Egypt, began a love affair with Rome that has survived separation by the Atlantic and several decades; he celebrates their abiding mutuality in his lovely memoir, "Roman Hours."

Collectively, the writings in *The Smiles of Rome,* like my books *Desiring Italy* and *For the Love of Ireland,* serve a double purpose. First, they provide a brilliant literary companion for readers and travelers alike. And second, they serve as a guide to the particular experience at the center of each selection. I've followed each one with a commentary, a mix of cultural, historical, and practical detail, to help the reader/traveler take the long meandering strolls that will connect you with the place evoked in each piece. Taking the walks, I've checked out how closely—or not—the writers' descriptions match the places we find today. That became the focus of each commentary: helping travelers/readers situate themselves along the writers' routes by providing a dash of relevant context.

Choosing the selections, I've made sure that taken together they point in the direction of Rome's most dramatic settings, and, at the same time, reflect the main historical periods. The writings about Ancient Rome feature the great ancient sites as the background of their impressions; those about Early Christian Rome some of the oldest churches and neighborhoods. The Renaissance and Baroque periods are represented, appropriately, by great artists— Michelangelo, his friend Vittoria Colonna, Bernini, and Artemisia Gentileschi—both in their own words and in stories about them. The Grand Tourists of the next three centuries speak for themselves about the places that give them pleasure, their enthusiasm one of the sparks that first kindled my own desire to know the Rome they bring to life.

Only a few of the Roman writers of the post–World War II period have their say in the final section of the book, but it's a strong sample of the torrent of writing and filmmaking that followed the overthrow of fascism, a culmination of one of the great national literatures of the twentieth century. The Roman writers present the "other" Rome that travelers might not encounter otherwise (except in the movies of Pasolini, De Sica, and Rossellini): the working-class neighborhoods, and the Jewish Ghetto, especially as seen through the fictional eye of Elsa Morante's magisterial epic, *History: A Novel,* one of the twentieth century's great books.

The luscious Roman cuisine, a culinary heritage that lives on in hundreds of simple trattorias and elegant restaurants, is featured on most of the itineraries with a few recommendations of places to eat that are convenient to the writer's neighborhood. This feature should make things easy for the traveler who's suddenly dizzy with hunger or whose feet hurt (like the husband in John Updike's story "Twin Beds in Rome"). But there are thousands of choices, and it's rare that you make a bad one.

There are more practical guides than this one. The *Rough Guide, Lonely Planet, Let's Go Rome, Fodor's,* each can answer the questions of any given day. Where to sleep. How much to tip. How to get an audience with the pope. How to say "please," a word every visitor should know: *Per favore,* pronounced *pear fa-VOR-ay.* (Sounds like *amore.*) The practicalities useful to the literary pilgrim walking the Rome of Henry James and Company are simple: besides this book, carry a street map (or don't), a water bottle in summer, and a few bus tickets (available in Tabacchi shops) for when the skies open or your legs give out. The Seven Hills are not steep, but they (and the domes) are meant to be climbed, their hilltop cafes and rooftop restaurants patronized: the views of the city from on high show off her beauty at its most harmonious. *Stupendissimo!* as Henry James used to cry out.

The large green information booths staffed by the Italian Tourist Board are helpful, depending on the mood of the person on duty the day you drop in. The booth in Viale Trastevere near Piazza Sonnino is always obliging, dispensing maps, printouts of bus routes to your destination, brochures about concerts, theater, and opera. There's also tourist information at the north end of Piazza Navona; in Stazione Termini; and at a large good-humored office facility in Via Parigi 5, near the Baths of Diocletian (tel 06 4889 9253). (Ask for a copy of *Here's Rome.*) The hours of openings and closings in Rome follow a pattern: except for the national monuments—the Colosseum, the Forum, the Capitoline museums, the Pantheon, etc., which are open all day—most places are open in the morning until noon or 1 P.M., close until 3:30 or 4:00 in the afternoon, and then stay open until about 7. Monday closings are common. You learn to organize your time accordingly because you have no choice. You learn the custom of the country: long midday meals in the piazza; a siesta behind closed shutters. Relaxing softens you, so that when you find a museum or church locked up tight when a sign says it should be open, you laugh. And go someplace else.

When I assembled the collection *Desiring Italy,* I discovered the enormous volume of writing about Rome that exists. Making the hard choices then—and now, as I've put together *The Smiles of Rome*—having to exclude so many wonderful testimonies, has induced a stoic realism. There's nothing else to be done. No one needs a travel anthology consisting of thousands of pages, no matter how engaging. But still there is regret. For there not being space to include writing by Pasolini; Dacia Maraini; Kate Simon; H. V. Morton; Bernard Malamud's "The Last Mohican"; Mary Gordon's "Sanctuary in a City of Display"; Alexander Stille's Roman chapters in *Benevolence and Betrayal;* Shelley's *The Cenci;* Byron's *Child Harolde* and other poets, Richard Wilbur, Louise Bogan, Alan Broughton, Wallace Stevens. Some writers on Rome are already widely anthologized, for example, Barbara Grizzuti Harrison who is included in "Overtures." Others—George Eliot's "Wedding Journey" from *Middlemarch,* Edith Wharton's story "Roman Fever," and Elizabeth Spencer's "The White Azalea"—can be found in the Rome section of *Desiring Italy.* James's *The Portrait of a Lady* is a world whole and entire. In some cases, and this is one of them, excerpting is a form of demolition.

In the end, what comes across in these pages, in a wide range of voices, is Rome's astonishing expressiveness. The silence of the Palatine. Bright mosaics, travertine, terracotta, pale pink brick, marble, peperino, so many stones. The light. Early morning in Piazza San Cosimato, the peaches in the market stalls. People, unpretentious, affectionate, the dazzle of their *sprezzatura.* Love of life, the imperfect world made new again, among the ruins of this old, old city.

SUSAN NEUNZIG CAHILL
Rome, 2004

OVERTURES

O Rome! my country! city of the soul!

—BYRON

But my letter would never end if I were to try to tell a
millionth part of the delights of Rome—it has such an
effect on me that my past life before I saw it appears a blank
and now I begin to live.

—MARY SHELLEY

Oh, the beautiful men and women and children here! And
the wonderful babies with such wise eyes! And the grand-
featured mothers nursing them!

—GEORGE ELIOT

Never have I enjoyed youth so thoroughly as I have in my
old age. . . . Nothing is inherently and invincibly young
except spirit. And spirit can enter a human being perhaps
better in the quiet of old age and dwell there more
undisturbed than in the turmoil of adventure. . . . In Rome,
in the eternal city, I feel nearer to my own past, and to the
whole past and future of the world, than I should in any
cemetery or in any museum. . . . Old places . . . when spirit
dwells in them, have an intrinsic vitality of which youth is
incapable; precisely the balance and wisdom that come from
long perspectives. . . .

—GEORGE SANTAYANA

Do you remember Rome, dear Lou? How is it in your
memory? In mine sometimes there will be only its waters,
those clear, exquisite, animated waters that live in its
squares; . . . its gardens' festiveness and the splendour of
great terraces; its nights that last so long, still and filled to
overflowing with great constellations.

—RAINER MARIA RILKE

Let the ruins rot!   —JAMES JOYCE

I feel happy here, for I learn something new every day: I try
to become impregnated with the unalterable beauty Rome
dispenses with such generosity.

—AUGUSTE RODIN

Rome became my home as soon as I saw it. I was born that
moment. That was my *real* birthday.

—FEDERICO FELLINI

What is Rome? Where is the real Rome? Where does it
begin and where does it end? Rome is surely the most
beautiful city in Italy, if not the world. But it is also the
most ugly, the most welcoming, the most dramatic, the
richest, the most wretched. . . . The contradictions
of Rome are difficult to transcend because they are
contradictions of an existential order. Rather than
traditional contradictions, between wealth and misery,
happiness and horror, they are part of a magma, a chaos.

—PIER PAOLO PASOLINI

I am happy here; when I or others have bruised my life, I
close my eyes against the hurt and think of Rome: as
possibility, and hope. . . . The world is loveable when the
world is Rome. . . . For the rest of my life I will love Rome
and think better of my life for having known Rome.

—BARBARA GRIZZUTI HARRISON

THE
SMILES *of* ROME

ANCIENT ROME

THE PALATINE HILL ❧ THE ROMAN FORUM ❧ CIRCUS MAXIMUS
THEATER OF MARCELLUS ❧ OSTIA ANTICA ❧ THE PANTHEON
HADRIAN'S TOMB ❧ HADRIAN'S VILLA ❧ THE COLOSSEUM

❧

Elizabeth Bowen ❧ *Georgina Masson* ❧ *Ovid* ❧ *Jane Alison*
Marguerite Yourcenar ❧ *Christopher Woodward*

*The melancholy of the antique world seems to me more profound
than that of the moderns, all of whom more or less imply that
beyond the dark void lies immortality. But for the ancients that
"black hole" is infinity itself; their dreams loom and vanish against
a background of immutable ebony. No crying out, no convulsions—
nothing but the fixity of the pensive gaze. . . .*

—FLAUBERT

ELIZABETH BOWEN

1899–1973

*Elizabeth Bowen grew up in Dublin, Bowen's Court in County Cork,
and London. A prolific novelist—*The Last September, The House in
Paris, The Death of the Heart—*who wrote in air-raid shelters during
the blitz, she traveled the world. When she arrived in Rome, commissioned
to write the city's portrait, she confessed a "monstrous" ignorance and confusion as she tried to find her way around. But getting lost was never a
waste of time. "Among Rome's splendours is its unexpectedness. . . . If one
cannot enjoy this, one enjoys nothing." Eventually, she walked the city into
her head, as she put it, and "kept it there." The elegant proof is* A Time
in Rome, *excerpted here, one of the most popular books ever written about
the city she called "my darling, my darling, my darling," when the time
came to say good-bye.*

From A TIME IN ROME

THE PALATINE HILL

People I met in Rome legitimately wanted to know what I was
doing.—Writing something?—Not while I was here.—No,
really?—Pity to stay indoors.—Sightseeing, simply?—Partly.—Ah,
gathering background for a novel to be set in Rome!—No.—No?
look at Henry James.—Yes.—Then a travel book: where was I
going next?—I was staying here.—Then, something in the way of
a gay guide-book?—I was afraid I should be no help to anyone
else.—Then it would have to be a book of impressions: but why
Rome?—What was the matter with Rome?—It was not Greece.—
I supposed not.—Did I, for instance, for an instant imagine that

Rome was old?—It was not too old.—Not too old for what?—
Me.—Then I did not care for antiquity?—Not in the abstract.—
What did I see in Rome, then?—Beginning of today.—That made
today long!—Today is being a long day.

But what did I like about Rome?—It was substantial.—And?—
Agreeable.—Once, or now?—Altogether.—Agreeable was hardly
the word for history.—Then there must be something in spite of
that.—Well, I should not find I got far with the ancient Romans.—
No?—No, they would not appeal to me.—Why not, specially?—
They were unimaginative.—They were, were they?—Yes, most
antipathetic.—I was not looking for friends.

I must look out, or Rome would ruin my style.

Oh?

Oh, yes! Attempts to write about Rome made writers rhetorical,
platitudinous, abstract, ornate, theoretical, polysyllabic, pompous,
furious.

Had this been so in all cases?

Too many.

Language seldom fails quietly, it fails noisily.

So went several conversations, or interrogatories. Curiosity in
Rome is a form of courtesy. The questions were disconcerting in
being too much to the point, to the point too soon. I was never
ready for them; accordingly I may well have sounded recalcitrant,
"clever," or plain stupid. I had nothing to hide, but also little to
show. I could not say what I intended doing, for that was not yet
known to myself; at the most I had a notion or suspicion, such as
one might form with regard to somebody else if one were to watch
their movements hourly, closely. Shyness, involved in any affair of
feeling, made me unforthcoming; also I never shook off my fear of
presumption in having "designs" on Rome, of whatever kind. The
idea of putting Rome into a novel not only did not attract me, it
shocked me—*background,* for heaven's sake! The thing was a major
character, out of scale with any fictitious cast. . . .

Troubling as it was to be asked questions, it led to my putting
them to myself. Omnivorous drifting cannot go on for ever; one
cannot continue to take in everything for the sake of nothing. Each

conversation left me with racing thoughts; after each, my rapid excited monologue, in beat with my excited solitary walking, took up again—and from a point further on. Often it took the character of an argument. I had noted, it had been borne in on me, that my loverlike ambiguous taste for Rome roused opposition; I seemed to be called upon to defend it. Rome in some roundabout way was not quite approved of. Deprecation—that was the attitude, on the whole. Naturally, that hardened me in my course. What my course was, I should discover from where it took me.

Looking in Rome for characters other than the city, I began by heading for those magnified by history, favourably or not. I began with the Emperors. These appeared to divide themselves, with regard to Rome, into makers and unmakers; a division which held good, looking further back, with outstanding figures of the Republic. Was it less true of millions who had blown away on the dust—can *any* person live and have no effect? Negativity, if there be any, is a form of destruction. Simply, to be a Somebody (that is, of position) involves more: it may not matter more but it counts for more. No wonder drama took for its figures kings, made the court the prototype of society; and no wonder history has learned from drama—persons not dramatizable are not recorded; they do not go for nothing but must appear to . . . Then again in Rome there had been the host of those represented by portrait busts, now in museums, labelled "unknown," or by just-legible names on outlying tombs—the sufficiently affluent and perhaps respectable. Below them, gradations of anonymity (with here or there a case of talent or scandal) down to mass-level. The Roman masses, I got the impression, simmered, sometimes just off boiling-point, placated by free entertainment, brutalizing in nature, and free corn. . . .

One of the merits of the Palatine, as a start, was its demarcation by individuals. There was no such thing as an "average" Roman emperor.

On the Forum side, the built-up Hill of the Caesars looks like a giant derelict hotel: a honeycomb of arches of keyhole narrowness, cavernous windows, gloomy vaulted apartments, ramps and galleries. The overhangingness and the staringness are unnerving. Sense of place and of a further dimension begins on the plateau at the top—or rather plateaux, for the levels are many. Here and there, also, grasslands tumble and spill downhill. Up-and-down winding walks and wooded hollows contrast with pavements splintered but formal. The Palatine as I found it in February seems still to be under the spell of mild late autumn. Birds utter solitary unmating notes; dusk emanates, any time of day, from humid underground corridors and successions of cavities without echoes. Now, out of season, there are few visitors; the custodians, wrapped in greatcoats and their own thoughts, interfere with nothing that is not forced upon their notice. Willing to act as guides, they are content not to. Out of their view, undeterred, one may penetrate past tangles of rusted wire into slippery understructures half-choked by rubble, or out on to heights barred by warnings: *pericoloso*. On the time-shorn Palatine, little rises above one: one assesses height, rather, by looking down, into the far-below vacant world of excavated series of halls of pleasure. The hill seems so riddled hollow, one asks oneself why it does not collapse. It seems most itself at an early springtime six o'clock in the evening, when to its atmosphere of evaporated pomp and residual danger is added one's risk of being locked in. How far it would be an ordeal to be there alone for a night, I was never certain: the draughty dark would be troubled by crepitations from the iron sheeting over the diggings, or the desiccated rustle of wintry ilexes; but the Palatine has not soul enough to be haunted. However, I was not put to the test. Veteran residents of Rome walk their dogs on the Palatine around sunset, and their calculation of time, down to the last possible of the darkening seconds, is infallible. They are the clocks to watch; when at last *they* turn to the gates, one is wise to follow.

The Palatine has a peculiar daylight, in which its shabby subtle colours appear. Here and there the black in the heaving pavements is more blotted out than the salmon pinks. And daylight is to be recommended for the taking of one particular way up, not generally used and I think rewarding. You *can* ascend, from the Forum, either by the Clivus Palatinus (the former Imperial route, still paved, now flanked by a convent wall and shady and naive as a country lane) or by letting the steps at the back of the Atrium of the Vestal Virgins conduct you into the upward zigzag of ramps and vaultings. But try, too, keeping round the base of the hill, at the Capitoline end, along under the wall of the Via di San Teodoro—past the butt end of the church, small locked gardeners' sheds and compost heaps of last year's scythed weeds and grass. This brings you out over the Circo Massimo. Here, where it looks across at the Aventine, over the trough of the circus, the Palatine is unkempt and steep, and across the face of the slope there run many dog-paths. Thin thornbushes, which flower sparsely and early, clutch at the soil between bosses of glossy serrated leaves—the architectural acanthus, more familiar to many when cut in stone. Foothold on any of the dog-paths is worth maintaining: you are taken along under the whole immense rampart-like frontage: porches launched into air, windows wide as gates. Finally comes the Septimus Severus structure's two-floored arcade and plum-coloured inner darkness— the lower passage, resembling some eerie subway of a moribund London railway station, must be followed: this has become your way from the outside into the inside of the Palatine. The sky once more, at the top, is like that of heaven.

The Palatine has been called the Cradle of Rome. Though from it, later, came the word "palace," there is something rebellious about its contours—legend, the primitive mysticism of the birthplace, outlives the succeeding tawdry story. Here, it is held, Romulus founded the original Rome; here were established the forefathers; here, stone by stone, came into being the fortified city of the Kings, altars dedicated to the protecting gods, who had not yet turned away their faces. Hymns rose from the templed corners of this island-like hill, coming to be answered, as time went on, by singers and lyres on the Aventine. Though the Palatine as it now is does not seem haunted, as it once was it had the power to haunt. Throughout the Rome that was to come to be ran the anguish set up by forfeited innocence, lost inspiration, corrupted purpose. Ruthless battles, predatoriness, everything that is harsh about an implanting, characterized those early days—which nevertheless assumed an undying light for the days after. The idea of redemption, with its power to fire, recurs throughout the history of Rome.

The Republic in its turn to survive as a moral memory, saw the growth of Rome out on to other hills. The Palatine then became residential, sought out by the eminent. Quiet with gardens, sanctified by their origin, these heights were favourable to the private hours of public figures and to the reflections of those who spoke to be heard. Cicero, Hortensius, Crassus, Catiline made their homes here; and it was, I suppose, such associations which first drew to the Palatine Octavius, Julius Caesar's great-nephew, who became Augustus when he was Caesar also. Alas, his choice brought no good to the hill, for on to it his dreadful successors followed him. Augustus himself lived on the Palatine with a well-known simplicity. Livia, whom he had desired, was his wife; she gave stylish enchantment to their modest surroundings. To her we owe the small sequence of painted rooms, lyrical, on two sides of a sunken courtyard—to enter the House of Livia* is to yield to it. It is near the square mound, topped by the grove of ilex, which once was the Temple of Cybele, Magna Mater. . . .

Augustus founded the line of Caesars known as the Julio-Claudian. With the last of them there expired (and none too soon) the idea of lineal descendency—of there being, *per se,* an imperial stock. "The hereditary principle, which," says Samuel Dill, "had been grafted on the principate of Augustus . . . inflicted on the world a succession of fools and monsters. The only hope lay in elevating the standard of virtue, and in the choice of a worthy successor by the form of adoption." The change was accomplished, but not before Caesarship had acquired a bad name; nor was there immediate improvement. Out of twelve who followed upon Augustus, seven died by violence. Their existences were nervous and ostentatious. They encaged the Palatine in marble, over which ran blood, more than once their own. The role impossible to fill was dangerous in its appeal to manias: man after man tottered under the

---

*Livia's gifts as interior decorator are exhibited in Palazzo Massimo. See page 210.

idea of godship—since the Emperor was *a* god, why not God?—inflicting the terrors that they felt. . . .

Though I love to walk about on the Palatine, there is something exhausting, because exhausted, about the place, which may cause a sudden fatigue of body. I often found myself sitting on the ground (for there is little else, there, to sit on) and each time I thought of King Richard II. The Emperors were not Shakespearean characters; not even Shakespeare could have made them so. Yet, they were designated chief actors, spotlit up to the moments of their dooms. The imperial predicament, as they knew it, had something in common with the royal. Their awfulness was the pollution of a tragedy; but there *was* a tragedy, somewhere, to be polluted.

> For God's sake, let us sit upon the ground
> And tell sad stories of the death of kings:
> How some have been depos'd, some slain in war,
> Some haunted by the ghosts they have depos'd,
> Some poison'd by their wives, some sleeping kill'd
> All murder'd: for within the hollow crown
> That rounds the mortal temples of a king
> Keeps Death his court, and there the antick sits,
> Scoffing his state and grinning at his pomp;
> Allowing him a breath, a little scene,
> To monarchize, be fear'd, and kill with looks,
> Infusing him with self and vain conceit
> As if this flesh which walls about our life
> Were brass impregnable; and humour'd thus
> Comes at the last, and with a little pin
> Bores through his castle wall, and farewell king!

And there the antick sat. . . . The Roman Empire, as an empire, was most *personally* tragic, within its first hundred years, because of a line of figures who were distorted. After that, one must not forget, there set in improvement, a continuous steadying on the destined course. The age of the Antonine Emperors was to be marked by humane, conscientious rule. One must be on guard against misconceptions, when trying to grasp the movement of the history of Rome—untruths are thieves, robbing us of a birthright. . . .

One dare not, all the same, minimize reigns of terror: the Republic had been aristocratic; the early Caesars altered the social landscape by exterminating or breaking the nobler families, as one might fell trees. Yet there were other times when they did no worse than give themselves over to wickedness in a vacuum. Suspiciousness was among the maladies from which they suffered; in this they resembled the common people—with whom, as was to be seen, they had tastes in common, and who possibly would have behaved much as did the Caesars had they felt free to and had the money. Surprisingly seldom do those showy neurotics seem to have been objected to by the populace, whom they not only entertained but made news for. Would we, ourselves, honestly, wish the Caesars to be missing from history? The Palatine, though burdened with hated memories, has shattered itself into the hill of Rome that is most lovely, consuming by its silence all those enormities. The ruins have been weathered and washed to all but innocence. . . .

The Palatine taught me what emptiness can be. Life has run out completely: one is alone there. Those existences, artificial as fireworks, have like fireworks died out on the forgetful dark. Of the Emperors, Nero seems to have lived longest, through having begotten a superstition; more than one are his fictitious "tombs," and a walnut tree had to be cut down because he infested it in the form of black, flapping birds. What was done to him, that he did this to Rome? I make off downhill, in the dusk, on the heels of the dog-walkers: night, floating with lights, is already into the city. . . .

FOR THE LITERARY TRAVELER

A delightful prelude to the long walk of discovery through Ancient Rome is to climb the **Palatine** and let Bowen introduce you. Enter from the Forum at the **Clivus Palatinus,** and find the benches overlooking the hill's southern slope. You look down on the **Circus Maximus** and beyond to the **Aventine.** Bowen's wide-ranging impressions coincide with this sweeping prospect on top of "the Cradle of Rome." Though tour guides coach their groups around the ruins—the **Houses of Flavia, of Livia, of Augustus, Domitian's Palace** and **Stadium**—this shady southwestern corner offers a tranquil retreat. You can be alone here to imagine not only the place where Rome began but a history more ancient. Inhabited from the Middle Palaeolithic era, some 100,000 to 35,000 years ago, the Palatine saw its first settlers by the ninth century B.C. Archaeology now confirms 754 B.C., Rome's legendary birth date, as the city's actual origin: Foundations found on the **Germalus,** the section of the hill where you're sitting, indicate that where tradition places the Hut of Romulus—according to legend, the brothers Romulus and Remus were raised in a cave by a wolf (the **Lupercal,** or Wolf's Grotto,* at the Palatine's northwestern corner, an unvisited and lovely part of the hill)—there was in fact a small settlement inhabited in the eighth century B.C. It wasn't called Rome, and there's no trace of Romulus, except in fiction and poetry, but this area was probably the site from which the city on the River Tiber did evolve.** As you wander around, it's easy to imagine the aristocratic neighborhood this hill became, and later as the place where emperors (and a pope) built their palaces. The Palatine gave its name to the word for the homes of megalomaniacs.

Today, the **Farnesina Gardens** (gone to seed), the rambling wild-flowers, the cedar groves and pines on the slopes, give the Palatine a poignancy at twilight, a good time to roam. Birds sing, the shadows lengthen, and the orangy pink of the *tufo* stone ruins—these hulking sculptures—almost glow in the golden air. You descend, Bowen in

---

*The legendary She-Wolf of Rome, in bronze, is the most famous relic of Etruscan Rome, on view in the **Captoline Museum,** in the **Sala della Lupa.** The figures of Romulus and Remus were added in the sixteenth century.

Archaeologists have turned up relics of the Palatine's pre-Roman residents, the Etruscans—eighth through fourth century B.C.—preserved in the beautiful **Villa Giulia museum (Piazzale di Villa Giulia 9), on the other side of the Borghese Gardens.

hand, understanding history as a continuum that is more than its cruelties and corruption. Imperfection may be the best we can hope for. But the last word up here belongs to time's beauty.

(*Skirting the Palatine's west end is Via di San Teodoro where the Etruscan She-Wolf was found beside the small sunken church of San Teodoro, its apse mosaic dated 600 A.D. Just off San Teodoro, the terraced restaurant,* **St. Teodoro** *at Piazza del Fienili 49–50 (tel 06 678 0933), is tucked away in this quiet storied corner of ancient Rome.*)

GEORGINA MASSON

1912–1980

Born Marion Johnson, the pseudonymous British writer Georgina Masson lived and traveled in Africa, Europe, and Asia before settling in Rome in the early forties. A historian of architecture, she wrote about Republican Rome, the Borgias, Queen Christina, Renaissance courtesans, Italian villas and gardens. But she's most remembered for her Companion Guide to Rome, *considered "the best guide to Rome" by many travelers, reviewers, and English-speaking residents of the city, all of whom agree that Masson knows her subject inside out. While she worked on it, she lived in the old stables of the Villa Doria Pamphili on the Janiculum.*

✎

From THE COMPANION GUIDE TO ROME

THE ROMAN FORUM

Just for a moment as we enter the **Forum** from the Via dei Fori Imperiali, let us try and picture something of its early days and the people who made it what it was. The Forum was originally a marshy valley or *marrana*, like many to be found in the *Campagna*, with a cemetery beside a rough highway. This last probably belonged to the Iron Age hut village that existed on the Palatine between the end of the ninth and the beginning of the sixth century B.C. The Romans identified the beginnings of the Forum with the legendary founding of their city by Romulus in 753 B.C. when the war with the Sabines of the Quirinal—touched off by the rape of their women—had ended.

These early Romans were a sober purposeful people, admiring the stoic virtues of discipline, industry and frugality, but from the first they seem to have possessed what we would call a community spirit, and also an aptitude for reasonableness and conciliation. *Clementia* was their word for it—and no doubt it was this *clementia* that brought about the peace between the Latins and the Sabines. Thus, as we would expect from such a people, the earliest identifiable sites in the Forum were of a religious and social nature—the Vulcanal and the Comitium; to these were added the Temple of Janus whose site has been lost, and whose doors were only opened in time of war—for these farmers who transformed Mars into a God of War were also born soldiers. To Numa, the second King of Rome's reign, tradition dates the building of the Regia and the Temple of Vesta; this accords with his reputation in later times as the alleged founder and coordinator of Roman state religion, and it is significant that the Regia continued to be associated with the high priest or Pontifex Maximus right through the Empire.

Though they revered it as the cradle of their institutions, the Romans continued to alter, add to and rebuild the temples and other buildings in the Forum. This was partly due to damage by fire and earthquake but also to their desire to make it worthy of the growing power of Rome. Augustus's pride in having found Rome a city of brick and transformed it into one of marble is typical of this attitude; the idea is still alive in Italian minds today—things are considered worthy or unworthy of the *decoro della città*.

The first building on our right as we enter the Forum, the **Basilica Aemilia,** affords a perfect illustration of this point of view that changed a market into a meeting place surrounded by palaces, for the porticoes and basilicas where the ordinary Roman men in the street met and did business were as rich in marbles and sculpture as any king's house. . . .

As basilicas are generally considered to be a peculiarly Roman contribution to architecture and certainly played a large part in Roman life, later even being taken as models for the great Christian churches, it is well worth our while to pause for a moment and study what they were really like. Basically they were great halls, with "aisles" divided by one or two rows of columns from the central "nave" which had a higher ceiling than the rest of the building and was lit by clerestory windows. Porticoes usually lined one or more of the outer walls of the building and were often connected to the great hall by an open colonnade. Caesar's Basilica Julia, on the other side of the Forum on the site of the old Sempronia, was built in this style; the Aemilia had an open portico at one end and the row of money changers' shops incorporated into the portico on the side facing the Forum. Later basilicas often had one or more apses in the side or end walls, like the last to be built in Rome, begun by Maxentius and completed by Constantine. The building in Rome today which gives us the clearest picture of what the interior of these ancient basilicas was like is the Christian one of San Paolo fuori le Mure.

The basilicas were built as general meeting places for business transactions, as in the case of the Aemilia, but also for use as law courts, like the Basilica Julia, and in time any city of the Empire worthy of the name had at least one basilica. The name basilica was, of course, derived from the Greek, and some eminent authorities consider that the building too was inspired by the Greek peristyles, but so far no one has explained why the Romans evolved the particular form they did; my personal belief is that the airless summer heat of the Forum supplies the explanation.

On a stifling August day buildings like the Basilica Aemilia would have been much cooler than any Roman tenement house, or than anything that exists in Rome today except their Christian counterparts. Perhaps it was this coolness combined with the belief that Rome was eternal—whatever happened in the world outside, Rome would continue—that persuaded the money changers to carry on business as usual on that fateful 23 August A.D. 410 with a Gothic army at the gates. Relics of their misplaced optimism can still be seen in the green stains which mark the Basilica Aemilia's marble pavement, for they are copper coins fused into the stone by the heat of the fire when the Goths, who entered the city during the night, sacked Rome. Nowhere else in the city is the scene brought so vividly before our eyes as by these few scattered coins. For six days the savage tribesmen sacked imperial Rome, the mistress of the world, and it must have seemed as if civilisation itself was crashing into ruins with the great basilica on that sultry August night. . . .

The superb fourth-century portico of the **Temple of Saturn** which soars up by the Vulcanal may well have had equally ancient beginnings, as according to legend the god was welcomed to Rome by Janus, and took up his residence at the foot of the Capitol. . . .

The Temple of Saturn was naturally the centre of the six days' celebrations of the December festival of the Saturnalia, or what was in effect the pagan Christmas. During this time schools were closed, all rank and formality were laid aside, and slaves sat at table with their masters or were even waited on by them. It was indeed a time of good will to all men, and presents were exchanged between people of all classes; the commonest were candles and, for children, clay dolls. A special fair was held by the makers of these during the festive season, which must have closely resembled the Advent fair in the Piazza Navona today.

Turning our backs on the Temple of Saturn, we walk down the western branch of the Sacred Way and find ourselves in the square which was the Forum proper. It is almost as difficult for a foreigner to understand what the Forum meant in the lives of the Romans as it is easy for a modern Italian, whose piazza is descended directly from it and plays very much the same part in his life. A few years ago an architectural critic said that Italians today pay little attention to the interior planning of their houses and, like the ancient Romans, have the smallest bedrooms, because they have the largest and finest "parlours," in the sense that a parlour is a place to meet and talk in, and that is exactly what a piazza is and what the Forum was, especially under the Empire. In Republican times the square had been the centre of every aspect of the city's life both grave and gay: the great religious ceremonies were held there, it was the scene of triumphs, sacrifices and important funerals, and was also a law court where the praetor, seated on his tribunal, gave judgment in full sight of the people. The early gladiatorial games were held there and sometimes sacrificial banquets; later it was the scene of elections and orators addressed the crowds, official communications of all kinds were posted up in it—edicts, prescription lists, the results of lawsuits and so on. But at the same time the Forum was the meeting place of everyone, from the briefless barrister in search of a client to the farmer up for a day from the country to sell his produce.

Today we see the Forum as an empty open space with grass growing among the paving stones and a few columns soaring up to remind us of what must have been. But let us half close our eyes and picture it surrounded with tall buildings and colonnades. It is not so difficult if we look at the temples at the far end, on the left that of Antoninus and Faustina, with its magnificent flight of steps which were the distinguishing feature of Roman temples as opposed to those of Greece, and on the right the three remaining columns of the Temple of Castor and Pollux. If we imagine the Basilica Aemilia on our left and the Basilica Julia on our right rising to a similar height, and the temples on the Capitol towering up behind us, we will quickly realise how small the open space of the Forum actually was, and readily understand why until the end of the Republic it was kept jealously clear. . . .

Turning our backs on the Forum and walking east, with the whispering clump of bay trees that marks the site of Caesar's temple on our left, we are confronted by the ruins of a small circular white marble temple whose rites remained immutable for over a thousand years in a changing world—the **Temple of Vesta.** The ruin that we see today has been recomposed from the fragments of the temple rebuilt after the fire of A.D. 191 by Septimius Severus and Julia Domna. Several previous temples on the same site had been destroyed by fire, but from reproductions on coins and literary descriptions we know that the temple had always been round, though its style and building materials had changed through the ages. According to Ovid it had originally been thatched and had walls of woven osiers. This is confirmed by the general archaeological opinion of today that the temple's circular shape dates right back to the huts of primitive Rome, like the thatched "house of Romulus" which was kept in continual repair beside the marble walls of the palaces on the Palatine.

The preservation of the original hut-form of the temple was consonant with the archaic simplicity which surrounded every aspect of the cult of Vesta and of the lives of the Vestal virgins who ministered to it. For the sanctity of the fire that burnt continually on the altar, and symbolised the perpetuity of the State, no doubt had its origins in far distant times when fire was a precious thing to be carefully tended and guarded—a task which naturally fell to young girls, the daughters, probably, of the king or tribal leader, in whose house it would have been kept for greater safety. This, at any rate, was the opinion of Frazer, author of *The Golden Bough*. It is borne out by the fact that the temple and the house of the Vestal virgins stand just beside the Regia, which was traditionally supposed to have been the house of the Priest-King Numa Pompilius and was certainly closely associated, possibly as a sort of office, with the Pontifex Maximus, who stood *in loco parentis* to the Vestal virgins.

The Vestals' house, or *Atrium Vestae* as it was called, owing to its being built in the patrician style round a rose-filled court or atrium, is without doubt the most evocative place in the whole of the Forum today. A short flight of steps beside the white marble shrine, which contained the statue of the goddess, leads us directly into what must have been a long and elegant garden court, surrounded by marble colonnades, with three pools in the centre. The existing house dates from the second century A.D. but it was built over an earlier and simpler one and there is no doubt that the origins of the Vestals' home date right back to the beginnings of the Forum. In atmosphere it must have resembled those austere convents for ladies of rank which grew up in Christian Rome, great walled enclosures grouped around tranquil cloisters, to which the noise of the city hardly penetrated. But even these cannot have equalled the style and grandeur in which the Vestals lived, at least in later times; the ground floor alone of their house comprises some fifty rooms and closets, and there were two or possibly even three upper floors. As in Roman palaces today, the Vestals probably lived on the first floor, while the ground floor would have been mainly given over to store-rooms and domestic offices—we can still see the remains of what were a kitchen, flour mill and bakery.

Its very spaciousness must have added to the sombre grandeur of the Vestals' house, for only six priestesses lived there, two of whom would have been quite young, even small, girls, as Vestals were re-cruited between the ages of six and ten. Like certain orders of nuns today, their hair was cut off when they entered the sisterhood and hung on the sacred lotus tree as an offering. When it grew again it was dressed in archaic style with six pads of artificial hair divided by narrow bands and adorned with a fillet resembling a diadem with pendent strips on either side. The Vestals were always dressed in long white robes, but when sacrificing had a curious insignia of their own—a white hood bordered with purple which was fas-tened on the breast with a brooch. This was the only ornament they were allowed as they were expected to be as austere in their dress as in their lives—Livy mentions the case of a Vestal being de-nounced and rebuked by the Pontifex Maximus for giving way to her taste for personal adornment.

The Vestals' lives were a curious mixture of extreme austerity and great privilege, but the benefits of the latter seem to have out-weighed the former, for although they could officially resign and marry, very few of them ever did so. For one thing they were very well off, being maintained by the State which provided them with a large dowry that they could spend as they wished. Socially they had precedence over everyone except the empress and only she and they were allowed to drive in Rome in carriages. The highest authorities—even consuls and praetors—made way for them in the street and special places were reserved for them in the theatres and at the gladiatorial games. They enjoyed enormous influence: a con-demned criminal could be reprieved simply by their asking if they passed him in the street, and their intercessions in general bore tre-mendous weight—for instance they saved Julius Caesar from Sulla's proscription—and wills and important documents of all kinds were entrusted to them for safe-keeping.

On the other side of the medal there was the penalty of being entombed alive if they transgressed their oath of thirty years' virginity, and the long intricate ritual that governed their whole existence and took ten years to learn. We do not know how long the watches were that the Vestals kept over the sacred fire, but it could never have been left for one instant, as its extinction was a national calamity which earned the attendant Vestal a scourging by the Pontifex Maximus. In the violent storms of wind and rain to which Rome is subject, its care could have been an anxious task in a small temple whose roof was pierced by a vent hole. In some secret hiding place in their house or temple the Vestals kept the sacred pledges of Rome's sway, one of which was the Palladium, reputedly a small wooden figure of Pallas Athene brought by Aeneas from Troy, another dire responsibility in a city so subject to devastating fires as ancient Rome.

Apart from these awe-inspiring responsibilities, the sacred duties of the Vestals were of a curiously housewifely character; they had to fetch water, carrying it on their heads from the fairly distant fountain of Egeria, and depositing it in a special marble tank. When used for ritual purposes this water was purified with salt, itself purified by being baked in an earthen jar in an oven. The Vestals also had the job of cooking special sacrificial salt cakes called *mola salsa* used in sacred ceremonies; these were made from the very first ears of ripened grain, pounded in archaic style in a mortar. The ritual cleaning of the temple with special mops was naturally one of their functions, also its decoration with bay or laurel which was changed once a year, on 1 March when the sacred fire was rekindled by the ancient method of rubbing a piece of wood against a plaque cut from a fruit tree. All these tasks had to be performed with the simplest of utensils, such as ordinary undecorated clay ware of the humblest kind.

The archaic simplicity of the Vestals' duties and their homely character confirms the supposition that their ritual was probably a survival of the domestic routine of early times. This is borne out by the fact that the religious functions at which they had to assist were connected with the oldest rites of primitive Italian agriculture, such as the harvest and vintage festivals and the Lupercalia.

So austere were the lives the Vestal virgins led and so great the esteem in which they were held that their order survived until A.D. 394, long after Christianity had become the religion of the emperors. . . .

For The Literary Traveler

The spaciousness of the **House of the Vestals** is striking amidst the crowded rubble of the **Roman Forum,** belying the constrictions of the virgins' lives and the cruelty of the consequences if they fell from grace. According to Plutarch, "The office of Pontifex Maximus, or chief priest"—usually the Emperor—"was to declare and interpret the divine law and to preside over sacred rites; . . . he was also guardian of the vestal virgins. . . . If the vestals commit any minor fault," continues Plutarch, "they are punishable by the high priest only, who scourges the offender, sometimes with her clothes off, in a dark place, with a curtain drawn between." (O chaste chief priest!) "But she that has broken her thirty-year vow of celibacy is buried alive near the gate called Collina"— in the "field of the wicked" **(Campus Scelleratus)** just outside the walls, in what is now Piazza dell'Indipendenza. "Under a little mound of earth a narrow room is constructed, to which descent is made by stairs; here they prepare a bed, light a lamp, and leave a small quantity of bread, water, a pail of milk; and some oil; so that body which had been consecrated and devoted to the most sacred service of religion might not be said to perish by such a death as famine. The culprit herself is put in a litter, which they cover over, and tie her down with cords on it, so that nothing she utters may be heard." (She was "gagged with leather straps," comments Barbara Grizzuti Harrison: "We are left to wonder at the persistence of male desire for the perfect priestess of the hearth.") Plutarch goes on: "They take her to the Forum; all people silently go out of the way as she passes, . . . and indeed, there is not any spectacle more appalling, nor any day observed by the city with greater gloom and sadness. When they come to the place of execution, the officers loose the cords, and then the high priest, lifting his hands to heaven, pronounces certain prayers to himself before the act; then he brings out the prisoner, being still covered, and placing her upon the steps that lead down to the cell, turns away his face with the rest of the priests; the stairs are drawn up after she has gone down and a quantity of earth is heaped up over the entrance to the cell. . . . This is the punishment of those who break their vow of virginity."

Recent scholars place the vestals within the history of sexuality in the chapter about sex and power. In return for their thirty-year vow of celibacy, the theory goes, the vestals received in exchange social status and legal independence. Similarly, according to Elizabeth Abbott in *A History of Celibacy,* later Christian virgins "recast the misogynist bachelor world of the Church Fathers into a splendid, challenging one where virgins were honorable and could also be powerful." As you contemplate the rose garden in the center of the House of the Vestals, you may or may not see the medieval Abbesses of the Rhine Valley, say, as splendid flowerings of the vestals' legacy.

Some consider the **Forum** the heart of Rome, though it's also been called a graveyard. ("Let the ruins rot," remarked James Joyce. After a guided tour through the Forum, he said, "Rome reminds me of a man who lives by exhibiting to travellers his grandmother's corpse.") Do not think of entering the Forum in summer without a large bottle of water (and a map). The direct sun can feel as flagellant as a Pontifex Maximus punishing a virgin's minor fault. One of the few shady spots, next to a water spigot, is beneath the Capitoline, near the **Temple of Saturn** at the western end of the **Via Sacra.** Saturn worship, as Robin Lane Fox explains in *Pagans and Christians,* did not end with the coming of Christianity; years after a Christian scholar had declared the great god dead, an inscription in his honor turned up in Africa, dated 323 A.D., and because he was believed to be a miracle worker, prayers continued to be offered to him as part of the "continuing pagan ceremonies."

(The Roman Forum is open 9 A.M. until dusk, and occasionally nights in summer. Maureen Fant, a New York Times *correspondent from Rome and author of* Dictionary of Italian Cuisine *(1998), recommends **La Piazzetta,** Vicolo del Buon Consiglio 23A (tel 06 699 1640; reservations necessary), a short walk from the Forum and the Colosseum.)*

OVID

(PUBLIUS OVIDIUS NASO)

43 B.C.–18 A.D.

Ovid, born in the Abruzzi, came to Rome to study law, a career chosen for him by his father. In love with poetry and the city—the parties, the circus, the fountains, the women—he gave up law and wrote verse. In The Art of Love (Ars Amatoria) *he delighted his readers with his lighthearted advice to men and women on the not-so-subtle strategies of seduction. Virgil's* Aeneid *had presented Rome's pious warrior-founder Aeneas as the son of Venus, the goddess of love. Ovid meant to inspire Romans to live true to their erotic roots. The poem is also a vivid portrait of the social life of ancient Rome. But the licentiousness he described without scruple or sermonizing antagonized the Emperor Augustus, who encouraged virtue as a hedge against civic unrest. Just after Ovid published his masterpiece, the* Metamorphoses, *Augustus banished the popular "Professor of Love" to the wilds of modern-day Romania, a Roman outpost on the Black Sea called Tomis.*

❧

THE ART OF LOVE

translated by ROLFE HUMPHRIES

This is a book for the man who needs instruction in loving.
Let him read it and love, taught by the lines he has read.
Art is a thing one must learn, for the sailing, or rowing,
  of vessels,
Also for driving a car: love must be guided by art. . . .

First, my raw recruit, my inexperienced soldier,
Take some trouble to find the girl whom you really can love.

Next, when you see what you like your problem will be
    how to win her.
Finally, strive to make sure mutual love will endure.
That's as far as I go, the territory I cover,
Those are the limits I set: take them or leave them alone.

While you are footloose and free to play the field at your
    pleasure,
Watch for the one you can tell, "I want no other but you!"
She is not going to come to you floating down from the
    heavens:
For the right kind of a girl you must keep using your eyes.
Hunters know where to spread their nets for the stag in his
    covert,
Hunters know where the boar gnashes his teeth in the glade.
Fowlers know brier and bush, and fishermen study the waters
Baiting the hook for the cast just where the fish may be found.
So you too, in your hunt for material worthy of loving,
First you will have to find out where the game usually goes.
I will not tell you to sail searching far over the oceans,
I will not tell you to plod any long wearisome road.
Perseus went far to find his dusky Indian maiden;
That was a Grecian girl Paris took over the sea.
Rome has all you will need, so many beautiful lovelies
You will be bound to say, "Here is the grace of the world!"
Gargara's richness of field, Methymna's abundance of vineyard,
All the fish of the sea, all the birds in the leaves,
All the stars in the sky, are less than the girls Rome can offer;
Venus is mother and queen here in the town of her son. . . .

Take your time, walk slow, when the sun approaches the lion.
There are porticoes, marbled under the shade,
Pompey's, Octavia's, or the one in Livia's honor,
Or the Danaids' own, tall on the Palatine hill.
Don't pass by the shrine of Adonis, sorrow to Venus,
Where, on the Sabbath day, Syrians worship, and Jews.

Try the Memphian fane of the Heifer, shrouded in linen;
Isis makes many a girl willing as Io for Jove.
Even the courts of the law, the bustle and noise of the
    forum,
(This may be hard to believe) listen to whispers of love.
Hard by the marble shrine of Venus, the Appian fountain,
Where the water springs high in its rush to the air,
There, and more than once, your counsellor meets with his
    betters,
All his forensic arts proving of little avail;
Others he might defend; himself he cannot; words fail him,
Making objections in vain; Cupid says, *Overruled!*
Venus, whose temple is near, laughs at the mortified creature,
Lawyer a moment ago, in need of a counsellor now.
Also, the theater's curve is a very good place for your hunting,
More opportunity here, maybe, than anywhere else.
Here you may find one to love, or possibly only have fun with,
Someone to take for a night, someone to have and to hold.
Just as a column of ants keeps going and coming forever,
Bearing their burdens of grain, just as the flight of the bees
Over the meadows and over the fields of the thyme and the
    clover,
So do the women come, thronging the festival games,
Elegant, smart, and so many my sense of judgment is troubled.
Hither they come, to see; hither they come, to be seen.
This is a place for the chase, not the chaste. . . .

Furthermore, don't overlook the meetings when horses are
    running;
In the crowds at the track opportunity waits.
There is no need for a code of finger-signals or nodding.
Sit as close as you like; no one will stop you at all.
In fact, you will have to sit close—that's one of the rules, at a
    race track.
Whether she likes it or not, contact is part of the game.
Try to find something in common, to open the conversation;

Don't care too much what you say, just so that every one
　　hears.
Ask her, "Whose colors are those?"—that's good for an
　　opening gambit.
Put your own bet down, fast, on whatever she plays.
Then, when the gods come along in procession, ivory, golden,
Outcheer every young man, shouting for Venus, the queen.
Often it happens that dust may fall on the blouse of the lady.
If such dust should fall, carefully brush it away.
Even if there's no dust, brush off whatever there isn't.
Any excuse will do: why do you think you have hands?
If her cloak hangs low, and the ground is getting it dirty,
Gather it up with care, lift it a little, so!
Maybe, by way of reward, and not without her indulgence,
You'll be able to see ankle or possibly knee.
Then look around and glare at the fellow who's sitting behind
　　you,
Don't let him crowd his knees into her delicate spine.
Girls, as everyone knows, adore these little attentions:
Getting the cushion just right, that's in itself quite an art;
Yes, and it takes a technique in making a fan of your
　　program
Or in fixing a stool under the feet of a girl.
Such is the chance of approach the race track can offer a
　　lover.
There is another good ground, the gladiatorial shows.
On that sorrowful sand Cupid has often contested,
And the watcher of wounds often has had it himself.
While he is talking, or touching a hand, or studying entries,
Asking which one is ahead after his bet has been laid,
Wounded himself, he groans to feel the shaft of the arrow;
He is a victim himself, no more spectator, but show. . . .

Young men of Rome, I advise you to learn the arts of the
　　pleader,
Not so much for the sake of some poor wretch at the bar,

But because women are moved, as much as the people or
     Senate,
Possibly more than a judge, conquered by eloquent words,
But dissemble your powers, and don't attempt to look learned,
Let your periods shun rancorous terms of abuse.
You would be out of your mind to go and declaim to your
     darling;
Even in letters beware using litigious terms.
Let the style you employ be natural, easy, familiar,
Coaxing, also, of course, so that she thinks you are there.
If she refuses to read, or sends back a letter unopened,
Hope that some day she will read, don't be discouraged.
     Someday! . . .

Don't be crimping your locks with the use of the curling iron,
Don't scrape the hair off your legs, using the coarse pumice
     stone;
Leave such matters as those to the members of Cybele's
     chorus,
Howling their bacchanal strains under the dark of the moon.
Men should not care too much for good looks; neglect is
     becoming.
Theseus, wearing no clasp, took Ariadne away,
Phaedra burned for his son, who was never exactly a dandy,
Adonis, dressed for the woods, troubled a goddess with love.
Let your person be clean, your body tanned by the sunshine,
Let your toga fit well, never a spot on its white,
Don't let your sandals be scuffed, nor your feet flap around in
     them loosely,
See that your teeth are clean, brush them at least twice a day,
Don't let your hair grow long, and when you visit a barber,
Patronize only the best, don't let him mangle your beard,
Keep your nails cut short, and don't ever let them be dirty,
Keep the little hairs out of your nose and your ears,
Let your breath be sweet, and your body free from rank odors,
Don't overdo it; a man isn't a fairy or tart. . . .

I was about to conclude, but—the hearts of the girls! How
    they differ!
Use a thousand means, since there are thousands of ends.
Earth brings forth varying yield: one soil is good for the
    olive,
One for the vine, and a third richly productive in corn.
Hearts have as many moods as the heaven has constellations:
He who is wise will know how to adapt to the mood.
Be like the Protean god, a wave, or a tree, or a lion,
Fire, or shaggy boar, shifting to any disguise.
Some fish are taken with spears, and others taken by trolling,
Some will rise to the fly, some must be hauled by the net.
Then there's the question of years, with experience also a
    factor;
Wary, naïve—you must choose which is the method to use.
If you seem coarse to a prude, or learned to some little
    lowbrow,
She will be filled with distrust, made to feel cheap in your eyes,
So she will run away from an honest man, and go flying
Off to the safer embrace of some inferior clown. . . .

Do not blame a girl for flaws of her nature or person:
Where's the advantage in that? Better pretend them away.
Andromeda, it would seem, was none too fair of complexion;
Perseus, the sandal-winged, never voiced any reproach.
All thought Andromache was much too big for a woman;
Only in Hector's eyes was she of moderate size.
If you like what you get, you will get what you like; love is
    captious
In our salad days, growing more mellow in time.
While the grafted shoot is new in the green of its growing,
Even the lightest breeze makes it shudder and fall,
But it will fasten with time, so even a gale cannot shake it,
Bear, on the parent tree, increase after its kind.
Time is a healer, and time removes all faults from the body;

What was a blemish of old comes to be nothing at all.
When we are children, we find the odor of leather obnoxious,
Hardly can stand it at all; when we are grown, we don't mind.
Words have a magical power to mitigate many shortcomings:
If she is blacker than tar, *tanned* is the term to employ.
Cross-eyed? She looks like Venus! Albino? Fair as Minerva!
Thin as a rail? What grace lies in her willowy charm!
If she's a runt, call her *cute;* if fat, a *full-bodied woman:*
Dialectic can make grace out of any defect. . . .

Now the bed has received two lovers; the bed seems to
     know it.
Now the door has been closed; linger, O Muse, at the door.
They will not need you, now, for the words they will whisper
     and murmur,
Nor will the left hand lie idle along the bed.
Fingers will find what to do in those parts where love plies his
     weapons:
Hector could use his hands in more endeavors than war,
So could Achilles, who lay with the captive from Lyrna beside
     him,
Tired from the wars, but a man in the soft ease of the bed.
Briseis did not object when his hands moved over her body,
Hands that had always known slaughter and Phrygian blood.
Or was it this, just this, that heightened her sense of
     excitement,
Feeling a conqueror's hands come to her secretest parts?
Take my word for it, love is never a thing to be hurried,
Coax it along, go slow, tease it with proper delay.
When you have found the place where a woman loves to be
     fondled,
Let no feeling of shame keep your caresses away.
Then you will see in her eyes a tremulous brightness, a glitter,
Like the flash of the sun when the water is clear.
She will complain, but not mean it, murmuring words of
     endearment,

Sigh in the sweetest way, utter appropriate cries.
Neither go too fast, nor let her get there before you;
Pleasure is best when both come at one time to the goal.
Slow is the pace to keep when plenty of leisure is given,
When you can dally at ease, free from the pressure of fear,
But when delay is not safe, it is useful to drive with full power,
Useful to give your mount spirited prick of the spur.

Here is the end of my work: be thankful, bring me the laurel,
Bring me the palm, young men, grateful for what I have
    taught.
The Greeks had their heroes of old, their specialists, Nestor in
    counsel,
Ajax, Achilles, in arms, wily Ulysses in guile,
Calchas, prophetic seer, and Podalirius, healer,
Automedon in his car—I am the master in love.
Give me your praises, men: I am your poet, your prophet;
Let my name be known, lauded all over the world.
I have given you arms, as Vulcan gave arms to Achilles,
Now that the gift is made, conquerors, go to the wars!
But if your shaft lays low your Amazonian victims,
Write on the votive spoil, "Ovid showed me the way."

Look! The girls are here, and asking me for some lessons.
You will be next, my dears . . .

Have your fun while you may, rejoice in the bloom of your
    springtime,
Years go by like the waves, rapidly streaming away.
Waves that are once gone by are past the hope of recalling,
Hours that are once gone by surely will never return.
Take advantage of time; time is a swift-footed glider,
Nor can the good days to come equal the ones that have
    fled.
Violets wither and fade; I have seen their color turn ashen,
Only the stems are left out of the garlands I wore.

There will come a day when you, the excluder of lovers,
Lie in the lonely night, cold, an old woman, alone.
No one will batter your door or break it with brawls in the
    nighttime,
You will not find in the dawn roses thrown down on the
    stone.
Most unhappily true—the body is furrowed with wrinkles,
Shining complexions lose all their bright radiant hues.
Those white hairs which you say you always had, from your
    girlhood,
Thicken and multiply fast, covering all of your head.
Serpents put off old age by sloughing their skins with the
    season,
Nor do the antlers lost tell the true years of the stag.
All our good things go, and we can do nothing about it,
Only gather the flower; soon the blossom will fall. . . .

Cultivation comes first, the proper care of the body—
From the well-tended vine comes the most exquisite wine.
Beauty's a gift from the gods, too rare for many to boast of:
Most of you (pardon me, dears) don't have so precious a boon.
So, take pains to improve the endowments nature has given;
With sufficient neglect, Venus would look like a hag.
If, in the olden days, girls took no care of their persons,
What did it matter? Of old, men were as crude and
    uncouth.
If Andromache wore a one-piece garment of burlap,
What was so strange about that? She was a warrior's spouse.
How would you like to be dressed like the wife of Ajax, in
    leather,
Seven layers of hide for your protection from cold?
Simple and rude, those days, but Rome, in our era, is
    golden,
Ruler of conquered tribes, holding the wealth of the world.
Look at the Capitol now, and see, in imagination,
What it used to be, home of a different Jove.

We have a Senate-house worthy of Caesar Augustus,
Fashioned, in Tatius' reign, out of wattles and clay.
On the Palatine Hill, where Apollo dwells with our princes,
What did there use to be? Pasture for oxen to browse.
Let others rave about those ancient days; I am happy
Over the date of my birth: this is the era for me.
Not because we mine the stubborn gold from the
    mountains,
Not because rare shells come from the farthest of shores,
Not because the hills decrease as we plunder the marble,
Not because sea walls bar raids of the dark-blue sea,
Not for reasons like these, but because our age has
    developed
Manners, culture and taste, all the old crudities gone. . . .

There are not many games which nature has fashioned for
    women,
Nothing like boxing or ball; men have the best of it here.
They can throw the swift spears, or get themselves up in their
    armor,
They can go riding around, taking the jumps in the field.
You have no place in all this, the ring, or the wrestling arena,
Nor where the rivers run, cold in the rush of the stream,
But you can walk at your ease by the shadowed arches of
    Pompey
When the August sun scorches the roofs of the town,
Visit the Palatine Hill, the temple of laurelled Apollo,—
His be the praise, whose power saved us from Egypt's design!
Visit the monuments of our leader, his wife, and his sister;
Look at the naval oak wreathing Agrippa's brow,
Visit the altars of Isis, steaming with incense from Memphis;
Theaters? All have good seats; choose any one of the three.
Go and look at the games, where the sands are sprinkled
    with crimson,
Go to the racecourse and watch chariots making the turn.

"Out of sight, out of mind"; and out of mind, out of
    longing.
What are good looks, unseen? Nothing is gained if you
    hide. . . .

I was about to omit the art of deceiving a husband,
Fooling a vigilant guard, crafty though either might be.
Let the bride honor, obey, pay proper respect to her husband,
That is only correct; decency says so, and law.
But why should you, set free, and not too long ago, either,
By the decree of the court, have to be kept like a bride?
Listen to me, and learn; though your watchers are there by
    the hundred,
If you will take my advice, you can get rid of them all.
How can they interfere or stop you from writing a letter?
What is a bathroom for? Tell them you have to go there.
Haven't you any close friend who knows how to carry a
    tablet
Under her arm, or perhaps tucked in the fold of a gown?
Isn't she able to hide a note in the top of her stocking,
Or, if that's apt to be found, in the instep of a shoe?
Is her guardian on to such tricks?—let her offer herself as a
    tablet,
Carry, in code, on her back, letters in lipstick of red.
For your invisible ink, use milk: it will show when you
    heat it;
Write with a stem of wet flax—no one will ever suspect. . . .

In our last lesson we deal with matters peculiarly secret;
Venus reminds us that here lies her most intimate care.
What a girl ought to know is herself, adapting her method,
Taking advantage of ways nature equips her to use.
Lie on your back, if your face and all of your features are
    pretty;
If your posterior's cute, better be seen from behind.

Milanion used to bear Atalanta's legs on his shoulders;
If you have beautiful legs, let them be lifted like hers.
Little girls do all right if they sit on top, riding horseback;
Hector's Andromache knew she could not do this: too tall!
Press the couch with your knees and bend your neck
    backward a little,
If your view, full-length, seems what a lover should crave.
If the breasts and the thighs are youthful and lovely to
    look at,
Let the man stand and the girl lie on a slant on the bed.
Let your hair come down, in the Laodamian fashion:
If your belly is lined, better be seen from behind.
There are a thousand ways: a simple one, never too tiring,
Is to lie on your back, turning a bit to the right.
My Muse can give you the truth, more truth than Apollo or
    Ammon;
Take it from me, what I know took many lessons to learn.
Let the woman feel the act of love to her marrow,
Let the performance bring equal delight to the two.
Coax and flatter and tease, with inarticulate murmurs,
Even with sexual words, in the excitement of play,
And if nature, alas! denies you the final sensation
Cry out as if you had come, do your best to pretend.
Really, I pity the girl whose place, let us say, cannot give her
Pleasure it gives to the man, pleasure she ought to enjoy.
So, if you have to pretend, be sure the pretense is effective,
Do your best to convince, prove it by rolling your eyes,
Prove by your motions, your moans, your sighs, what a
    pleasure it gives you.
Ah, what a shame! That part has its own intimate signs.
After the joys of love, a girl who will ask for a present
Surely is wasting her time: that's not a nice thing to do.
Don't let the light pour in, with all of the windows wide
    open—
It is more fitting to keep much of your body concealed.

———

So our sport has an end: our swans are tired of their harness:
Time for their labors to rest, time to step down from our
     car.
As the young men did, now let the girls, my disciples,
Write on the votive spoil, "Ovid showed us the way."

FOR THE LITERARY TRAVELER

Caesar's adoptive son, Octavian, who as emperor re-named himself Augustus ("Reverend"), was not amused by Ovid's do-it-yourself guide to sexual politics. His penalty, exile from the city that was the poet's life's blood, could not have been more cruel, a permanent drip of living death. The Christian Middle Ages had a better sense of humor. Ovid's poetry was part of the Latin curriculum of monasteries and universities. Chaucer put *The Art of Love* in the library of the Wife of Bath's fifth husband, and in *The Canterbury Tales* he salutes the racy author: "Venus clerk, Ovyde,/ That hath y-sowen wonder-wyde/ The grete god of loves name." Ovid's poem gives the sexual dance a number of local sightings, the Capitoline, the Forum, the fashionable Palatine, Octavia's Portico (now in the Jewish Ghetto), . . . but the sharpest details belong to the **Circus Maximus.** There, where the charioteers performed before audiences ranging from 150,000 to 385,000, frenzy and aggression marked the tenor of the place. The Circus was vast, as it still is today: three stadiums long (1,875 feet) and one wide (600 feet). The grandstands—you can still see some remains on the eastern end—were ringed by eateries, bars, and shops, by the booths of prostitutes and gamblers, and at the straight end, by the stalls for the horses and charioteers. In the midst of the races, and the contests between wild beasts or athletes, or, when the arena was flooded, during mock sea battles, the opportunities for casual pickups presented themselves at every wreck of a chariot or roar of the crowd. Some historians date the Circus to 600 B.C., in the time of the Etruscans, but the first written reference is in 329 B.C. There were other circuses in Rome, but the Circus Maximus, sunk in the valley between the Palatine and the Aventine, was the most fantastic. And from their seats on the south side, Ovid and his friends could look up at the Palatine, where Ovid lived. The Imperial Box, built by Augustus in

10 B.C., also faced the Palatine, affording direct communication with the palaces on top of the hill. (As Hadrian tells us in his *Memoirs,* he was a Circus regular. See page 48.)

These days the Circus is always open, and you can sit on the grass and look up at the splendid southside views of the Palatine. At sunset the runners take it over, on weekends, political and sports rallies. Whatever the gathering, the games of love—and of boldface sexual harassment—continue. Yesterday, today, and tomorrow, Ovid lives.

JANE ALISON

1961–

Why was Ovid, the most popular poet of his day, banished from Rome? In The Love-Artist, *novelist and classicist Jane Alison imagines the story behind Ovid's exile. Elaborating on one of the hypotheses about his punishment—Ovid was implicated in a scandal involving the Emperor Augustus's promiscuous granddaughter Julia, whom Augustus also banished (along with her mother)—she creates a love story in which the ancient city becomes a passionate presence. In the novel's Prologue, which follows here, Ovid's love for Rome feels like a fire in the brain, the loss of it a fatal wound.*

⊱

From THE LOVE-ARTIST

Prologue

Now the word is given, the horses are lashed, and the wagon jolts down the dark street, a helmeted soldier seated at each side and Ovid, the exile, between them. Flames glare through the eyes and mouths of stone lanterns, and the blue night air swirls about him like water. The Palatine, crusted with villas, floats off to his left, the Capitoline with its glowing temples to his right; his own house dissolves far behind. His cold hands are clasped together upon his satchel, and he stares, his eyes like the eyes of the lanterns, that word still incomprehensible. *Exile.*

The soldiers came to his house only an hour ago. They stood in the overgrown atrium, in their dazzling armor, and when they told him why they'd come, Ovid—tall and lean, pen in hand—noticed the red wall near his arm gently waver. It was late. "I see," he said, but all he could hear was a humming. "Tomis." He touched the wall with his fingertip to still it. "The Black Sea, you say. *Exile*"— as if in his own voice it might become clear. "But I may bring what I want. My writing things, my books." He watched as his index finger drew a damp line on the wall, from the hoof of a stag to the white teeth of a dog. Then, unaccountably, he felt his mouth stretching into a grotesque hyena grin; he actually heard himself laugh. "Does that mean I can bring *Rome*?"

The soldiers, of course, didn't answer. They placed themselves at either side of the door and waited for him to pack. So Ovid found himself turning slowly, underwater, moving through the red and gold and black walls of his house, his shocked eyes falling upon the familiar bronze, marble, and papery surfaces, with that terrible grin stretching his face, with that terrible word incomprehensible. He stood swaying slightly in his bedroom, on the mosaic skeleton that danced upon the floor. He put some warm clothes, a few tablets, and a stylus in his satchel. Then another pair of shoes, and Carus's book. He stood there, looking around; he knelt and fastened his boots. He walked back into the wet green atrium, past Persilla with her streaming old eyes, past poor Lazar hiding his face in the shadows. "I'm sorry, goodbye," he heard himself say, as if he had been a bad guest. Then he passed for the last time through his own door into the cool spring night, and stepped into the wagon, a soldier on either side.

The blue night swirls by, and there's a dim roar of Rome all around. The wagon has reached the green stretch between the two hills and passes over the cloaca; it threads around the circular temple and, climbing, skirts Marcellus's theater. It would be lit inside now, Ovid realizes. The stage would be glowing saffron red, and there would be the murmur of all the voices, and the intricate hairstyles, and the bare shoulders, and the messages flying, and the swift appreciative glances, and the limb-weakening applause, which has often been for him . . .

The theater drifts by. They reach the river with its marshy spring air, and as the horses break into a gallop Ovid is thrown against one of the soldiers. He's jolted; his heart pounds.

"The thing is," he says—and he's shocked by his voice, how suddenly it flies from his throat—"the thing is, I didn't do anything."

The soldier's gaze shifts his way, and light glances from his helmet, a reflection of the city going by.

"I didn't. I thought Augustus believed me." But Ovid's voice seems to be drifting away. "You see," he says, concentrating with effort, "it was a mistake. I didn't know what Julia was doing. How could I have known?"

The soldier turns. It has nothing to do with him. His instructions were simple: arrest Ovid, remove him from Rome, place him on the ship bound for Tomis, the Black Sea. It's someplace up and over, he vaguely knows, at the edge of the world. A Roman outpost, very cold, always under siege. Uncivilized. Not likely that anyone speaks Latin up there, not even much chance of fresh fruit. What a place for this swan, he thinks, this poet with his tall, gray elegance, his finely arched nose, his feverish look, his leanness. Women were said to rush him on the streets, their dresses flying, bare arms lifted, eyes dilated, delirious to know him . . . *Tomis.*

Ovid has fallen silent, realizing that his words do not matter. The wagon jolts along more slowly, one of thousands rolling through the city, their wooden wheels groaning upon the granite roads. He gazes at the faces passing by—hard faces of fishermen and farmers, their wagons full of octopus, artichokes, and quail, the minor delights of Rome that he won't taste again. A merchant's daughter looks up as she passes, and her mouth falls open in recognition. She covers it with a startled hand.

Now the Aventine is rising to the left, its great black form blocking out the stars, giving off a scent of cypress. They turn onto the Via Ostiensis, swing south. Ovid has become aware of the pain in breathing; he keeps his teeth tightly clenched. They trot by a place that is discreetly marked, but he knows it at once: it's where the Vestals are buried alive when they break their vows to be virgins. Something runs through him, and he finds an arm flying; he finds himself almost laughing.

"He may as well just do that," he cries. "Give me a lamp and food for a day and pack me underground."

The soldier to his left grips Ovid's wild arm. He himself supervised hundreds of suicides some years back, when Augustus was cleaning out the senate, not to mention the swift executions when they didn't go willingly. Exile seems to him rather mild. "It's not the end of the world," he says.

Ovid looks away, sobered. "It is," he says. "I've been there."

Although in his mind he amends himself. He hasn't been there, exactly, not Tomis. Not the western side of the Black Sea, where he is bound now. But the eastern shore he has certainly seen, for that is where he found *her*, Xenia, only a year ago. When he set out blindly on the trip that has ruined him.

Suddenly he feels it streaming behind him, this world that he is leaving. This great city and all that it's made of—the finest things men have created and all the texture of cultured life, books and art and buildings and music, whispers in a marble square, sun shining through an amethyst dress, a glance on the street, sleek onyx statues standing in a row, the flare of recognition in intelligent eyes, the piercing spur of rivalry, the pleasure of praise, the thunder of the crowd as the horses gallop by, a translucent white vase in a garden, walls all figured with myth, the rooms where conversation flies like torches, and everywhere, everywhere, the subtle net of language, whose strands he himself has woven so finely that veils upon veils of meaning have hovered . . . He is going where there will be nothing: only the silent ground and the hard sky, alone.

The wagon rattles on. He clenches his teeth as the darkened walls roll by, and no one sees or comes.

Where is everyone? Where are the women who were inflamed by his *Loves*—the one who drew him a message in wine on a dinner-party tablecloth, that one who stood before him in an afternoon bedroom, nude? Where are the grand old patricians who clapped him on the back, their eyes wet from the sheer knowing beauty of his *Metamorphoses*? Where are the ox-eyed young men with their groomed dark heads, reading his *Art of Love* for advice? And the old women, keyholes to bedrooms, and the tarty slave girls with their slippery tongues? And the Greek booksellers, who know literature when they see it! Where is Carus? Where are his friends?

All the doors are closed, the shutters drawn for the night, this, his last night in Rome.

Julia?

No, what's he thinking: she's already gone. Augustus's own granddaughter—she had to be gotten rid of. Adultery is the official charge, as Augustus doesn't want known what she's really done. She's been packed off like her mother to a remote island, to live and die, alone. You are a boil, Augustus said. I want you out of my sight.

And *she,* that other, that Xenia? Where exactly is she? She left nothing behind but that jungle in the atrium, a few withered things in the window, and those two chilling lines . . . She even took her door handle.

At the thought of those two lines and all that is lost, a quiver runs through him. "Witch," he whispers. The word flies from his mouth, and his eyes dart up to the night sky with it, as if he expects to see her there, wheeling like the gulls against the lopsided moon. Only blue clouds drift by. She could be anywhere. In the sea—in the grass—for all he knows, laughing right now in his satchel. He looks down at it sharply, then closes his eyes and passes a damp hand over them.

Palm trees hurry by, and lemon trees, and an illuminated temple. A door to a house opens upon a bright hum of voices and color, and two drunken men come out, laughing. They look up with blurred recognition at Ovid as he is borne by.

Guilt and remorse fan slowly through him, like blood let in a bath. The sickening sense washes up his throat, flows salty into his mouth, but when it reaches his teeth he bites down. No: Xenia did it to herself. She could have given him what he wanted, when he begged her, and he would have undone everything—he would have burned the precious thing himself. If she had only told him what she alone was able to *see,* what he so desperately wanted to know.

Whether his work would last. Whether he'd be immortal.

How much could it have cost her to tell?

If only, as Ovid is carried from Rome, the world would draw

back its veils and show itself the way Xenia could see it! If only he could see what was to become of him, of his name and his bright, mercurial poems—the palaces and villas that will rise up hundreds of years later all over these famous hills, their ceilings and walls made brilliant with frescoes, and the stately galleries of paintings, the halls of marble sculptures . . . all glorying *him* and his clever, alchemical stories. If he could see the scholars and monks illuminating his verses with tiny images of girls becoming trees, of boys with feathery wings, of cool statues blushing to life. *I'll write about bodies transfigured* . . . He has hoped and begged for this so fervently that his nails have pierced his lean dry palms, as iron nails will pierce other palms only a few years from now; he has forced the blood to pounding behind his eyes with the sheer aching pressure of his ambition; he has, finally, done what he's done, in the terrible force of his desire.

To be *known.* To be *remembered.* To live forever.

Now they've come to the bottom of Rome; they're approaching the Ostian gate. This is it, then. Nothing will stop this steady movement, he's helpless. The wagon keeps rolling forward; the gate rises up with its huge brick arches and all its engraved inscriptions. With a sudden darkness, a smell of damp, the wagon passes under the arch and they're through, out in the stretching fields, the straight road lined with tombs.

Beside him, the soldiers relax. They are out of Rome now. Ovid is gone.

FOR THE LITERARY TRAVELER

Alison's Prologue maps Ovid's last Roman carriage ride, a *passeggiata* toward exile that will haunt him forever.

From the Palatine, he follows the Tiber, passing the **Cloaca Maxima,** the still functional main sewer built by the Etruscans in the sixth century B.C., enabling engineers to drain the marshy Forum; he sees the **Temples of the Forum Boarium**—the cattle market and landing stage (near Tiber Island) that later developed into the Portus Tiberinus, the oldest of Rome's river ports. The Temples in this Forum include the

Circular Temple, which Ovid notes, a Corinthian sanctuary with twenty fluted columns you can still visit; Bramante copied it in his renowned Tempietto on the Janiculum. Up the hill—in ancient times, the hills near the Tiber were steeper than they are now—the **Theater of Marcellus** "drifts by." Built by His Eminence Augustus in 11 B.C., between the Tiber and the Capitol, its twenty thousand seats, open to the sky, might have been empty the night Ovid saw it for the last time, since some historians say the Romans satisfied their love for theater during the day. Now the Theater of Marcellus serves the pleasure of concertgoers on summer nights. While you listen to Schubert under the stars, you see not only the Theater but the three columns of the Temple of Apollo, rising under the moonlight. The benevolent sun god determined the site for the theater: the special games played in his honor included theatrical spectacles. (Tickets are sold the night of the concerts, at the gate in the Via del Teatro di Marcello before 9 P.M.)

Ovid looks up at the **Aventine,** "rising to the left, its great black form blocking out the stars, giving off a scent of cypress." The last of the traditional seven hills to be included in the city, the Aventine still shows from its crest a line of black cypresses and umbrella pines as you head toward the Ostian Gate (later renamed St. Paul's Gate or Porta San Paolo) along Via Marmorata, through Testaccio, and then south along Via Ostiense toward **Ostia,** Rome's main port for six hundred years; the ruins of the ancient city of **Ostia Antica** are undergoing extensive excavations. After Pompeii and Herculaneum, it's Italy's best preserved Roman town, and according to legend, where Aeneas, forefather of the Latins, landed. This port that was Ovid's most dreaded destination is now the most interesting day excursion from the city. (*A thirty-minute train ride from Stazione Ostiense, across the road from Porta San Paolo; follow the signs for Ferroviere Roma-Lido; open 9–1 hour before sunset, Tues–Sun.*)

Roman roads, along with bridges, aqueducts, and sewers, the engineering marvels of Ovid's time, connected the towns throughout the Empire in a network of fifty thousand miles. They all lead to Rome, of course, except on this night, the darkest of the poet's soul: the ancient **Via Ostiense** carried him in the wrong direction. Today the bus route along the Via Ostiense is ugly without relief, like whatever it was that drove the censorious Augustus to impose exile on Rome's best beloved poet ten years after *The Art of Love* was published. Alison's novel, along with the stories we have about Augustus's two wayward Julias (the daughter picked up men in the Forum), makes you wonder. The anti-democratic and sexist thrust of his moral reforms—he initiated codes against adultery aimed only at wives, leaving husbands free of prohibi-tions, and left on the books a law allowing a man to kill an unfaithful wife though he might legally house a concubine or visit prostitutes—was it Ovid's sophisticated even-handedness, his inclusion of women's pleasure in *The Art of Love,* that made Augustus (who'd had three wives of his own in succession) fear for his empire's morality? What if, under the Ovidian influence, dutiful Roman matrons abandoned their hearths, the virgins their House of Vesta? According to Gilbert Highet's *Poets in a Landscape,* that's exactly what made Augustus declare Ovid persona non grata: "In 8 A.D. Ovid was banished for seeming to recommend moral laxity when the emperor was trying to raise moral standards."

But *The Love-Artist* is most of all the love story of Ovid and Xenia in which ancient Rome's sexual politics plays as context. We see the lovers in the city's crowded forums, Ovid reclining at feasts served by slaves, making secret visits to Julia on the Palatine. For Ovid, Rome is love's body. In exile he wrote *Tristia,* Book of Sorrows:

> *Cum subit illius tristissima noctis imago,*
> *quod mihi supremum tempus in urbe fuit,*
> *cum repeto noctem, qua tot mihi cara reliqui,*
> *labitur ex oculis nunc quoque gutta meis.*

When I remember that most sorrowful night, my last few hours in Rome, when I look back on that night, when I left so much that was dear to me, even now my eyes fill with tears.

MARGUERITE YOURCENAR

1903–1987

Born Marguerite de Crayencour in Brussels of a French father and Belgian
mother, Yourcenar was as widely traveled as the emperor she portrays in
Memoirs of Hadrian. *Author of some twenty books ranging from art and*
literary criticism to novels, drama, poetry, and translation, Yourcenar became
the first woman elected to the prestigious French Academy. Her most fa-
mous work, excerpted here, is written in the form of a farewell letter from
the Emperor Hadrian to his successor, the young Marcus Aurelius. She
called it a meditation upon history inspired by a letter of Flaubert, which
Yourcenar discovered in 1927:

The melancholy of the antique world seems to me more
profound than that of the moderns, all of whom more or
less imply that beyond the dark void lies immortality. But
for the ancients that "black hole" is infinity itself; their
dreams loom and vanish against a background of immutable
ebony. No crying out, no convulsions—nothing but the
fixity of the pensive gaze. Just when the gods had ceased to
be, and the Christ had not yet come, there was a unique
moment in history, between Cicero and Marcus Aurelius,
when man stood alone. Nowhere else do I find that
particular grandeur.

From MEMOIRS OF HADRIAN

They accuse me of caring little for Rome. It had beauty, though, during those two years when the State and I were feeling our way with each other, the city of narrow streets, crowded Forums, and ancient, flesh-colored brick. Rome revisited, after the Orient and Greece, was clothed with a strangeness which a Roman born and bred wholly in the City would not find there. I accustomed myself once more to its damp and soot-grimed winters; to the African heat of its summers, tempered by the refreshing cascades of Tibur and by the Alban lakes; to its almost rustic population, bound with provincial attachment to the Seven Hills, but gradually exposed to the influx of all races of the world, driven thither by ambition, enticements to gain, and the hazards of conquest and servitude, the tattooed black, the hairy German, the slender Greek, and the heavy Oriental. I freed myself of certain fastidious restraints: I no longer avoided the public baths at popular hours; I learned to endure the Games, where hitherto I had seen only brutal and stupid waste. My opinion had not changed; I detested these massacres where the beast had not one chance, but little by little I came to feel their ritual value, their effect of tragic purification upon the ignorant multitude. I wanted my festivities to equal those of Trajan in splendor, though with more art and decorum. I forced myself to derive pleasure from the perfect fencing of the gladiators, but only on the condition that no one should be compelled to practice this profession against his will. In the Circus I learned to parley with the crowd from the height of the tribune, speaking through heralds, and not to impose silence upon the throngs save with deference (which they repaid me hundredfold); likewise never to accord them anything but what they had reasonably the right to expect, nor to refuse anything without explaining my refusal. I did not take my books with me, as you do, into the imperial loge; it is insulting to others to seem to disdain their joys. If the spectacle revolted me, the effort to bear it out was for me a more valuable exercise than the study of Epictetus.

Morals are matter of private agreement; decency is of public concern. Any conspicuous license has always struck me as a tawdry display. I forbade use of the baths by both sexes at the same time, a custom which had given rise to almost continual brawling; I returned to the State treasury the colossal service of silver dishes, melted down by my order, which had been wrought for the hoggish appetite of Vitellius. Our early Caesars have acquired an odious reputation for courting inheritances; I made it a rule to refuse both for myself and for the State any legacy to which direct heirs might think themselves entitled. I tried to reduce the exorbitant number of slaves in the imperial household, and especially to curb their arrogance, which leads them to rival the upper classes and sometimes to terrorize them. One day one of my servants had the impertinence to address a senator; I had the man slapped. My hatred of disorder went so far as to decree flogging in the Circus for spendthrifts sunk in debt. To preserve distinction of rank I insisted that the toga and senatorial robe be worn at all times in public, even though these garments are inconvenient, like everything honorific, and I feel no obligation to wear them myself except when in Rome. I made a practice of rising to receive my friends and of standing throughout my audiences, in reaction against the negligence of a sitting or reclining posture. I reduced the insolent crowd of carriages which cumber our streets, for this luxury of speed destroys its own aim; a pedestrian makes more headway than a hundred conveyances jammed end to end along the twists and turns of the Sacred Way. For visits to private homes I took the habit of being carried inside by litter, thus sparing my host the irksome duty of awaiting me without, or of accompanying me back to the street in the heat of the sun, or in the churlish wind of Rome.

I was again among my own people: I have always had some affection for my sister Paulina, and Servianus himself seemed less obnoxious than before. My mother-in-law Matidia had come back from the Orient already revealing the first symptoms of a mortal disease; to distract her from her suffering I devised simple dinners, and contrived to inebriate this modest and naïve matron with a harmless drop of wine. The absence of my wife, who had retreated to the country in a fit of ill humor, in no way detracted from these family pleasures. Of all persons she is probably the one whom I have least succeeded in pleasing; to be sure, I have made little effort to do so. I went often to the small house where the widowed empress now gave herself over to the serious delights of meditation and books; there I found unchanged the perfect silence of Plotina. She was withdrawing gently from life; that garden and those light rooms were daily becoming more the enclosure of a Muse, the temple of an empress already among the gods. Her friendships, however, remained exacting; but all things considered, her demands were only reasonable and wise.

I saw my friends again, and felt the subtle pleasure of renewed contact after long absence, of reappraising and of being reappraised. My companion in former pleasures and literary pursuits, Victor Voconius, had died; I made up some sort of funeral oration, provoking smiles in mentioning among the virtues of the deceased a chastity which his poems belied, as did the presence at the funeral of that very Thestylis, him of the honey-colored curls, whom Victor used to call his "fair torment." My hypocrisy was less blatant than might appear: every pleasure enjoyed with art seemed to me chaste. I rearranged Rome like a house which the master intends to leave safe in his absence; new collaborators proved their worth, and adversaries now reconciled supped together at the Palatine with my supporters in former trials. At my table Neratius Priscus sketched his legislative plans; there the architect Apollodorus explained his designs; Ceionius Commodus, a wealthy patrician of Etruscan origin, descended from an ancient family of almost royal blood, was the friend who helped me work out my next moves in the Senate; he knew men, as well as wines. . . .

Some of the great works of construction were nearing completion: the Colosseum, restored and cleansed of reminders of Nero which still haunted its site, was no longer adorned with the image of that emperor, but with a colossal statue of the Sun, Helios the King, in allusion to my family name of Aelius. They were putting the last touches to the Temple of Venus and Rome, erected likewise on the site of the scandalous House of Gold, where Nero had grossly displayed a luxury ill acquired. *Roma, Amor:* the divinity of the Eternal City was now for the first time identified with the Mother of Love, inspirer of every joy. It was a basic concept in my life. The Roman power was thus taking on that cosmic and sacred character, that pacific, protective form which I aspired to give it. At times it occurred to me to identify the late empress with that wise Venus, my heavenly counselor.

More and more the different gods seemed to me merged mysteriously in one Whole, emanations infinitely varied, but all equally manifesting the same force; their contradictions were only expressions of an underlying accord. The construction of a temple of All Gods, a Pantheon, seemed increasingly desirable to me. I had chosen a site on the ruins of the old public baths given by Agrippa, Augustus' son-in-law, to the people of Rome. Nothing remained of the former structure except a porch and a marble plaque bearing his dedication to the Roman citizens; this inscription was carefully replaced, just as before, on the front of the new temple. It mattered little to me to have my name recorded on this monument, which was the product of my very thought. On the contrary, it pleased me that a text of more than a century ago should link this new edifice to the beginning of our empire, to that reign which Augustus had brought to peaceful conclusion. Even in my innovations I liked to feel that I was, above all, a continuator. Farther back, beyond Trajan and Nerva, now become officially my father and my grandfather, I looked for example even to those twelve Caesars so mistreated by Suetonius: the clear-sightedness of Tiberius, without his harshness; the learning of Claudius, without his weakness; Nero's taste for the arts, but stripped of all foolish vanity; the kindness of Titus, stopping short of his sentimentality; Vespasian's thrift, but not his absurd miserliness. These princes had played their part in human affairs; it devolved upon me, to choose hereafter from among their acts what should be continued, consolidating the best things, correcting the worst, until the day when other men, either more or less qualified than I, but charged with equal responsibility, would undertake to review my acts likewise.

The dedication of the Temple of Venus and Rome was a kind of triumph, celebrated by chariot races, public spectacles, and distribution of spices and perfumes. The twenty-four elephants which had transported the enormous blocks of building stone, reducing thereby the forced labor of slaves, figured in the procession, great living monoliths themselves. The date chosen for this festival was the anniversary of Rome's birth, the eighth day following the Ides of April in the eight hundred and eighty-second year after the founding of the City. Never had a Roman spring been so intense, so sweet and so blue.

On the same day, with graver solemnity, as if muted, a dedicatory ceremony took place inside the Pantheon. I myself had revised the architectural plans, drawn with too little daring by Apollodorus: utilizing the arts of Greece only as ornamentation, like an added luxury, I had gone back for the basic form of the structure to primitive, fabled times of Rome, to the round temples of ancient Etruria. My intention had been that this sanctuary of All Gods should reproduce the likeness of the terrestrial globe and of the stellar sphere, that globe wherein are enclosed the seeds of eternal fire, and that hollow sphere containing all. Such was also the form of our ancestors' huts where the smoke of man's earliest hearths escaped through an orifice at the top. The cupola, constructed of a hard but lightweight volcanic stone which seemed still to share in the upward movement of flames, revealed the sky through a great hole at the center, showing alternately dark and blue. This temple, both open and mysteriously enclosed, was conceived as a solar quadrant. The hours would make their round on that caissoned ceiling, so carefully polished by Greek artisans; the disk of daylight would rest suspended there like a shield of gold; rain would form its clear pool on the pavement below; prayers would rise like smoke toward that void where we place the gods. . . .

From the top of a terrace on the night following these celebrations I watched Rome ablaze. Those festive bonfires were surely as brilliant as the disastrous conflagrations lighted by Nero; they were almost as terrifying, too. Rome the crucible, but also the furnace, the boiling metal, the hammer, and the anvil as well, visible proof of the changes and repetitions of history, one place in the world where man will have most passionately lived.

FOR THE LITERARY TRAVELER

The sources for the reign of Hadrian (117–138) are so skimpy that whether you're reading traditional histories or the *Memoirs of Hadrian* you're actually reading lots of fiction. In the *Memoirs*, the aging and sickly Hadrian, facing death, wants to understand himself more fully before he dies. He looks back on his life as a passionate world traveler, before and after he became emperor, admitting his failures, triumphs, the ruthless abuses of power. Readers become an intimate of "the man who accepts all experience." We come to know his young Greek lover, the "favourite" Antinous who drowned in the Nile in 130 A.D. (His statue—and Hadrian's—is in the Capitoline Museum.)

Through Hadrian's eyes we see the monuments in Rome he had built to replicate the splendors of his beloved Greece and Egypt.

First, **The Pantheon.** The word comes from the Greek *pan* (all) and *theos* (god). "A temple of All gods," as Hadrian called it, expressing his sense that "the different gods . . . merged mysteriously in one Whole, emanations infinitely varied, but all equally manifesting the same force. . . ." The most magnificent architectural work of antiquity stuns you the first time you come upon it in the heart of the *Centro Storico*—Historical Center—in ancient times known as the Campus Martius or the Field of Mars, the flat ground east of the loop formed by the Tiber, north of the Capitoline, and west of the Via del Corso; you can see it clearly on the large *Pianta* (map) *di Roma*. Military exercises, games, and races were conducted on the grassy plain where Hadrian built (or rebuilt on Agrippa's orginal structure) the temple you see today. The light of the great domed interior, the Rotunda, suggests a harmony of heaven and earth, the oculus—the great open hole in the center of the cupola—Hadrian's belief in the all-seeing eye of the gods. Wherever you see architectural genius in Rome, it's possible it was the dome of the Pantheon that first inspired the architect's imagination: Bramante, Michelangelo, Palladio. Brunelleschi studied it as he planned the dome of the Duomo in Florence.

Sitting outside a cafe or on the steps around the obelisk, you can contemplate the Pantheon, and the Piazza della Rotonda it commands so magisterially. Except for the accidentals of decoration, the temple's interior and the outdoor scene have not changed much since ancient times. Then there were fishmongers and live chicken hawkers and gypsies; now there are souvenir vendors and cameras and tour guides waving orange flags and shouting it's time for gelato or espresso.

(*The caffè Rienzo is fine, but the best coffee in Rome is minutes away, at Tazza d'Oro, just off the piazza on Via degli Orfani 84; and at Caffè Sant'Eustachio in Piazza Sant'Eustachio 82, a short walk in the direction of Piazza Navona.*)

The legend of St. Eustachio dates from Hadrian's reign. When Eustachio, a Christian solder, refused to offer sacrifice to Jupiter after a military victory, Hadrian ordered him and his wife and two sons roasted alive inside a brazen bull. The first-century martyr is buried with his family in the third-century church of Sant'Eustachio, built on the site of his home. There's a stag's head over the entrance. Whether Hadrian's contempt for Christians, expressed in the *Memoirs,* ever took such a maniacal form is not known; history does record his treatment of the Jews, for whom he also had contempt. After his brutal military campaign in Judea in the 130s, Hadrian was cursed in the rabbinical literature as the most destructive enemy the Jews had yet known. The tolerance expressed in Hadrian's Pantheon didn't extend to his foreign imperial projects. Yourcenar attributes to Hadrian the conqueror the same attitude expressed in Caligula's favorite saying: *"Oderint dum metuant"*—"Let them hate as long as they fear."

There's more of Hadrian's architectural legacy back in the direction of the Valley of the Colosseum. **The Temple of Venus and Roma**—the largest temple ever built in Rome—now under excavation near the Arch of Constantine, was his tribute in honor of the Mother of Love as the Mother of Rome, the "inspirer of every joy . . . wise Venus, my heavenly counselor." (Roma spelled backwards is *amor.*) Walking back, toward Piazza Venezia, you see **Trajan's Column** rising above Trajan's Forum,

Hadrian's tribute to the Emperor Trajan, his adoptive father, and like him, a Spaniard. The spiralled column of carved reliefs, which were once colored—an almost perfectly preserved spiral frieze depicts Trajan's military victories in Romania—dominates Trajan's Forum, between the Greek and Latin libraries, buildings that Trajan's widow, the wise Empress Plotina—whom Hadrian considered "my sole friend among women"— called "the dispensary of the soul." The Forum of Augustus adjoins Trajan's. Both are open for thrilling nighttime guided tours. (*Climb the stepped Via Magnanapoli to the entrance in Via Quattro Novembre.*)

The most dramatic approach to **Hadrian's Tomb** or the **Mausoleum of Hadrian** on the left, or west, bank of the Tiber is to walk from the Pantheon through the *Centro Storico.* The streets of medieval Rome could not be less like a grid so you'll get completely lost. But lost and walking in circles, you'll learn the labyrinthine city, get it into your head, where it will wind on forever. When you see the massive tomb that Hadrian built for himself (now the **Castel Sant'Angelo**), you can approach it on the same bridge Hadrian designed to lead straight to it from the Campus Martius: the Pons Aelius, now called the **Ponte Sant'Angelo,** along which copies of Bernini's ecstatic angels gyrate, and the view of St. Peter's is superb.

As you climb the long spiral ramp of the cavernous tomb, you'll pass the only writing of Hadrian that survives, inscribed on the wall that once held the urn of his ashes and those of his unloved wife, the "vexatious Sabina." Byron translated, entitling the lines "Address to His Soul":

> animula, vagula, blandula,
> hospes comesque corporis,
> quae nunc abibis in loca,
> pallidula, rigida, nudula,
> nec ut soles dabis jocos

> Ah! gentle, fleeting wavering Sprite,
> Friend and associate of this clay
> To what unknown region borne
> Wilt thou, now, wing thy distant flight?
> No more, with wonted humor gay,
> But pallid, cheerless and forlorn.

The ascent takes you through the papal apartments, their erotic frescoes revealing the private lives of Renaissance pontiffs; Clement VII's highly decorated bathroom; the torture chambers of prisoners, the prison cells of Beatrice Cenci, and of Benevenuto Cellini who wrote about the castle during the Sack of Rome in 1527 in his *Autobiography.* Up, up, up you climb. There's a scenic terrace, with bar, along the way, but the cruelty of the prison's history hangs in the air. "Compared with S. Angelo, the Tower of London is almost a happy place," H. V. Morton commented in *A Traveller in Rome.* At the top—the setting of the last act of Puccini's *Tosca*—the view is one of the most glorious in Rome. There below, inside the loop of the Tiber, is Hadrian's Pantheon.

In the distance you see the rolling Alban Hills, where he built his country retreat, **Hadrian's Villa.** "The tomb of my travels, the last encampment of the nomad, the equivalent, though in marble, of the tents and pavilions of the princes of Asia."

(*By public transport, take Metro linea B to* **Rebibbia;** *from there take the COTRAL bus to Tivoli, twenty miles from Rome. Before Tivoli, ask to be let off the bus at the "Bivio Villa Adriana," walk fifteen minutes along a well-marked byroad to the entrance. Or take a coach tour, air-conditioned in summer, but allowing for only hour-long tours of the Villa. Schedules of Carrani Group Tours leaving from Via Orlando 95 [near Piazza Repubblica] are available at that office and in hotel lobbies. Tel 06 474 2501. E-mail: www.carrani.viaggi@tiscali.it-info@carranitours.com. Or Green Line Tours, Via Farini, 5A–00185, Roma. Tel 06 482 7480.*)

The largest Imperial villa in the Roman Empire offers cool sanctuary on summer afternoons, a place to picnic, or read Yourcenar's masterpiece. The three hundred acres are shaded by pines and cypresses, planted with olive groves, the sweet-smelling laurel thick, especially in the **Valle di Tempe,** named after the valley Hadrian loved in Greece where according to legend Daphne escaped Apollo's pursuit by turning into a laurel tree. The ruins are stunning, dreamlike. They include two libraries, some nine hundred rooms, and copies of Greek and Egyptian pools and temples. (The sculpture found on the grounds is now in the Vatican and Capitoline Museums: see the **Salle delle Colombe** on the Capitoline's first floor, the room named after the lovely small mosaic of four doves at a fountain; and in the **Sala del Gladiatore,** there's the

"Satyr Resting," the Marble Faun of Nathaniel Hawthorne's novel, also found at Hadrian's Villa. See pages 171–74.) "Tibur," as Hadrian called his home, "where to the very end I am assembling whatever pleasures life has. . . ." He describes for Marcus Aurelius (the future emperor and author of the self-reliance classic *Meditations,* whom Hadrian thought should loosen up) the rituals he instituted in memory of his young lover: "Around that chapel of Canopus where his cult is celebrated in Egyptian fashion, I have encouraged the establishment of various pleasure pavilions. . . ."

Around the **Cento Camerelle** are underground tunnels and small rooms, the soldiers' quarters, according to a guidebook. "Those were the slave quarters," declared a tour guide, in a voice that carried. "How much *work* it must have taken to run this place . . . just *cooking* for Hadrian's huge entourage. . . ."

The tour guide recited the human cost of Hadrian's sophisticated taste. Ancient Rome was a slavocracy, and Hadrian's Villa a slave plantation, a coercive system perpetuated by the rampages of the Empire seizing its human spoils: people who were kidnapped and brought back in chains to serve the pleasure of the masters. The Stoic Seneca described the duties of a household slave in his *Epistles:*

> When we recline at a banquet, one slave mops up the disgorged food, another crouches beneath the table and gathers up the leftovers of the tipsy guests. . . . And he must remain awake throughout the night, dividing his time between his master's drunkenness and lust; in the chamber he must be a man, at the feast a boy.

In Rome, male slaves were called *puer,* or "boy," the same designation used for a male slave in the American South, according to Michael Parenti's *The Assassination of Julius Caesar: A People's History of Ancient Rome.* "Against a slave everything is permitted," said the slave-owning Seneca. Hadrian, whose household staff at the Villa numbered in the hundreds, considered human cruelty another inevitability of the essentially self-interested human condition. "A hundred slaves a hundred enemies," is a Roman proverb that might have crossed his mind while he strolled as an insomniac among the pines, after a late-night banquet.

(*In summer, the Villa's nighttime concerts begin at 9 P.M.—the New*

York City Ballet; Lorin Maazel conducting Mozart; Aprile Millo singing Puccini—in the Grandi Terme [Baths] and the Maritime Theater. Shuttle bus: Rome/Hadrian's Villa-Tivoli/Rome pick up at Stazione Termini, Via Marsala, with booking at tel 06 68 80 91 07. Restaurant/Bar at Hadrian's Villa; next to it is Hotel Ristorante Adriano at Via di Villa Adriana 194.)

CHRISTOPHER WOODWARD

1969–

Christopher Woodward, English art historian and world traveler, has achieved a masterpiece, according to critics, in this meditation on time past and crumbling, entitled In Ruins. *The first chapter, "Who Killed Daisy Miller?," excerpted here, focuses on the Colosseum. The title comes from Henry James's novella,* Daisy Miller, *about a young American woman who caught her death inside the Roman ruin at night, an ambiguous tale about the clash of cultures and their sexual politics that is open to multiple interpretations. With a delightful erudition, Woodward's interpretation of this story's setting deepens one's sense of a monument that has become one of the great clichés of the Ancient Rome itinerary.*

❧

From IN RUINS

WHO KILLED DAISY MILLER?

In the closing scene of *Planet of the Apes* (1968) Charlton Heston, astronaut, rides away into the distance. "What will he find out there?" asks one ape. "His destiny," replies another. On a desolate seashore a shadow falls across Heston's figure. He looks up, then tumbles from his horse in bewilderment. "Oh my God! I'm back. I'm home. Damn you all to hell! . . . You maniacs. They did it, they finally did it, they blew it up!" The shadow is cast by the Statue of Liberty. She is buried up to her waist, her tablet battered, and her torch fractured. The planet of the apes is Earth, he realises, destroyed by a nuclear holocaust while the astronauts were travelling in space. He is the last man, and the lone and level sands stretch far away. . . .

When we contemplate ruins, we contemplate our own future. To statesmen, ruins predict the fall of Empires, and to philosophers the futility of mortal man's aspirations. To a poet, the decay of a monument represents the dissolution of the individual ego in the flow of Time; to a painter or architect, the fragments of a stupendous antiquity call into question the purpose of their art. Why struggle with a brush or chisel to create the beauty of wholeness when far greater works have been destroyed by Time? . . .

It is the shadow of classical antiquity which is the deepest source for the fascination with ruins in the western world. Every new empire has claimed to be the heir of Rome, but if such a colossus as Rome can crumble—its ruins ask—why not London or New York? Furthermore, the magnitude of its ruins overturned visitors' assumptions about the inevitability of human progress over Time. London in Queen Victoria's reign was the first European city to exceed ancient Rome in population and in geographical extent; until the Crystal Palace was erected in Hyde Park in 1851, the Colosseum (or Coliseum) remained the largest architectural volume in existence. Any visitor to Rome in the fifteen centuries after its sack by the Goths in A.D. 410 would have experienced that strange sense of displacement which occurs when we find that, living, we cannot fill the footprints of the dead.

A second shadow falls on the same ground. This is the Christian doctrine that man's achievement on earth is a fleeting transience, that pyramids and houses and skyscrapers will crumble into oblivion at the sound of the Last Trump. The apocalyptic finale is not exclusive to the Christian religion, but what is unique is the conjunction of the cult's holy shrines with the greatest ruins of classical civilisation. The two greatest influences on the mind of Europe share the same circle of hills above the River Tiber. So the Eternal City is the place to begin an investigation into the feelings of pleasure and fear which ruins suggest.

In A.D. 400 Rome was a city of eight hundred thousand people

glittering with 3,785 statues of gold, marble and bronze. Its encir-
cling walls were 10 miles in length with 376 towers, and vaulted by
nineteen aqueducts carrying fresh spring-water to 1,212 drinking
fountains and 926 public baths. There is no evidence that any
writer or painter imagined its future ruin, and the poet Rutilius
Namatianus expressed his contemporaries' view that Rome was as
eternal as the universe itself:

> No man will ever be safe if he forgets you;
> May I praise you still when the sun is dark.
> To count up the glories of Rome is like counting
> The stars in the sky.

In A.D. 410 the Visigoths seized and plundered the city, and in 455
the Ostrogoths. By the end of that century only a hundred thousand citizens remained in Rome, and the rich had fled to Constan-
tinople or joined the Goths in their new capital at Ravenna. In the
sixth century the Byzantines and the Goths contested the city three
times and the population fell to thirty thousand, clustered in
poverty beside the River Tiber now that the aqueducts had been
destroyed and the drinking fountains were dry. The fall of Rome
came to be seen by many as the greatest catastrophe in the history
of western civilisation. . . .

And nowhere was the lesson of *Sic transit gloria mundi* more evident than in the Colosseum. It had served as a quarry, a private
fortress and a bull-ring: earthquakes had struck in 422, 508, 847,
1231 and 1349 A.D. Its external arcades, littered with dunghills,
were full of beggars and occupied by shopkeepers who slung their
awnings on poles slotted into the holes where clamps of bronze
had once held the marble cladding in place. Even inside you could
smell the cabbages from the surrounding farms.

> Quamdiu stat Colyseus, stat et Roma:
> Quando cadet Colyseus, cadet et Roma:
> Quando cadet Roma, cadet et Mundus.

As Byron translated the words of the Venerable Bede:

> While stands the Coliseum, Rome shall stand
> When falls the Coliseum, Rome shall fall
> And when Rome falls—the world.

It is oval in plan, 617 feet in length and 513 feet in width and 187 feet high. The arena was built by Emperor Vespasian and opened in A.D. 80, when it was welcomed as "the eighth wonder of the world" by the poet Martial. It contained fifty thousand spectators. For naval battles the arena was flooded, and when gladiators fought lions, panthers, elephants and ostriches it was redecorated as a jungle or a rocky desert. Christians were fed to the lions from the earliest days of the arena, and it was they who banned the gladiatorial games in A.D. 404.

The Christian Emperor Constantine had deliberately placed the principal Christian shrines—such as St. Peter's and the Lateran Palace—at a discreet distance from the temples of the classical gods. In the Colosseum a clash of the two religions was unavoidable, however, and the sand impregnated with the blood of martyrs became a place of pilgrimage. At the beginning of the eighteenth century it was formally consecrated to the martyrs, and pilgrims processed round the Stations of the Cross erected at the rim of the arena, or kissed the tall black cross in the centre for 100 days' indulgence. The more intrepid pilgrims climbed the tangled, slippery terraces to plant crosses at the grassy summit. A hermitage was built into the tiers of the amphitheatre; one occupant was fined for selling hay he had grown in the arena. The Colosseum showed the Romans at their mightiest but also at their cruellest, so a visit was a dilemma for any Christian with a classical education. The ambivalence is best expressed by Charles Dickens in his *Letters from Italy* (1846). The faces of Italians changed as he entered Rome:

> Beauty becomes devilish; and there is scarcely one
> countenance in a hundred, among the common people in
> the streets, that would not be at home and happy in a

renovated Coliseum to-morrow. . . . [Inside the arena] its
solitude, its awful beauty, and its utter desolation, strike
upon the stranger, the next moment, like a softened sorrow;
and never in his life, perhaps, will he be so moved and
overcome by any sight, not immediately connected with his
own affections and afflictions.

To see it crumbling there, an inch a year; its walls and arches
overgrown with green; its corridors open to the day; the long
grass growing in its porches; young trees of yesterday, springing
up on its ragged parapets, and bearing fruit: chance produce of
the seeds dropped there by the birds who build their nests
within its chinks and crannies; to see its Pit of Fight filled up
with earth, and the peaceful Cross planted in the centre; to
climb into its upper halls, and look down on ruin, ruin, ruin,
all about it . . . is to see the ghost of old Rome, wicked
wonderful old city, haunting the very ground on which its
people trod. It is the most impressive, the most stately, the most
solemn, grand, majestic, mournful sight, conceivable. Never, in
its bloodiest prime, can the sight of the gigantic Coliseum, full
and running over with the lustiest life, have moved one heart,
as it must move all who look upon it now, a ruin. GOD be
thanked: a ruin! . . .

The arena demanded drama of its visitors. Its sand was as resonant
as the wooden planking of the stage, and at night its empty stalls
were a hushed, dimmed auditorium; the Colosseum had the loud-
est echo in the world. On a night of bright moonlight in 1787
Goethe watched the beggars who had bivouacked under the arches
light a fire in the centre, and the phenomenon of the smoke swirling around the bowl gave rise to one of the most celebrated visions
in *The Italian Journey* (1816):

Presently the smoke found its way up the sides, and through
every chink and opening, while the moon lit it up like a cloud.
The sight was exceedingly glorious. In such a light one ought
also to see the Pantheon, the Capitol, the Portico of St Peter's,

and the grand streets and squares. And thus the sun and the
moon, as well as the human mind, have here to do a work
quite different from what they produce elsewhere—here where
vast and yet elegant masses present themselves to their rays.

Perversely, Henry James used the arena's amplification to place
in scale the littleness of human transactions. It is here that he set the
final act of his 1878 novella, *Daisy Miller.* At eleven o'clock in the
evening Nigel Winterbourne is wandering through the city struggling to clarify his confusions over Daisy, a capricious American
heiress. When he enters the arena his first response is to murmur
the lines from Byron's drama *Manfred,* which had become the most
celebrated description to nineteenth-century tourists:

> When I was wandering,—upon such a night
> I stood within the Coliseum's wall,
> Midst the chief relics of almighty Rome!
> The trees which grew along the broken arches
> Waved dark in the blue midnight, and the stars
> Shone through the rents of ruin; from afar
> The watchdog bay'd beyond the Tiber; and
> More near from out the Caesars' palace came
> The owl's long cry . . .
> Ivy usurps the laurel's place of growth;—
> But the gladiators' bloody Circus stands,
> A noble wreck in ruinous perfection!

The Colosseum is filled with mist, a miasma released into the air by
recent excavations in the sewers. Seated at the base of the cross are
Daisy and Giovanelli, a handsome Italian who is his sly rival. For
Winterbourne the composition has a sudden, welcome clarity:
"She was a young lady about the *shades* of whose perversity a foolish puzzled gentleman need no longer trouble his head or heart.
That once questionable quantity *had* no shades—it was a mere
little black blot." His mind resolved, he speaks only to instruct
her that the miasma is a danger to her health. She protests: "I never

was sick, and I don't mean to be! I don't look like much, but I'm healthy! I was bound to see the Coliseum by moonlight—I wouldn't have wanted to go home without that . . ." Their last words are exchanged in the tunnel of the entrance as, driving away in a cab, she turns to cry out: "I don't care whether I have Roman fever or not!" A week later she is dead of malaria. . . .

Poor Daisy Miller—it was the excavations that released the fatal vapours from the sewers.

The sewers and underground service corridors have remained exposed ever since, as bald as the foundations of a modern construction site. I cannot find a single writer or painter who has been inspired by the Colosseum since 1870, and only one exception to a general rule: the failed painter, Adolf Hitler, and his architects.

"Rom hat mich richtig ergriffen!" ["Rome completely bowled me over!"] His first sight was on a state visit in 1938. Mussolini prepared a ceremonial progression from the railway station at the Pyramid of Caius Cestius to Palazzo Venezia, his palace at the foot of the Capitoline Hill. Hitler's train arrived by night, and the proudest monuments of Imperial Rome were illuminated by 45,000 electric lamps linked by 100 miles of cabling. The Colosseum was lit from inside by red lamps so that, as if ablaze, it cast a bloody glow on to the grass and the ruddy brick ruins on the surrounding slopes. Heavy rain in the days which followed led to military displays being cancelled, and Hitler took the opportunity to return to the Colosseum and spend several hours alone studying designs for the new Congress Hall in Nuremberg. This was amphitheatrical in form: his architect Albert Speer had discussed Goethe's speculation that in the Colosseum the crowd became a single spirit, swaying forward and back in mesmerised loyalty. Hitler saw an even more chilling moral in the structure: the construction of these "imperishable symbols of power" depended on slaves brought from conquered, "uncivilized" territories.

On his return to Germany Hitler introduced an official policy, the *"Teorie von Ruinwert."* Steel and ferro-concrete could no longer be used in the construction of official Nazi buildings because they were too perishable. The use of marble, stone and brick alone would ensure that at the fall of the 1,000-year Reich they would resemble their Roman models. As Speer explained in his memoirs:

> Ultimately, all that remained to remind men of the great epochs of history was their monumental architecture, he recalled. What then remained of the emperors of the Roman Empire? What would still give evidence of them today, if not their buildings. . . . So, today the buildings of ancient Rome could enable Mussolini to refer to the heroic spirit of Rome when he wanted to inspire his people with the idea of a modern imperium. Our buildings must speak to the conscience of future generations of Germans. With this argument Hitler also understood the value of a durable kind of construction.

Speer even presented Hitler with sketches in which he imagined the marble colonnade of the Zeppelinfeld at Nuremberg as a romantic, ivy-clad ruin of the future. And in the Cabinet Room at the Reichstag Hitler hung views of the Forum painted by the French artist Hubert Robert in the eighteenth century. Should Hitler's obsession with ruins deter us from enjoying them ourselves? No; the opposite rather. To Hitler the Colosseum was not a ruin but a monument, a bottle that was half-full rather than half-empty as it were. He was attracted to the endurance of the masonry and the physical survival of an emperor's ambitions; to the lover of the ruinous, by contrast, the attraction is in the sight of transience and vulnerability. Poets and painters like ruins, and dictators like monuments. . . .

Today it is the most monumental bathos in Europe: a bald, dead and bare circle of stones. There are no shadows, no sands, no echoes and if a single flower blooms in a crevice it is sprayed with weedkiller. The monument is open to the public from nine-thirty A.M. to six P.M., when the gates are locked.

FOR THE LITERARY TRAVELER

"Mai visto in vita mia qualcosa di cosi brutto come il Colosseo."

"Never saw such an ugly thing as the Colosseum in my life," exclaimed John Ruskin on sight of Rome's most visited monument.

A party atmosphere swirls outside the gates. Crowds mill and queue to buy tickets to the hour-long tours. Mimes on stilts perform; goofy Romans dressed as gladiators cavort and flirt. The organizers of the various tours compete for customers, buttonholing bystanders. If you decide to straggle along with a group, following the guides of the "Discover Rome Tours," say, you're in for an hour of sound bites and an instant laugh track. According to these stand-up comics, the **Colosseum** is all about the movie *Gladiator. Here's where Russell Crowe dropped his spear . . . do you remember the part where Commodus . . . they really packed in the crowds back then, the Romans loved a good show!*

The tour guides, like Hollywood, play fast and loose with history. The Colosseum, even for Roman historians, was the setting for the triumph of evil.

In *Daisy Miller,* Henry James's most popular novel (1878), his innocent and beautiful American heroine, whose only strengths, in the words of Italo Calvino, "are her lack of culture and her spontaneous vitality," catches her death here in the form of malaria, carried on the diseased air from the marshes of the Campagna. The malaria represents the moral pestilence that surrounds her in Rome, a city controlled by the puritans and pagans who condemn her to be sacrificed "right in the middle of the Colosseum"; for James it's a reminder of the history of human cruelty and the slaughter of the innocents.

Slaves, who built it, were the usual victims in Ancient Rome. The gladiators who entertained audiences of fifty thousand were slaves, and prisoners of war. (They trained just to the east, across the road, in the **Ludus Magnus.**) Slaves made up between 30 and 40 percent of the population of Italy, with a slightly smaller percentage in Rome.

Sometimes, to warm up the crowd at the Colosseum, emperors ordered fat women and cripples to fight one another. To celebrate his slaughter of the Dacians, Emperor Trajan sent ten thousand gladiators and eleven thousand animals, mostly from Africa, into the arena. In a single day, five thousand wild animals were massacred. The moralistic Emperor Augustus, who sent Ovid into exile presumably for sexual depravity, was said to enjoy the "games," the torture and shredding of human bodies, the butchery of panthers, tigers, lions, zebras, elks, elephants, rhinoceros, hippos, giraffes, leopards, crocodiles, and ostriches. Emperor Domitian added a theatrical prologue, directing prisoners to plunge into fire, and to be crucified.

Your tour guide will point out the seating arrangements for these spectacles: women, slaves, and the poor sat on wooden benches at the top, though up there it was mostly standing room only; foreigners sat in the section below. Further down were middle-class men, then the ranks of the wealthy, then the senators, in white togas with red borders. The ringside seats were reserved for the emperor and the Vestal Virgins.

One historian connects this culture of carnage with the practice of empire: the visible sign of the Roman will to power was Roman cruelty. Christopher Woodward ends his piece with a story about how much Hitler admired the Colosseum and how proud Mussolini was to show it off.

(These days, in Easter season, the pope presides over a re-enactment of the Stations of the Cross around the Colosseum, at 9 P.M. on Good Friday.)

Emperor Vespasian built it in 70 A.D., to celebrate his victory over the Jews and the destruction of Jerusalem; the gold and silver he took from the Temple paid for it. It's also thought he used it to distract the populace from Neronian atrocities. Nero's house, **Domus Aurea**—Golden House—now excavated and open to the public, is just across (northeast) from the Colosseum, off Via Labicana up a driveway (Viale Domus Aurea) into Parco Oppio, a public park, about a ten-minute walk. After the fire of 64 A.D., Nero began to represent himself as the Sun and as the initiator of a new golden age. His residence, built on land appropriated from aristocrats, became the royal palace of the Sun, the whole house covered with gold and gems, the frescoes and stuccoes done in gold leaf. Moving in, the man who had killed his pregnant wife with a savage kick after having had his mother battered to death by sailors and his first wife bound and drowned in a bath, with her veins cut, declared, "Now at last I can begin to live like a human being."

The informative tour of Domus Aurea (open 9–7:45, closed Tues) leaves you gaping: at the incredible **Octagonal Hall,** the dining room where mad Nero entertained; at the Homeric friezes in the **Room of Hector and Andromache.** And much more. Here, and everywhere in Ancient Rome, you come to sense how Henry James looked on the ruins: "The appeal seems ever to rise out of heaven knows what depths of ancient trouble."

(You can take the long view of the ancient sites from the roof-top restaurant of the **Hotel Forum,** *Via Tor de' Conti 25–30—off Fori Imperiali and Trajan's Forum. Tel 39 06 6792446. Open for lunch and dinner, reserve for dinner. Web site: www.hotelforumrome.com. For as long as you like, you can sit overlooking the Forum, the honeyed Palatine rising behind it, the Colosseum off to the left, the Capitoline to the right, adjacent to it another megalomaniacal monument, the white Victor Emmanuel, honoring Italy's first king. From up here—possibly the setting of Edith Wharton's brilliant story "Roman Fever"—the ruins look mythic, outside time, the pain of their particular stories forgotten for now, washed in sunlight, or the dark blue night.)*

EARLY CHRISTIAN ROME

❧

St. Peter ❧ St. Paul ❧ Margaret Visser

*For all God's beloved in Rome, who are called to be saints:
Grace to you and peace from God our Father and the Lord Jesus
Christ. . . . For I long to see you. . . . I am eager to preach the
gospel to you who are in Rome. . . . There will be . . . glory and
honor and peace for every one who does good, the Jew first and also
the Greek. For God shows no partiality.*

—St. Paul, Letter to the Romans

ST. PETER

?–67

When he was a fisherman in Judea, an outpost of the Roman Empire, Peter had been known as Simon. The Aramaic title Kepha—Peter, meaning rock—was given to him by his friend Jesus, the carpenter and prophet from Nazareth, who was crucified around 31 A.D. by order of Judea's Roman governor, Pontius Pilate.

Some years later, Peter is believed to have traveled from Jerusalem to Rome as a missionary. He preached an unrestricted love, the main message of Jesus. His converts welcomed the scum of Rome to their gatherings, slaves, immigrants, prostitutes, cripples, children, women, and Jews, a wrinkle considered subversive of the Roman system of rigid class boundaries. And like the Jews and unlike the Romans, the new Christians believed in only one god, not many gods. For their refusal to sacrifice before the statue of the emperor, they were reviled as atheists.

As the following letter shows, Peter advised his people to keep a low profile as citizens; when obedience to Roman law would not require the betrayal of their faith, by all means, obey. Despite their careful behavior, when Nero needed scapegoats after the great fire of Rome in 64 A.D.—which he himself was suspected of starting—he turned on the new community and instigated the persecutions. According to tradition, Peter and Paul, Peter's coworker in Rome, were among the thousands who were murdered. Inspired by the blood of the martyrs, Christians made Rome their "Holy City," the destination of pilgrims for two thousand years.

From I PETER

THE FIRST LETTER OF PETER

I

Peter, apostle of Jesus Christ, sends greetings to all those living among foreigners in the Dispersion of Pontus, Galatia, Cappadocia, Asia and Bithynia, who have been chosen, by the provident purpose of God the Father, to be made holy by the Spirit, obedient to Jesus Christ and sprinkled with his blood. Grace and peace be with you more and more.

Blessed be God the Father of our Lord Jesus Christ, who in his great mercy has given us a new birth as his sons, by raising Jesus Christ from the dead, so that we have a sure hope and the promise of an inheritance that can never be spoilt or soiled and never fade away, because it is being kept for you in the heavens. Through your faith, God's power will guard you until the salvation which has been prepared is revealed at the end of time. This is a cause of great joy for you, even though you may for a short time have to bear being plagued by all sorts of trials; so that, when Jesus Christ is revealed, your faith will have been tested and proved like gold—only it is more precious than gold, which is corruptible even though it bears testing by fire—and then you will have praise and glory and honour. . . .

Free your minds, then, of encumbrances; control them, and put your trust in nothing but the grace that will be given you when Jesus Christ is revealed. Do not behave in the way that you liked to before you learnt the truth; make a habit of obedience: be holy in all you do, since it is the Holy One who has called you, and scripture says: Be holy, for I am holy. . . .

You have been obedient to the truth and purified your souls until you can love like brothers, in sincerity; let your love for each other be real and from the heart—your new birth was not from any mortal seed but from the everlasting word of the living and eternal

God. All flesh is grass and its glory like the wild flower's. The grass withers, the flower falls, but the word of the Lord remains forever. What is this word? It is the Good News that has been brought to you. . . .

2

. . . I urge you, my dear people, while you are visitors and pilgrims, to keep yourselves free from the selfish passions that attack the soul. Always behave honourably among pagans so that they can see your good works for themselves and, when the day of reckoning comes, give thanks to God for the things which now make them denounce you as criminals.

For the sake of the Lord, accept the authority of every social institution: the emperor, as the supreme authority, and the governors as commissioned by him to punish criminals and praise good citizenship. God wants you to be good citizens, so as to silence what fools are saying in their ignorance. You are slaves of no one except God, so behave like free men, and never use your freedom as an excuse for wickedness. Have respect for everyone and love for our community; fear God and honour the emperor.

Slaves must be respectful and obedient to their masters, not only when they are kind and gentle but also when they are unfair. You see, there is some merit in putting up with the pains of unearned punishment if it is done for the sake of God but there is nothing meritorious in taking a beating patiently if you have done something wrong to deserve it. The merit, in the sight of God, is in bearing it patiently when you are punished after doing your duty.

This, in fact, is what you were called to do, because Christ suffered for you and left an example for you to follow the way he took. He had not done anything wrong, and there had been no perjury in his mouth. He was insulted and did not retaliate with insults; when he was tortured he made no threats but he put his trust in the righteous judge. He was bearing our faults in his own body on the cross, so that we might die to our faults and live for holiness;

through his wounds you have been healed. You had gone astray like sheep but now you have come back to the shepherd and guardian of your souls.

3

In the same way, wives should be obedient to their husbands. Then, if there are some husbands who have not yet obeyed the word, they may find themselves won over, without a word spoken, by the way their wives behave, when they see how faithful and conscientious they are. Do not dress up for show: doing up your hair, wearing gold bracelets and fine clothes; all this should be inside, in a person's heart, imperishable: the ornament of a sweet and gentle disposition—this is what is precious in the sight of God. That was how the holy women of the past dressed themselves attractively—they hoped in God and were tender and obedient to their husbands; like Sarah, who was obedient to Abraham, and called him her lord. You are now her children, as long as you live good lives and do not give way to fear or worry.

In the same way, husbands must always treat their wives with consideration in their life together, respecting a woman as one who, though she may be the weaker partner, is equally an heir to the life of grace. This will stop anything from coming in the way of your prayers. . . .

No one can hurt you if you are determined to do only what is right; if you do have to suffer for being good, you will count it a blessing. There is no need to be afraid or to worry about them. Simply reverence the Lord Christ in your hearts, and always have your answer ready for people who ask you the reason for the hope that you all have. But give it with courtesy and respect and with a clear conscience, so that those who slander you when you are living a good life in Christ may be proved wrong in the accusations that they bring. And if it is the will of God that you should suffer, it is better to suffer for doing right than for doing wrong.

For The Literary Traveler

Peter's Rome begins in **Trastevere** ("across the Tiber," *trans Tiberim,* on the left bank), the first and oldest Jewish community in Rome—dating from 200 B.C.—and the oldest in Europe. The first Christians in Rome were Jews, who accounted for 10 percent of the Roman Empire's population. Workers and foreigners—Greeks, Africans, Jews, Gauls, Britons, who disembarked from the ships that sailed up the Tiber from the Mediterranean—lived in this poor neighborhood that would have been the place where Peter landed and began to build his new community.

There's evidence of the ancient Jews and Jewish Christians in the main piazza, in the portico of the **Church of Santa Maria in Trastevere,** one of the oldest—possibly the oldest—church in Rome and the first dedicated to Mary (Miriam in Hebrew). Fragments of stone grave markings are mounted on the wall. You can see the *shofar,* the ram's horn used in Jewish ritual, and the *etrog,* a heart-shaped fruit with a stem, symbolizing a Jew known for learning and good works. You also see the doves that marked the graves of the Jews who joined Rome's first Christian community, which probably began in the fourth decade of the first century. A Jewish catacomb was discovered in Trastevere, but was demolished in the 1930s; the Trastevere railway station was built on the site. The six Roman Jewish catacombs discovered elsewhere in the city in the seventeenth century held the graves of 100,000 Jews buried between the second and fourth centuries A.D.

There were no formal churches in Peter's time. In what is now the church of **Santa Pudenziana**—a five-minute walk from Santa Maria Maggiore, down Via Agostino Depretis and to the left onto Via Urbana—Peter is thought to have enjoyed the hospitality of his friend Pudens, a Roman senator, in his house on this site. The church, which is sinking—you descend 124 steps to the entrance—is dedicated to Pudens's daughter, Pudenziana, who, with her sister Prassede, was converted by Peter. (Prassede has her own church, in the same neighborhood as her sister's; see page 166.) Pudenziana's apse mosaic (390 A.D., the earliest of its kind in Rome) depicts "Christ Enthroned," with two women and two apostles, in togas, dressed like senators. An altar in a north aisle chapel encloses a piece of the legendary table on which Peter offered the Eucharist, the Christian love feast.

Peter's work in Rome came to a horrific end in 67 A.D., when during Nero's reign, he was crucified upside down at his own request, refusing to imitate the death of Jesus too closely. (Caravaggio's paintings of the "Crucifixion of St. Peter" and the "Conversion of St. Paul" are in the church of Santa Maria del Popolo.)

The Roman historian Tacitus provides the details of the early Christians' "farcical deaths":

> Dressed in wild animals' skins, they were torn to pieces by dogs, or crucified, or made into torches to be ignited after dark as substitutes for daylight. Nero provided his Gardens for the spectacle, and exhibited displays in the Circus, at which he mingled with the crowd—or stood in a chariot dressed as a charioteer. . . . the victims were pitied. For it was felt that they were being sacrificed to one man's brutality rather than to the national interest.

Peter's body was buried on **Vatican Hill**—il Vaticano—north of Trastevere on the Tiber's left—west—bank, in the vicinity of Nero's gardens and racetrack, where he died. (The bodies of Peter and Paul were temporarily deposited in the Catacomb of St. Sebastian.) The Emperor Constantine began the building of **St. Peter's Basilica** on this same hill; the first-century tomb of St. Peter, immediately beneath the high altar, may be visited in the **necropolis** beneath the basilica. The burial grounds were discovered in excavations in 1940. Today visitors file through the narrow red-stone passageways, crouching down, whispering, noting the ancient iconography along the dusky maze: Christ as sun-god; the image of a heavy-set fisherman. For many travelers, whether students of history or religious pilgrims, the *scavi* is subterranean Rome at its most affecting, an experience of the mystery of the great city's soul.

*(The entrance to the ticket office for the one-hour tour is to the left of St. Peter's, through the Arco delle Campane, where Swiss Guards stand at attention. Groups are limited to fifteen people. For tickets, apply in writing or in person to the **Ufficio Scavi**, Mon–Fri, 9–5. Tel 06*

6988 53 18. Off season, you have a better chance of joining a tour with-out advance planning. If Peter McQuirk happens to be your tour guide, you're in luck.)

After visiting the *scavi,* if you want to return to Trastevere, where Roman Christian history began, it's a twenty-minute walk south, down the Lungotevere, then to the Via della Lungara—the Tiber is on your left—to the **Porta Settimiana.** You'll pass the **Regina Coeli** prison where Italian and German fascists tortured prisoners in World War II, and where Pope John XXIII visited prisoners on Christmas morning. Re-entering Trastevere's narrow, scruffy, cobble-stoned streets, it's not hard to imagine that in this neighborhood of small ancient stone houses and winding alleys at every turn, many Jews were hidden during the Nazi oc-cupation of 1943. (See page 273.)

An outdoor table at Caffè di Marzio, in **Piazza Santa Maria in Trastevere,** directly across from the Judeo-Christian lapidary in the church's portico, is a good place to stop. (Though Galeassi and Sabatini are more popular with the glitterati). A fountain surges into the air, the church's mosaics of Mary and the Foolish Virgins sparkle on high; ocher and salmon-pink palazzos shelter this lovely space that on summer nights rocks with music and bambini who don't have a bedtime. Inside the magnificent church, the lay Community of St. Egidio, founded in 1968 to carry out the gospel imperatives of peace and justice in the spirit of the early Christians, welcomes visitors to their prayer service, sung every night at 8:30 P.M.

(*For dinner, the* **Paris** *restaurant in the square just off Piazza Santa Maria—through the arch—features fine classic Roman cuisine in a serene atmosphere. [Piazza San Calisto 7A, tel 06 581 5378, reserva-tions necessary, closed Mon.] In the nearby Piazza San Cosimato [32],* **Corsetti's,** *serves excellent salmone alla griglia, and other fine seafood.*)

You can take a beautiful scenic walk from here back to the Vatican, the City of the Church Triumphant, which, depending on your religious affiliation, you may or may not see as part of Peter's Roman legacy. Re-turn to Porta Settimiana, turn left into Via Garibaldi, which takes you up the **Janiculum Hill.** At the first stopping point, just off the road to the right—or, up a flight of stairs—in the piazza of **San Pietro in Monto-**

rio (St. Peter on the Mountain), you see, next to the church, the spot long considered the most sacred in Rome: Bramante's **Tempietto,** a small circular Renaissance temple, where St. Peter was thought to have been (but wasn't) crucified. Inside the church is a painting of Christ's Passion, which Peter may have witnessed in Jerusalem: "The Flagellation" by Sebastiano del Piombo, made to a drawing by Michelangelo.

Climbing higher, you come to the monumental **Acqua Paola** fountain and a beautiful view of the city, the red-tile roofs of Trastevere below, the domes of the great churches—there's Sant'Andrea della Valle where *Tosca* begins—the Villa Medici (or French Academy) across on the Pincian Hill, and Hadrian's Pantheon. On summer nights, concerts are held in the small theater behind the fountain; as music fills the air, the sun sets, and in the distance, Rome turns pink, orange, dark violet. (Tickets at the top of the steps, behind the fountain.)

The ascent continues in two directions: to the right, along a lonely avenue of plane trees and sycamores—the **Passeggiata del Gianicolo**—to the promenade dominated by Garibaldi on his horse and a view of Rome unsurpassed; farther along is Anita Garibaldi on her horse, in one hand holding a gun, in the other her nursing baby. Continue on to see the view of the city and the dome of St. Peter's from the Lighthouse. *Bellissima!* even Romans exclaim.

The other route, beyond the Acqua Paola fountain, continues straight up the road to the **Porta San Pancrazio** at the top. Opposite the gate, at the **Bar Gianicolo,** Joseph Brodsky and other writers-in-residence at the nearby American Academy have enjoyed the coffee; a poem by Brodsky hangs on the wall.

(*In the same small piazza,* **Antico Arco,** *Piazzale Aurelia 7, tel 06 581 5274, closed Sun, and* **Al Tocco,** *Via San Pancrazio 1, closed Mon, are both excellent restaurants, reservations required.*)

From Porta San Pancrazio, continue straight toward the parkland of the **Villa Doria Pamphili,** the umbrella pines rising into the sky, a shelter for joggers, children, couples, dogs. On April 30, 1849, these gardens saw Garibaldi's soldiers and *ragazzi* repel the French, whom Pope Pius IX had summoned to defend him and the Vatican from the forces of Italian unification. In the end, Pio Nono and the French won that round. Garibaldi retreated to Staten Island. Twenty years later he returned, this time a conquering hero. Pio Nono retreated to the Vatican.

To return to St. Peter's from the top of the Janiculum, imitate Rome's stout-hearted first missionary and walk. Via Fornaci cuts straight down to Piazza San Pietro; or return to the Lighthouse, descend the steps at St. Onofrio, and you'll eventually end up in the neighborhood where you started out and where St. Peter died.

ST. PAUL

?–67 A.D.

*Saul, born a Jew in Tarsus, the capital of the Roman province of Cilicia,
persecuted the followers of Jesus in Jerusalem. Caravaggio's painting "The
Conversion of St. Paul" depicts the experience that turned him upside
down, probably around 35 A.D. Struck by spiritual lightning on the road to
Damascus, Saul—his Roman name was Paul—was knocked off his horse
and blinded. Then, as a voice and a great light came out of the heavens, he
experienced a radical change of heart. As a missionary, Paul traveled the
Mediterranean and Aegean, making converts, writing letters to the friends
and communities he encountered on his journeys, again and again getting
arrested and beaten and jailed for causing trouble. A prisoner of the Empire, he asserted his right as a Roman citizen to be tried under Roman law,
after a hearing before the emperor, who happened to be Nero. He was transported in chains, disembarking at Puteoli on the coast of Italy. He walked
to Rome, with his fellow prisoners and slaves, along the Appian Way, the
military road built by slaves for the purpose of their own transport and
where six thousand slaves had been crucified after the failed slave revolt led
by Spartacus. For a long time Paul had promised to visit the Christians in
Rome, possibly on his way to Spain. He'd already written and sent ahead
from Corinth a letter to the Romans, his most important epistle of all, a
part of which follows here. There's no record of how much time he spent in
the city. When Nero presided over the first persecution of the new religion,
Paul, as a Roman citizen, was spared the ignominy of crucifixion. As a
courtesy, they cut off his head.*

From ROMANS

THE LETTER OF PAUL
TO THE CHURCH IN ROME

1

From Paul, a servant of Christ Jesus who has been called to be an apostle, and specially chosen to preach the Good News that God promised long ago through his prophets in the scriptures.

This news is about the Son of God who, according to the human nature he took, was a descendant of David: it is about Jesus Christ our Lord who, in the order of the spirit, the spirit of holiness that was in him, was proclaimed Son of God in all his power through his resurrection from the dead. Through him we received grace and our apostolic mission to preach the obedience of faith to all pagan nations in honour of his name. You are one of these nations, and by his call belong to Jesus Christ. To you all, then, who are God's beloved in Rome, called to be saints, may God our Father and the Lord Jesus Christ send grace and peace. . . .

12

Think of God's mercy, my brothers, and worship him, I beg you, in a way that is worthy of thinking beings, by offering your living bodies as a holy sacrifice, truly pleasing to God. Do not model yourselves on the behaviour of the world around you, but let your behaviour change, modelled by your new mind. This is the only way to discover the will of God and know what is good, what it is that God wants, what is the perfect thing to do.

In the light of the grace I have received I want to urge each one among you not to exaggerate his real importance. Each of you must judge himself soberly by the standard of the faith God has given him. Just as each of our bodies has several parts and each part has a separate function, so all of us, in union with Christ, form one body, and as parts of it we belong to each other. Our gifts differ according to the grace given us. If your gift is prophecy, then use it as your faith suggests; if administration, then use it for administration; if teaching, then use it for teaching. Let the preachers deliver sermons, the almsgivers give freely, the officials be diligent, and those who do works of mercy do them cheerfully.

Do not let your love be a pretence, but sincerely prefer good to evil. Love each other as much as brothers should, and have a profound respect for each other. Work for the Lord with untiring effort and with great earnestness of spirit. If you have hope, this will make you cheerful. Do not give up if trials come; and keep on praying. If any of the saints are in need you must share with them; and you should make hospitality your special care.

Bless those who persecute you: never curse them, bless them. Rejoice with those who rejoice and be sad with those in sorrow. Treat everyone with equal kindness; never be condescending but make real friends with the poor. Do not allow yourself to become self-satisfied. Never repay evil with evil but let everyone see that you are interested only in the highest ideals. Do all you can to live at peace with everyone. Never try to get revenge; leave that, my friends, to God's anger. As scripture says: Vengeance is mine—I will pay them back, the Lord promises. But there is more: If your enemy is hungry, you should give him food, and if he is thirsty, let him drink. Thus you heap red-hot coals on his head. Resist evil and conquer it with good.

13

You must all obey the governing authorities. Since all government comes from God, the civil authorities were appointed by God, and so anyone who resists authority is rebelling against God's decision, and such an act is bound to be punished. Good behaviour is not afraid of magistrates; only criminals have anything to fear. If you want to live without being afraid of authority, you must live honestly and authority may even honour you. The state is there to serve God for your benefit. If you break the law, however, you may well have fear: the bearing of the sword has its significance. The authorities are there to serve God: they carry out God's revenge by punishing wrongdoers. You must obey, therefore, not only because you are afraid of being punished, but also for conscience' sake. This is also the reason why you must pay taxes, since all government officials are God's officers. They serve God by collecting taxes. Pay every government official what he has a right to ask—whether it be direct tax or indirect, fear or honour.

Avoid getting into debt, except the debt of mutual love. If you love your fellow men you have carried out your obligations. All the commandments: You shall not commit adultery, you shall not kill, you shall not steal, you shall not covet, and so on, are summed up in this single command: You must love your neighbour as yourself. Love is the one thing that cannot hurt your neighbour; that is why it is the answer to every one of the commandments.

Besides, you know "the time" has come: you must wake up now: our salvation is even nearer than it was when we were converted. The night is almost over, it will be daylight soon—let us give up all the things we prefer to do under cover of the dark; let us arm ourselves and appear in the light. Let us live decently as people do in the daytime: no drunken orgies, no promiscuity or licentiousness, and no wrangling or jealousy. Let your armour be the Lord Jesus Christ; forget about satisfying your bodies with all their cravings. . . .

15

It is not because I have any doubts about you, my brothers; on the contrary I am quite certain that you are full of good intentions, perfectly well instructed and able to advise each other. The reason why I have written to you, and put some things rather strongly, is to refresh your memories, since God has given me this special position. He has appointed me as a priest of Jesus Christ, and I am to carry out my priestly duty by bringing the Good News from God to the pagans, and so make them acceptable as an offering, made holy by the Holy Spirit.

I think I have some reason to be proud of what I, in union with

Christ Jesus, have been able to do for God. What I am presuming to speak of, of course, is only what Christ himself has done to win the allegiance of the pagans, using what I have said and done by the power of signs and wonders, by the power of the Holy Spirit. Thus, all the way along, from Jerusalem to Illyricum, I have preached Christ's Good News to the utmost of my capacity. I have always, however, made it an unbroken rule never to preach where Christ's name has already been heard. The reason for that was that I had no wish to build on other men's foundations; on the contrary, my chief concern has been to fulfil the text: Those who have never been told about him will see him, and those who have never heard about him will understand.

That is the reason why I have been kept from visiting you so long, though for many years I have been longing to pay you a visit. Now, however, having no more work to do here, I hope to see you on my way to Spain and, after enjoying a little of your company, to complete the rest of the journey with your good wishes. . . .

16

I commend to you our sister Phoebe, a deaconess of the church at Cenchreae. Give her, in union with the Lord, a welcome worthy of saints, and help her with anything she needs: she has looked after a great many people, myself included.

My greetings to Prisca and Aquila, my fellow workers in Christ Jesus, who risked death to save my life: I am not the only one to owe them a debt of gratitude, all the churches among the pagans do as well. My greetings also to the church that meets at their house.

Greetings to my friend Epaenetus, the first of Asia's gifts to Christ; greetings to Mary who worked so hard for you; to those outstanding apostles Andronicus and Junias, my compatriots and fellow prisoners who became Christians before me; to Ampliatus, my friend in the Lord; to Urban, my fellow worker in Christ; to my friend Stachys; to Apelles who has gone through so much for

Christ; to everyone who belongs to the household of Aristobulus; to my compatriot Herodion; to those in the household of Narcissus who belong to the Lord; to Tryphaena and Tryphosa, who work hard for the Lord; to my friend Persis who has done so much for the Lord; to Rufus, a chosen servant of the Lord, and to his mother who has been a mother to me too. Greetings to Asyncritus, Phlegon, Hermes, Patrobas, Hermas, and all the brothers who are with them; to Philologus and Julia, Nereus and his sister, and Olympas and all the saints who are with them. Greet each other with a holy kiss. All the churches of Christ send greetings.

I implore you, brothers, be on your guard against anybody who encourages trouble or puts difficulties in the way of the doctrine you have been taught. Avoid them. People like that are not slaves of Jesus Christ, they are slaves of their own appetites, confusing the simple-minded with their pious and persuasive arguments. Your fidelity to Christ, anyway, is famous everywhere, and that makes me very happy about you.

FOR THE LITERARY TRAVELER

Paul the traveler made friends on his journeys. His letter to the Romans mentions them by name. Prisca, whom he calls a "fellow worker in Christ Jesus," a woman he'd met in Corinth, along with her husband, Aquila, were leaders of their house-church high on the Aventine Hill, now the **Church of St. Prisca** (a short climb from Viale Aventino/Piazza Albania). "Salute, Prisca and Aquila," Paul wrote, "and the church that is in their house." The early Christians, including Peter, who may have baptized Prisca and Aquila, would have gathered here to listen to Prisca's preaching and to share the bread and wine of their love feast. Prisca's colleagues included other women whom Paul mentions in *Romans*. He describes Tryphaena, Tryphosa, and Persis as "working hard in the Lord"; they're ministers having authority within the community. Another woman, Junia, he characterizes as "outstanding among the apostles" (Romans, 16:7). Later translators sex-changed Junia; she became the masculine "Junius." Paul's friendly acceptance of his female coworkers raises the question of the misogyny and sexism of which he is often accused. In *Eunuchs for the Kingdom of Heaven: Women, Sexuality and the Catholic Church,* Catholic theologian and feminist Uta Ranke-Heinemann defends Paul; so does Karen Armstrong in *The Spiral Staircase:* he's been misrepresented, mistranslated, and taken out of context. They cite examples. Accused of telling women to keep quiet in church, Paul actually reports "that women preached during the liturgy just as men did" (1 Corinthians, 11:5). Current biblical scholarship says he didn't write 1 Timothy, which urges women to be silent and submissive. Rather, Paul tells of women "prophesying," which means "preaching." He calls his coworker Phoebe "a deacon," or minister, which is how he describes his own role.

Michele Roberts's wonderful novel *Impossible Saints* presents a virile Paul, a man charged not only with spiritual vision and a love of travel but with sexual energy and a passion for a woman named Thecla. (The apocryphal *Acts of Paul and Thecla* describe him as bald, bowlegged, and with a rather large nose.) Whatever his appearance, the Roman state must have found the fearless Paul a grave threat. "No longer Jew or Greek, slave or free, male or female, for we are all one in Christ Jesus," he wrote to the Galatians (3:28). It was never in the Roman stars that such an egalitarian could survive within the belly of the empire, a system made to preserve and defend every conceivable pattern of master-slave domination. Pagan writers (Pliny, Lucius Apuleius, Galen) commented that the freedom and initiative allowed to early Christian women were subverting the Greek and Roman order of women's roles.

It is said Paul lived under house arrest for two years before he died, that he (and Peter) were imprisoned in the **Mamertine Prison,** which can be visited beside the Roman Forum. It is also thought that Paul and Peter must have worked together, meeting at the gatherings of Jewish Christians in Trastevere. But because the early Christians came mainly from the lower classes, the gentlemen historians of the ancient world largely ignored them. Early Roman Christianity remains pretty anonymous, most of it buried, along with the history of women and of slavery, under centuries of indifference.

Paul's presence in Rome is commemorated mostly in places connected with his death. According to some Christian historians, if you leave Rome through St. Paul's Gate, or **Porta San Paolo,** along the Via Ostiense—on bus 23—you're following the route he took on the way to his martyrdom on the site of the abbey of **Tre Fontane.** The gate was not yet built in his time, but he would have seen the Pyramid of Cestius, built in 18–12 B.C. as the tomb of Cestius, praetor (chief magistrate), tribune of the plebs, and a state priest in charge of banquets honoring Jupiter. The pyramidal design, indicating he probably served in Egypt, shadows the beautiful Protestant Cemetery (see page 228).

Though Paul's last journey is believed to have ended at what is now the Trappist Abbey of the Three Fountains in Laurentina, you can detour along the way to visit **San Paolo fuori le Mura** or the basilica of St. Paul Outside the Walls on Via Ostiense, built to hold Paul's body, supposedly buried in a vineyard on this site along the ancient Ostian Way, by a Roman woman named Lucina. There's a large necropolis, as yet unexcavated, beneath this basilica, which, more than any other in Rome, has the size and feeling of the pagan basilicas reproduced in the Christian models. It's a cold place, a vastness which only tourists' kids, chasing and sliding across the marble floors on a hot summer Sunday, seem to like. ("This could be a dance hall!") The chill also pervades the large gift shop, operated by grumpy veiled clerks. When you enter the **Cloister,** however (the entrance is from the gift shop), you enter another world. Whereas the austere basilica freezes you out, this twelfth-century columned space invites us in. You can imagine George Herbert here, writing his poem, "Love bade me welcome . . ."

From a square opposite the basilica's north transept, on Via Placido Riccardi, take bus 761 out to Via Laurentina, where you get off and immediately cross the road to the entrance to **Tre Fontane.** The driveway, bordered by a forest of eucalyptus trees, leads to the medieval gatehouse where you can see a portion of the old Roman road which Paul, according to tradition, traveled on the way to his execution in 67 A.D. The Church of the Three Fountains—the site of his beheading, according to the story—is named after the report that Paul's decapitated head bounced three times and at each place where it did a fountain of water sprang up. On weekends Tre Fontane is crowded with Italian pilgrims.

After the tour buses depart, however, this legendary crime scene becomes an oasis, the fragrance of roses, eucalyptus, and pines, the sounds of cooing pigeons and flowing water soothing in the summer heat. Inside the gatehouse, a gift shop offers eucalyptus liqueurs, honey, and chocolate, made by monks.

MARGARET VISSER

1940–

In The Geometry of Love, *classicist, world traveler, and award-winning Canadian author Margaret Visser explores the significance of the church building and reads the ancient church of Sant'Agnese fuori le Mura— St. Agnes Outside the Walls—as if it were a text. For travelers to Rome, whether believers or not, she performs a helpful service. For Rome is a city of churches. A writer whose knowledge spans art and ecclesiastical architecture, theology, and history and folklore is a resource to treasure.*

❧

From THE GEOMETRY OF LOVE:
SPACE, TIME, MYSTERY, AND MEANING IN AN ORDINARY CHURCH

I.
THE DOOR SWINGS OPEN:
THRESHOLD

The church stands with its back to the road. It turns away, quietly guarding its secret.

For more than 1,350 years it has stood by the road, and around it once stretched open fields and vineyards. The massive brick walls and towers that encircled the city of Rome were clearly and unforgettably visible, cutting across the landscape to the south.

If you arrive today, say by bus—a two-kilometre ride from Termini Station—you will have to cross the busy road you came on, from the bus stop near a fountain captured in stone. *Acqua Marcia* is inscribed on it, in memory of Rome's first important aqueduct, constructed in 144 B.C. Within the last hundred years or so, the view from here of the city walls has been blocked as the area became first a suburb and then a fairly central district of modern Rome.

Having reached the pavement opposite the bus stop, you look through an iron gate with a walkway leading to a closed door under a porch. To the left of it stands the brick back of the church and its medieval tower—not by any means a spectacular tower, but a strong and graceful one nonetheless. The building not only conceals what it contains, it also marks the spot.

To find an entrance to the building, you can take a small descending side road on your right to a break in the wall on the left; this gateway is invisible from the main street. Or you must walk along the pavement, as I did the first time I came here, and brave a small porch with an arch on columns and a painting over the door, at number 349 Via Nomentana; it lets you into a solid medieval monastery building with yellow ochre walls. Once you have crossed into the precinct, you must traverse a courtyard, then walk through the vaulted space that supports another medieval tower, and enter a door on your right. You find yourself at the top of a broad staircase, forty-five steps in all, descending into the church. You realize, with a shock, that the church floor is deep down; the building is much higher inside than it looks from the street. For almost a millennium, until the year 1600, the church was half buried. Only its upper level rose above ground.

The floor level is the same as one of the levels of the catacomb into which the church has been built. These narrow tunnels, with graves cut one above the other into their earthen sides, snake out underneath all of the area hereabouts. There is another, much larger catacomb almost adjoining this one; its entrance is just a street block away. The entrance to a smaller, uninvestigated warren has also been discovered. The thundering main road outside, carrying the bus or car you arrived in, passes over a section of the catacombs. There are thousands of graves—in 1924, 5,753 of them had been counted—and several kilometres of tunnelling, not all of which has yet been explored.

A single grave among all the rest gives its name to this catacomb and to the church sunk into it: the grave of Agnes, a twelve-year-old girl who was murdered in A.D. 305. She has never been forgotten; the building remembers her. . . .

Audiences: Church and Theatre

Memory, in a church, is not only individual, but also collective: the building is a meeting house for a group of people who agree with each other in certain important respects. They come together to express solidarity, and they do this by participating in an intensely meaningful performance known as a ritual.

The closest relative of a church is a theatre, where people also come together to witness a scripted performance. There is a stage in a church, and seats for the audience; in both theatre and church, people come in order to live together through a trajectory of the soul. They come to be led by the performance to achieve contact with transcendence, to experience delight or recognition, to understand something they never understood before, to feel relief, to stare in amazement, or to cry. They want something that shakes them up—or gives them peace. Successful drama, like a well-performed ritual, can provoke an experience of transcendence: through feeling, for example, two contradictory emotions at once. Aristotle spoke of *katharsis*—"purification"—as the aim of tragedy. Catharsis, he said, is achieved by undergoing two opposing movements of the soul—pity (feeling for, and therefore drawing close) and fear (longing to move out of the danger's range)—at the same time.

In a theatre the audience is the receiver of a play, and essential to a play. At an ancient Greek drama the audience was indeed part of the spectacle. The form of the theatre, a huge horseshoe shape, ensured that this was so. The Greek theatres that survive today allow us to imagine what it must have been like, sitting in a vast crowd of fellow citizens with everyone spread out in full view, in broad daylight, fanning out to embrace the round dancing-floor below them. Actors say that an audience can draw out of them their best performances, just through the quality of its attention, its intentness.

A theatre is like a church—not the other way round. "Church" or "temple" is the main category, and "theatre" a division of it. Historically, drama grew out of religious performance (and never entirely left it) in a process wherein the play gradually separated itself from the crowd watching. The distance between watcher and watched is essential to theatrical experience. ("Theatre" comes from Greek *theatron,* a place for viewing.) People come together in a church, however, not to view but to take part. The word "church" comes from Greek *kyriakon,* "house of the Lord"; it is a place of encounter between people and God.

It is perfectly possible to be moved at a spiritual level at the theatre; one can open oneself and be brought to mystical insight, as Aristotle showed us, through attentive watching. (Such experiences, however, can occur anywhere, at any time—indeed, they seem to prefer arriving when we are least expecting them, at times and places we would be least inclined to call "appropriate.") But a performance in a church is permitted to involve people to an extent that the theatre traditionally avoids. People come to participate in it, to join in, and then allow the realization to enter them and work upon them. The whole point of the proceedings is to help them change the orientation of their souls, even though they are also confirming the foundation of their beliefs. They have come to meet, to make the ceremony, and to respond, at a level that may include but goes well beyond the aesthetic. But a church can go on "working" even when there is no performance and no crowd. A person can come into a silent church in order to respond to the building and its meaning. This can produce an experience as profoundly moving as that of attending a performance. The same thing cannot be said of visiting an empty theatre.

Meaning and Response

A church like Sant'Agnese fuori le Mura (Saint Agnes Outside the Walls) vibrates with intentionality. It is meaningful—absolutely nothing in it is without significance. Even if something is inadvertently included that has no meaning to start with, a meaning for it will be found, inevitably. A church stands in total opposition to the narrowing and flattening of human experience, the deviation into the trivial, that follow from antipathy towards meaning, and especially meaning held in common. Meaning is intentional: this building has been made in order to communicate with the people in it. A church is no place to practise aesthetic distance, to erase content and simply appreciate form. The building is trying to speak; not listening to what it has to say is a form of barbarous inattention, like admiring a musical instrument while caring nothing for music. . . .

The Light and the Life: The Catacombs

After traversing the dim passage through the maze of catacomb galleries, a visitor today standing underneath the church before the grave of Agnes and Emerentiana* may (if he or she wishes) consider many things, remember many a moment of insight. The silver coffin with the bones of two young women inside it can embody and recall, for example, a person's deepest desire, or a specific experience of grace in the life of the beholder at the end of a long "dark night of the soul." It can remind the visitor of seventeen centuries of faithful memory, of the long history of this place, and of the story of the death of Agnes.

It will certainly recall to Christians the words of Jesus: "I tell you, most solemnly, that unless a wheat grain falls on the ground and dies, it remains only a single grain; but if it dies, it yields much fruit." Because of the story of Agnes, the little grave caused an oratory to be built, then a church, and then this basilica, just as the Christian community grew from small, poor, and unpromising beginnings. The whole building is rooted in this coffin, just as the Church lives still out of the spiritual conviction, the courage, and the generosity of its members—out of the choice, continually to be made by Christians just as it had to be made by Agnes and Emerentiana, of love over hatred, greed, selfishness, and violence.

---

*Agnes's sister.

For The Literary Traveler

The ride out along Via Nomentana to **Sant'Agnese fuori Le Mura**—buses 36, 37, 60, 136, or a taxi to the cross street, Via di S. Costanza—passes **Porta Pia,** the gate designed by Michelangelo in 1561 which later admitted liberators: in 1870 the army fighting for a united Italy, under Garibaldi's command, which ended the temporal power of the papacy; in 1944, the American Allies, ending the German occupation.

Visiting Sant'Agnese in this ancient neighborhood where St. Peter is said to have performed baptisms, you've left behind the popular routes of most tourists. The quiet detachment of Visser's narrative suits the subdued atmosphere of Sant'Agnese. The tour of the **Catacombs of Sant'Agnese,** considered the best preserved in Rome, is also uncrowded and intense. "Reading" this church, guided by Visser's excavations of hidden meanings, prepares you for the often obscure language of Rome's other earliest churches. What becomes evident as you visit them is that the ruins of private Rome, as opposed to the public Forum or the Colosseum—the houses, mausoleums, tenements, the meeting places of the pagan cults—are often to be found beneath these early Christian houses of worship. What follows here is a selection of these ancient layered houses, each memorable for an atmosphere, or a striking detail that comes back long after you've left the city behind. "It seemed to me hopeless to make a methodical round of all Rome's churches," said Elizabeth Bowen.

San Clemente. (A ten-minute walk east of the Colosseum, up Via San Giovanni In Laterano, past the Ludus Magnus, on the left.) According to lovers of Rome who are given to reciting their "favorites" when they bump into other *romanistas* around the world, the apse of this medieval church has the loveliest mosaic your eyes will ever rest upon. Below the church you descend into the cool damp of a first-century Roman house (the House of Clemens, freedman), and below that into a well-preserved and creepy second-century B.C. Mithraeum (*mitreo* in Italian), the sacred space of the Mithraic pagan cult, open to military males only. To fortify their commitment to war, they drank bull's blood, after killing the bull. Deep in the underground of San Clemente, you hear the rushing water of a stream that once flowed through this neighborhood and to this day flows into the drainage system—the Cloaca Maxima built by the Etruscans—that empties into the Tiber. The sound of the stream in these hidden cellars brings to mind the currents of all the buried under-grounds, where the past makes itself present. On summer nights, con-certs of Mozart, Vivaldi, and Bach stir the heart in San Clemente's lovely colonnaded layered courtyard (tickets at the door).

(**Caffè San Clemente,** *across from the side entrance, serves light fare before and after concerts. There's a taxi stand in front of the nearby hotel on Via Labicana, parallel to Via San Giovanni in Laterano*).

Santa Maria in Cosmedin. (Five minutes from the Circus Maximus, down the hill on Via Del Circo Massimo / Via Di Greca, in Piazza Della Bocca Della Verità.) It's the darkness that makes this church compelling at first, then the apse. As the tourists who stop to see the stone Bocca della Verità—Mouth of Truth—in the portico suddenly rush the nave, then the gift shop, it turns carnivalesque. When the tour buses roar off, you again stand awed by the stillness, the language of a house of prayer. In the crypt are columns of an altar dedicated to Hercules; the side walls belong to the sixth-century Christian welfare center (*diaconia*) that preceded the eighth-century church. You can see Cosmedin's gra-cious seven-story campanile from the Tiber bridges and the Janiculum.

Santa Sabina. Some find this Dominican church on the Aventine Hill cold; others name it a favorite, "perhaps the most beautiful basilica in Rome," according to Alta Macadam's *Blue Guide*. (Ten minutes uphill from the Circus Maximus; or, a prettier, more pastoral climb, on the Clivo Di Rocca Savelli from the Lungotevere Aventino.) The carved doors bear the first known image of the crucifixion of Christ. In the side chapel of St. Hyacinth or San Giacinto, with dismal frescoes by the Zuccari brothers, there's a painting of the Madonna and Child, glorious in after-noon sunlight. The artist's name, Renaissance painter Lavinia Fontana, appears in none of the guidebooks or on the postcard of the painting sold in the gift shop. St. Dominic's room, now a chapel, overlooks the cloister of Santa Sabina; a Dominican friar or the friendly nuns residing in the convent will admit you, if they're at home. (Ring at the reception desk.) The adjoining Parco Savello, planted with orange trees, has one of the finest views of St. Peter's dome in the city.

*(The famous keyhole of the Knights of Malta is at the other end of Via di Santa Sabina, next to the Benedictine St. Anselm's where Edith Wharton attended Vespers; Gregorian chant is sung at Sunday Mass at 9:30. Wandering the quiet residential streets of the Aventine, supposedly the site of a temple of the goddess Diana, you'll come to the Hill's only restaurant, **Apuleius.** The worship of Diana, according to the owner, took place in what is now the rear dining room, used for banquets.)*

Santa Maria Maggiore or St. Mary Major. (A half-hour walk from San Giovanni in Laterano—St. John Lateran—down Via Merulana, a broad tree-lined street, originally named Via Gregoriana. Henry James liked Maggiore, one of the four patriarchal basilicas. The others are St. Peter's, the Lateran, and St. Paul Outside the Walls. Maggiore's fifth-century nave mosaics are splendid, the campanile is the tallest in the city, on weekends the side chapels and high altar are cacophanous with sung and shouty liturgies, hideously miked, a heteroglossic orgy. (Maggiore's newly appointed archpriest is Cardinal Bernard Law, formerly of Boston.)

*(Near Via Merulana is the acclaimed restaurant **Agata e Romeo,** Via Carlo Alberto 45, tel 06 446 6115; **I Buoni Amici,** Via Aleardo Aleardi 4, tel 06 704 91993, is a good inexpensive trattoria; **Ornelli,** Via Merulana 224, is a wonderful bar / gelateria—offering twenty-eight flavors— a favorite with Romans and the many pellegrini [pilgrims] walking between the Lateran and Maggiore.)*

Santi Giovanni e Paolo. (From the Colosseum, this off-the-beaten-track architectural gem is about a fifteen-minute walk up the Caelian Hill on Via Claudia, heading southeast.) "No spot in Rome can show a cluster of more charming accidents," said Henry James. For a fee, the sacristan will take you down to the complex of rooms and frescoed walls from the second and third centuries. Above ground, the ancient portico and the Romanesque dark red campanile date the church as early Christian. Beside it, a two-thousand-year-old narrow street called the Clivus Scauri, or Clivio di Scauro, runs downhill beneath medieval arches. Descending, you see the slopes of the Palatine, a forest of cypresses, rising in front of you.

(Along the Clivio, near the church of St. Gregorio Magno, is the entrance to a walled park of flowers, a boat fountain, and a children's

playground, **Villa Celimontana,** *formerly a private estate, now a well-kept secret hideaway. Free concerts are held here in summer.*)

Sant'Eustachio. Sitting outdoors at one of the cafes in the Piazza of Sant'Eustachio, opposite the church, looking up at the rooftop stag's head and the campanile, you're on ancient ground. The piazza is sinking, for one thing. From Camilloni à Sant'Eustachio Caffè you can see Borromini's campanile on the church of St. Ivo (See page 150.)

San Lorenzo fuori le Mura. Begun by Emperor Constantine in 330. Everything about this sanctuary is moving, including the memory of its bombardment in World War II and the neighborhood's poor who suffered hundreds of civilian casualties after the Allied bombing of 1943. (Their target was the nearby Tiburtina train station.) This is the world of Elsa Morante's *History: A Novel.* (See pages 276–92.)

Santa Maria in Trastevere. (See page 77.)

Santa Prassede. (See page 166.)

Santa Maria Sopra Minerva. (See page 251.)

"Creative fictions," Margaret Visser's phrase for the stories of the Roman martyrs, might apply to everything we think we know about ancient and early Christian Rome. Next door to St. Agnes Outside the Walls stands another building, rich in stories, scant on facts.

It goes by two names: the **Mausoleum of Constantia;** and the **Church of Santa Costanza** (St. Constance). Constantia was the elder daughter of Emperor Constantine who, having made Christianity the state religion during his lifetime, was baptized a Christian on his deathbed. Constantia built this round tomb for herself, her sister Helena, and maybe her husband. She's variously described as a Christian lady, a nun, and a nasty, grasping bourgeois. Whatever her virtue or vices, her tomb's interior is exquisite, a perfect setting for Roman weddings, those extravaganzas of flowers, families, and rambunctious ringbearers celebrated regularly here throughout the summer. Georgina Masson declares the decorative vaulting—San Clemente *afficionadas,* take note—"probably the most beautiful mosaics in Rome, graceful and free . . . absolutely devoid of Christian content." Against a white background, brightly colored cupids, sheep, and peacocks play amid the flowers and fruits of the vines; the making of wine is represented as ritualized pleasure, you can almost hear the flutes piping in the background. Rome's "most lyrical mosaics," said Elizabeth Bowen.

Visiting Sant'Agnese and Constantia's tomb on the same day (the tomb is across a garden and up a wide path), you realize the intertwining of the Rome of pagan antiquity and of Catholic Rome, a coexistence still in play, the very texture of the movies of Fellini.

(*If you'd like to see how Rome looked before the Christian era, and then in the time of Constantine, there are two plaster scale models in the Museum of Roman Civilization at **EUR** [Universal Exhibition of Rome], a hugely ugly white marble complex—built in 1938 to show the glories of fascism—about nine miles [thirty minutes] from the city center. Take the 714 and 761 bus, along the Via Cristoforo Colombo to Piazza Agnelli 10; or take the Metro, linea B, or a taxi, for about $9.00. Enter through the right wing [9–6:45; 9–1:30 Sun; tel 06 59 26041; closed Mon; www.romaeur.it/ing/musei/home.htm]. The famous model of Constantinian Rome is in the opposite—left—wing across the colonnaded piazza.)*

RENAISSANCE AND BAROQUE ROME

❧

*Michelangelo ❧ Vittoria Colonna ❧ Sigmund Freud
Susan Vreeland ❧ Simon Schama*

*The Renaissance . . . which was only one of many results of a
general excitement and enlightening of the human mind . . . the
care for physical beauty, the worship of the body, the breaking down
of those limits which the religious system of the middle age imposed
on the heart and the imagination . . .*

—WALTER PATER, *THE RENAISSANCE*

MICHELANGELO BUONARROTI

1475–1564

Rome wouldn't be Rome without Michelangelo, the sculptor, architect, and painter who brought the Renaissance from Florence, where it started, to Rome, where papal patronage made it flourish. Travelers track his art with a passionate thoroughness, though in "The Love Song of J. Alfred Prufrock," T. S. Elliot makes the passion feminine, and passive: "In the room the women come and go / Talking of Michelangelo."

Michelangelo was also the most powerful lyric poet of the Italian Renaissance, which few visitors realize. His 300 sonnets and songs, sometimes written down on the margins of his sketches, have the "sweetness and strength" that Walter Pater defines as the character of the "Michelangelesque." The most famous poems—which follow here—concern the painting of the Sistine Chapel (though he liked to say he was no painter); the art of sculpture (which he called his "true profession"); and his "chaste autumnal love" for the poet Vittoria Colonna. Their intense friendship began in 1542, when he was almost seventy (see page 112).

🦎

I' ho Già Fatto Un Gozzo In Questo Stento,*

> This comes of dangling from the ceiling—*
> I'm goitered like a Lombard cat
> (or wherever else their throats grow fat)—
> it's my belly that's beyond concealing,
> it hangs beneath my chin like peeling.
> My beard points skyward, I seem a bat
> upon its back, I've breasts and splat!
> On my face the paint's congealing.

---

*The title of each poem is translated in the first line of each poem.

Loins concertina'd in my gut,
I drop an arse as counterweight
and move without the help of eyes.
Like a skinned martyr I abut
on air, and, wrinkled, show my fate.
Bow-like, I strain towards the skies.

No wonder then I size
things crookedly; I'm on all fours.
Bent blowpipes send their darts off-course.

Defend my labour's cause,
good Giovanni, from all strictures:
I live in hell and paint its pictures.
(Girardi, 5, 1509–10.)

Colui che fece, e non di cosa alcuna,*

(To Tommaso Cavalieri?)

The Creator, who from nothingness could make*
all Time and every creature in the void,
divided Time: He kept the sun employed
by day, the moon He set in night's dark lake.
Thus fortune, chance and fate are all awake
to fix for each what no man can avoid;
to me they give that time of sun devoid,
a dark which at my birth set up the stake.
And like a shadow which must imitate
itself, as night advancing darker grows,
so I in sin advancing grieve and mourn.
Some consolation yet this gift creates:
your sun is born for me whose brightness shows
through my dark night and ushers in the dawn.
(Girardi, 104, 1535–41?)

Non Ha L'ottimo Artista Alcun Concetto*†

To Vittoria Colonna

No block of marble but it does not hide*
the concept living in the artist's mind—
pursuing it inside that form, he'll guide
his hand to shape what reason has defined.
The ill I flee, the good I hope to find
in you, exalted lady of true pride,
are also circumscribed; and yet I'm lied
to by my art which to my will is blind.
Love's not to blame, nor your severity,
disdainful beauty, nor what fortune shows,
or destiny: I fixed my own ill course.
Though death and mercy side by side I see
lodged in your heart, my passion only knows
how to carve death: this is my skill's poor force.
(1538–41/4.)

A L'alta Tuo Lucente Diadema

To Vittoria Colonna

To your resplendent beauty's diadem*
no one may hope to rise, O Lady,
except by long and steep ascent—the way
on high is by your gentle courtesy.
My strength is failing me, I spend
my breath half-way—I fall, I stray,
and yet your beauty makes me happy
and nothing else can please my heart
in love with everything sublime
but that, descending here to me

---

†This is Michelangelo's most famous poem.

on earth, you are not set apart.
It comforts me meantime,
forseeing your disdain, that this my crime
pardons in you the bringing of such light
down so closely from your hated height.
(Girardi, 156)

Com'esser, donna, può quel c'alcun vede*

To Vittoria Colonna

How chances it, my Lady, that we must*
from long experience learn that what endures
in stone is but the image it immures
though he who liberates it turn to dust?
This cause to its effect will so adjust
that our fine work defeat of time ensures.
I know this true and prove it in my sculptures:
art lives forever, death forfeits its trust.
Therefore, long life in colours or with stone,
in either form, I give to you and me
and our own two resemblances devise,
and for a thousand years when we have gone
posterity will find my woe, your beauty
matched, and know my loving you was wise.
(Girardi, 239, 1545?)

For The Literary Traveler

Michelangelo made a sketch of himself to accompany this first sonnet:
The flat-nosed Florentine, scrunched but standing inside the scaffolding
he'd designed to hold him, his paintbrushes and pigments, sixty feet
above the floor of the **Sistine Chapel,** within arm's length of the
12,000-square-foot ceiling he'd been commissioned to paint by *il papa
terribile,* Julius II. Working for four years (1508–1512) in this tortuous
position, Michelangelo did in fact develop the goiter he refers to in the

poem. The subject matter of the vault, he told his biographer, Ascanio Condivi, was also of his own devising. Julius gave him free rein "to do what I liked." What he liked was to give a heroic shape, in the boldest mix of color and light, to his vision of cosmic time: creation itself—the subject of the second poem, "The Creator"—culminates in Christ who is the alpha and omega of history, a point of view appropriate for this first chapel of Catholic Christendom in which popes, the lords of the kingdom, are still elected in secret conclave. The more than 300 figures and 150 separate pictures you lean back and look up at are considered "the greatest pictorial decoration in Western art," by every art historian under the sun, a rather textbookish take on the splendor up there. The creamy-golden blush of the Cumaean Sibyl. The magisterial Hebrew prophets. The expectancy of Adam as he reaches out for life. (Yet, there is poor abject Eve! "Take the snake, the fruit-tree and the woman from the tableau," said Elizabeth Cady Stanton, and "the bottom falls out of Christian theology.")

On the east wall, at the far end, above the altar is "The Last Judgment," commissioned and created years later (1535–1541), after Martin Luther's revolt had changed the mood of the Church forever. If certain clergy had been repelled by the *ignudi* on the Sistine ceiling—the pairs of muscular male nudes—the swirling nudity in the altar painting that Michelangelo called the "Resurrection"—318 bodies have been counted—aroused their wrath. The infamous Pope Paul IV, who in 1555 established the Jewish Ghetto (see page 277), would denounce it as "a stew of nudes." Then, in 1564, the Counter-Reformation's Council of Trent ordered a cover-up. A student of Michelangelo was commissioned to "dress" the fresco, a travesty the artist didn't live to see.

In the reactionary culture that demanded breeches on Michelangelo's saints and sinners, Walter Pater felt a loss of soul, a spiritual death from which Catholic Christendom has never recovered:

The "new catholicism" had taken the place of the Renaissance. The spirit of the Roman church had changed: in the vast world's cathedral which [Michelangelo's] skill had helped to raise for it, it looked stronger than ever. . . . The opposition of the reformation to art has been often enlarged upon; far greater was that of the

Catholic revival. But in thus fixing itself in a frozen orthodoxy, the Roman Church had passed beyond him, and he was a stranger to it.

"The nearer painting approaches sculpture, the better it is," Michelangelo said in a letter. In his third poem—"No block of marble but it does not hide"—he put the meaning of his sculptural art into words just as Michelangelo the sculptor struggled to bring life to blocks of stone.

Leaving the Sistine Chapel, visit the **Pio-Clementino Museum** and **Cortile Ottagono,** the largest collection of ancient sculpture in the world; it includes pieces that Michelangelo loved: the **Laocoon** group and the **Belvedere Torso,** found in Rome and installed by Julius II in the original Vatican Museums around the time Michelangelo was working on the ceiling. In the agonized contortions of the Laocoon and the musculature of the Torso, you see the bodies of the Sistine frescoes. In the Gabinetto dell'Apollo, you'll find the most famous work of ancient sculpture in the world, the Apollo Belvedere, an emblem of ideal beauty in "The Wedding Journey" chapters of George Eliot's *Middlemarch.*

(*It helps to arrive at the **Vatican Museums** at 8:45 A.M., when they open. Closings at 4:45 Mon–Fri, 1:45 Sat in Mar–Oct; Nov–Feb, 1:45 every day. The later you get there, the longer the lines, at least in summer. A shuttle bus from Piazza San Pietro to the entrance on Viale Vaticano leaves half past the hour. Seeing the Museums in one visit can feel like punishment. "Staid in Vatican till closed," Herman Melville wrote in 1857. "Fagged out completely, and sat long time by the obelisk, recovering from the stunning effect. . . ." But if you only have time for one visit, head straight for the Sistine Chapel when the Museums open. Outside the entrance vestibule, Quattro Cancelli, there's a cafe, with benches on the outdoor terraces; in summer, a small cafe is open near the Sistine Chapel. High on his scaffold, Michelangelo was said to ignore the stifling summer heat as well as the constant pestering of his "Holy Lord" Julius about how much longer the work was going to take. "It will be finished," he said, "when I shall have satisfied myself in the matter of art."*)

From the Museums, it's a twenty-minute walk back to **St. Peter's.** Inside the basilica, at the front of a small chapel on your right, behind glass, the white Carrara marble of Michelangelo's **Pietà** expresses the tenderness and sorrow of the young woman wrapped in silence, her son in the stillness of death. It's possible to see the Pietà alone, if you arrive early or just before closing (7 A.M.–7 P.M.; Oct-Mar, 7 A.M.–6 P.M.).

On a bright day, the generous light from Michelangelo's **Dome,** rising above the site of St. Peter's tomb, falls in spangled patterns on the colored marble floor of the nave. Some visitors marvel at the basilica's superheroic statuary, or Bernini's baldacchino, but none of these compare with the light pouring down from the Dome: The entrance, via lift and stairway, is outside the basilica, at the right end of the portico, open 8 A.M. until one hour before closing. As you walk around the inside of the Dome, or stand in the gallery that circles the sixteen-ribbed drum, looking down over the church from this great height, Michelangelo's poems—in particular the friends to whom he dedicated them, young Tommaso Cavalieri and the middle-aged widow, Vittoria Colonna—come to mind. His desire to rise above earthly passions, expressed in his idealization of those friends, up here, it all feels of a piece. As a youth in Florence, he'd been taught the value of abstinence and chastity from the Platonist Marsilio Ficino. In his private life Michelangelo loved passionately, but from a distance. There is no evidence that he ever consummated his love for either his male or female friends. In *Michelangelo and the Pope's Ceiling,* Ross King quotes his views on sex as told to his biographer: "If you want to prolong your life, practice it not at all, or the least that you can."

> This abstemious philosophy was behind his depiction of the Virgin in the Pietà which came in for criticism because it appeared to show a mother much too youthful to have an adult son. . . . "Don't you know," [Michelangelo] asked . . . "that women who are chaste remain much fresher than those who are not? How much more so a virgin who was never touched by even the slightest lascivious desire which might alter her body?"

Though he never saw it completed, he dedicated the Dome of St. Peter's to the Madonna and the people of Rome. A year after he began to work on it, in 1546, Vittoria Colonna died; according to one biographer, he almost went mad with grief. For the rest of his life he wrote poetry, in which he revealed how deeply he had loved her piety.

You can ascend higher. Either by stairway or lift, you can reach the roof of St. Peter's, stand at the balustrade next to the gigantic statues of the apostles, feeling dwarfed as you look down on the Piazza. And then comes the grand finale. Another stairway, narrower this time, takes you farther up, and around, slowly, coming out at last onto the highest balcony that encircles the Lantern. Goethe said so, travelers who take the time to make the climb agree: The view of Rome from the lantern of St. Peter's is never to be forgotten, the city a haphazard sprawl, the Tiber looping through her, on the horizon a curve of blue Alban hills.

Again, Walter Pater:

In Michelangelo's lifelong effort to tranquillise his vehement emotions by withdrawing them into the region of ideal sentiment, . . . the significance of Vittoria is that she realises for him a type of affection which even in disappointment may charm and sweeten his spirit.

Up here, close to the sky, the real city so far away, seems the perfect setting for Michelangelo's "region of ideal sentiment," the dreamy Christian Platonism that holds ideas superior to facts, the invisible soul to the physical body. And yet, as an artist, he realized the incarnate beauty of human flesh.

(*On the ground, when you line up to enter the basilica from the Piazza in summer, young clothing police out of* The Sopranos—*as cold-eyed and nasty as Christopher—inspect the exposed flesh of visitors. Even if yours is safely covered, you can't avoid noticing the women in sleeveless dresses and tops being told—rudely, coldly, contemptuously—to scram because their upper arms are showing. Inside Bernini's Colonnade gypsies sometimes sell chiffon shawls. You can recover your equilibrium in the nearby rooftop restaurant of the* **Atlante Star Hotel,** *Via Vittelleschi 34, tel 06 687 3233; or farther away, and less expensively, in the markets on Via Cola di Rienzo.* **Gelateria Pellacchia** *at Cola di Rienzo 105 has tables outside, and gelato worth walking for. Or take the Metro to Ottaviano or Risorgimento.*)

If you do cross the Tiber at St. Peter's, avoid the Corso del Vittorio Emanuele II leading from the bridge and look for the gracious **Via Giulia,** to the right of and parallel to the Corso. Julius II commissioned it, wanting a dramatic and straight approach to the Vatican from the Ponte Sisto, at the far end. To quote Anya Shetterly's informative *Romewalks,* "Via Giulia could be a set design for an Italian Renaissance play." From the top, you can enjoy a full view of the straightest street in the city, off limits to cars, all the way to the far end, where it's framed by an arched bridge, the work of Michelangelo performing as architect. He meant it to connect the rear garden of the **Palazzo Farnese** (turn left off Via Giulia at the Mascherone Fountain, which on feast days flowed with wine, toward Piazza Farnese) with the Villa Farnesina (see page 159), on the other side of the Tiber in Trastevere. Michelangelo worked on the Palazzo Farnese, unanimously considered the finest Renaissance palace in Rome. The two bathtub fountains in the piazza were taken from the Baths of Caracalla.

*(Perpendicular to the Farnese, now the French Embassy, there's opulent dining at **Camponeschi,** tel 06 687 4927, reservations required, closed Sun. The wine bar to the right, also called Camponeschi, is excellent. Directly across on the right of the square is the small church and convent of **Santa Brigida** [St. Bridget], the site of the Swedish saint's death in 1373; guest rooms are available here; Piazza Farnese 96, tel 39 06 686 5721; book far in advance. Off Via Giulia, back in the direction of the Vatican, **Hostaria Giulio,** Via della Barchetta 19, tel 06 688 06466, is small and quiet. The good restaurant **Pierluigi** is tucked into the charming Piazza de Ricci 144, tel 06 686 1302, closed Mon.)*

The architectural legacy of the Renaissance Michelangelo brought to Rome dominates these streets off Piazza Farnese. They're also living proof of the rivalry that fueled Renaissance popes and cardinals and nobles as they competed to mount their family crest on the grandest palazzo in the neighborhood. The hypocrisy of official Christendom was not lost on Martin Luther, who visited its Holy City in 1510; at the time, Michelangelo, contorted inside his scaffold, was working the miracle of the Sistine ceiling.

VITTORIA COLONNA

1490–1547

*She grew up a Colonna, the oldest of all the patrician families of Rome,
first mentioned in the city's annals in the ninth century. The Colonna, the
Orsini, the Savelli, the Conti, the Frangipani, the Annibaldi were enemies, constantly waging war, poisoning and strangling one another, getting
their blood elected to the papacy. Married at seventeen, left on her own by
a soldier husband who died when she was thirty-five, Vittoria turned to religion and writing. She loved St. Francis of Assisi, whose habit she sometimes wore; she and Michelangelo read Dante together. Her poetry shows
what she thought of the warring tyrant families she knew from the inside,
and she had no use for the degenerate papal autocracy the families were
hand and glove with. Michelangelo felt blessed by the "meditative sweetness" of their friendship, which, like their mutual religious passions, flowed
with its own chaste erotic current. They first met in 1537, but their frequent
meetings didn't begin until 1542. When she died, he grieved that in death
he had kissed only her hand.*

On the Church

When the breath of God that moved above the tide
Fans the embers of my smouldering state,
And the winds of God begin to dissipate
The fetid stench of the church, his bride,
Then the swaggering knights prepare to ride.
The war begins. They gloat and cannot wait.
They think they are the masters of their fate
And would display their valor far and wide.
Then within they hear God's trumpet blow,

And they, whose gods were goblets and a crest,
Appalled by death, their headlong charge arrest.
They cannot lift the vizier to the rays
Which penetrate the heart beneath the vest.
Would they but discard their gear and ways!

On Justification by Faith

One cannot have a lively faith I trow
Of God's eternal promises if fear
Has left the warm heart chilled and seer
And placed a veil between the I and Thou.
Nor faith, which light and joy endow
And works, which in the course of love appear,
If oft some vile, deep dolor drear
Injects itself into the here and now.
These human virtues, works and these desires
All operate the same, are but a shade,
Cast as a shadow, moving or at rest,
But when the light descends from heaven's fires
Kindling hope and faith within the breast
Then doubt and fear and dolor, these all fade.

The Annunciation

Blessed angel with whom the Father swore
The ancient covenant now sealed anew.
Which gives us peace and shows the pathway true
To contemplate his gifts for evermore.
For this holy office held in store
With soul inclined and mind in constant view
By his high embassy he did imbue
The virgin's heart, which joyful I adore.
I beg you now behold the face and hands,
Humble response, tinged with chaste dread,

The ardent love and faith with pulsing beat
Of her, who come from out no earthly lands,
With humble heartfelt yearning, sweet desire replete,
Greets, adores, embraces all God said.

FOR THE LITERARY TRAVELER

After a Saturday morning visit to **Palazzo Colonna: The Gallery** (the only time it's open, 9–1), it's clear why a learned daughter of the Colonna dynasty with a mind of her own would have looked elsewhere for satisfaction. (From Piazza Venezia, walk up Via Quattro Novembre and turn left, into Via della Pilotta, which is spanned by four overhead arches connecting the Palazzo Colonna with the Villa Colonna above, on the west slope of the Quirinal Hill.) The entrance at number 17 is plain. But up a spiral staircase and through a small antechamber you'll find Rome's most amazingly extravagant interior, the perfect setting for Audrey Hepburn as sacrificial princess in the movie *Roman Holiday.*

The palazzo dates from the late thirteenth century. In the next century, Petrarch visited. From 1424 onward, Oddone Colonna, who became Pope Martin V, lived here. By Vittoria's time, the family owned seven palazzos in Rome, parts of which were incorporated into this baroque Galleria, the vast architectural complex begun by one of the many Cardinal Colonnas in the 1650s.

The Room of the Battle Column, in red marble, is the first of the three rooms comprising the gallery itself, which displays one of the finest collections in the city: Tintoretto, Andrea del Sarto, Hieronymous Bosch, Botticelli, Veronese, Caracci's "The Bean Eater," anticipating Van Gogh's "The Potato Eaters." As you face the doorway (through which you entered this room) and the huge painting of Venus, you'll see to the left of it, in the corner, a portrait believed to be Vittoria Colonna's, by Bartolomeo Cancellieri. She wears a dress of green silk, a simple strand of pearls, and a widow's headdress. Serious dark eyes and a self-possessed gaze define the most famous woman poet of her day, who declined to enter a convent because she saw too little difference between the Renaissance Church and her arrogant family. (A picture of her also hangs in the entrance hall of another Colonna palazzo, now a high school named after her in Via dell'Arco del Monte 99, on the right as you approach Ponte Sisto.) Her poetry appears in the bilingual collections *The Defiant Muse: Italian Feminist Poems from the Middle Ages to the Present* (1986) and *Women Poets of the Italian Renaissance* (1997).

The lower room, The Great Hall, celebrates Marcantonio Colonna's victory for the pope over the Turks at the naval battle of Lepanto in 1571 after which he brought home 170 Turkish prisoners: the motif of the palazzo's decorations—the pedestals holding up tables, the chair backs—is the Turkish slave, the gilded pagan Other, chained, wretched, dark.

Around the corner from Via Pilotta, to the left—continue up on a winding Via Quattro Novembre and left into Via Ventiquattro Maggio, ascending toward the **Piazza del Quirinale**—is Vittoria's soul's home, **San Silvestro al Quirinale.** She belonged to the "Oratory of Divine Love," which met here, its educated members interested in church reform and a reconciliation with Lutheranism; they took seriously the Protestant doctrine of justification by faith (as one of her poems shows). A free thinker, and under suspicion for her "new opinions," Vittoria was said to have narrowly escaped the persecution of the Inquisition. She once had to leave Rome for two years. Michelangelo, whose piety deepened as he grew older, joined her here. (As a youth in Florence, he'd admired Savonarola, the reformer priest who was burned at the stake for heresy in 1498.) They read their poetry to each other, and listened to a theologian's talks about St. Paul's Epistle to the Romans (see pages 82–87).

Ring the bell at number 10, the door to the right of the church entrance; a sacristan or porter will admit you, 9–1, every day, and show you upstairs to the newly restored frescoes in the church's apse and vault, bright with the biblical characters and stories Vittoria loved. Like Michelangelo, she was devoted to Maria, the Mother of Jesus: "The virgin's heart, which joyful I adore." Beyond the north transept is a door leading to a rooftop terrace and courtyard, a lovely secluded space (*in restauro* in 2003), where the two friends used to sit. She cherished the crucifix he carved for her. The black chalk "Pietà" he made for her is now in the Isabella Stewart Gardner Museum in Boston. Today, the view from San Silvestro looks over a cityscape similar to what they saw, Trajan's Forum, a jumble of domes and red tile roofs, cupolas, balconies trailing vines and flowers. Pietro, the kindly old porter, guides you through the church and onto the terrace with a fervent enthusiasm, in the spirit of the famous friendship.

Outside, continuing up the hill toward **Piazza del Quirinale,** you'll pass more of the family's palatial property on the left, fronting the gardens of **Villa Colonna.** Then you come into the Piazza itself, a favorite of Elizabeth Bowen: "There is . . . a suddenness about the entire burst of sky, Rome and space." The huge **Palazzo del Quirinale**— "of a yellow no other Roman yellow approaches; it has a melon underglow"—was built here ten years after Michelangelo died, as the pope's summer residence. Nearby is Bernini's oval gem of a church, **Sant' Andrea al Quirinale** (8–12, 4–7, closed Tues), of all his works in Rome, the one he liked best. The pink and gray marble interior dazzles, like the piazza outside, golden at high noon, at midnight, a gleaming flood of moonlight, St. Peter's dome in the distance. Coming into the Quirinale for the first time—this Roman moment never fades.

(*Near Palazzo Colonna at the corner of Piazza SS. Apostoli, the interior and al fresco dining at Ristorante **Abruzzi** [Via del Vaccaro 1, tel 06 6793 897] is a pleasure. The Roman poet Trilussa ate here. His picture, along with prints of the city, hangs on the walls. To the right off the Piazza, at Via S. Marcello 19, Romans enjoy the midday meal at **Peroni,** Via S. Marcello 19, a large, inviting place.*)

SIGMUND FREUD

1856–1939

After Pope Julius II commissioned Michelangelo to sculpt his tomb—it was to be the largest monument in Christendom—il papa terribile made it impossible for him to do the job. The Sistine Chapel was only one of the many interruptions that drove Michelangelo to anguish over "the tragedy of the sepulchre." Finally, after working on it on and off for thirty years, he did finish it, but only in parts, and long after Julius died. Michelangelo considered the seven-and-a-half-foot-high Moses, holding the tablets of the Ten Commandments and flanked by Leah and Rachel, his most important work.

Freud was obsessed with the founder of Judaism. And Rome figures as a seductress haunting his subconscious in The Interpretation of Dreams *(1900). He saw the Moses for the first time in 1901, on his first visit, "after," in the words of biographer Peter Gay, "he had overcome his crippling inhibition against seeing Rome. Thereafter, whenever he spent time in Rome . . . , he made a pilgrimage to 'his' Moses." He considered it the greatest work of art in the world, and Rome "one of the summits of his life."*

❧

From THE MOSES OF MICHELANGELO*

I may say at once that I am no connoisseur in art, but simply a layman. I have often observed that the subject-matter of works of art has a stronger attraction for me than their formal and technical qualities, though to the artist their value lies first and foremost in these latter. I am unable rightly to appreciate many of the methods used and the effects obtained in art. I state this so as to secure the reader's indulgence for the attempt I propose to make here.

Nevertheless, works of art do exercise a powerful effect on me, especially those of literature and sculpture, less often of painting. This has occasioned me, when I have been contemplating such things, to spend a long time before them trying to apprehend them in my own way, i.e., to explain to myself what their effect is due to. Wherever I cannot do this, as for instance with music, I am almost incapable of obtaining any pleasure. Some rationalistic, or perhaps analytic, turn of mind in me rebels against being moved by a thing without knowing why I am thus affected and what it is that affects me.

This has brought me to recognize the apparently paradoxical fact that precisely some of the grandest and most overwhelming creations of art are still unsolved riddles to our understanding. We admire them, we feel overawed by them, but we are unable to say what they represent to us. I am not sufficiently well-read to know whether this fact has already been remarked upon; possibly, indeed, some writer on aesthetics has discovered that this state of intellectual bewilderment is a necessary condition when a work of art is to achieve its greatest effects. It would be only with the greatest reluctance that I could bring myself to believe in any such necessity.

---

*[The following footnote, obviously drafted by Freud himself, was attached to the title when the paper made its first, anonymous, appearance in *Imago*:

"Although this paper does not, strictly speaking, conform to the conditions under which contributions are accepted for publication in this Journal, the editors have decided to print it, since the author, who is personally known to them, moves in psycho-

I do not mean that connoisseurs and lovers of art find no words with which to praise such objects to us. They are eloquent enough, it seems to me. But usually in the presence of a great work of art each says something different from the other; and none of them says anything that solves the problem for the unpretending admirer. In my opinion, what grips us so powerfully can only be the artist's *intention,* in so far as he has succeeded in expressing it in his work and in getting us to understand it. I realize that this cannot be merely a matter of *intellectual* comprehension; what he aims at is to awaken in us the same emotional attitude, the same mental constellation as that which in him produced the impetus to create. But why should the artist's intention not be capable of being communicated and comprehended in *words,* like any other fact of mental life? Perhaps where great works of art are concerned this would never be possible without the application of psycho-analysis. The product itself after all must admit of such an analysis, if it really is an effective expression of the intentions and emotional activities of the artist. To discover his intention, though, I must first find out the meaning and content of what is represented in his work; I must, in other words, be able to *interpret* it. It is possible, therefore, that a work of art of this kind needs interpretation, and that until I have accomplished that interpretation I cannot come to know why I have been so powerfully affected. I even venture to hope that the effect of the work will undergo no diminution after we have succeeded in thus analysing it.

Let us consider Shakespeare's masterpiece, *Hamlet,* a play now over three centuries old. I have followed the literature of psycho-analysis closely, and I accept its claim that it was not until the material of the tragedy had been traced back by psycho-analysis to the Oedipus theme that the mystery of its effect was at last explained. But before this was done, what a mass of differing and contradictory interpretative attempts, what a variety of opinions about the hero's character and the dramatist's intentions! Does Shakespeare

---

analytic circles, and since his mode of thought has in point of fact a certain resemblance to the methodology of psycho-analysis."]

claim our sympathies on behalf of a sick man, or of an ineffectual weakling, or of an idealist who is merely too good for the real world? And how many of these interpretations leave us cold!—so cold that they do nothing to explain the effect of the play and rather incline us to the view that its magical appeal rests solely upon the impressive thoughts in it and the splendour of its language. And yet, do not those very endeavours speak for the fact that we feel the need of discovering in it some source of power beyond them alone?

Another of these inscrutable and wonderful works of art is the marble statue of Moses, by Michelangelo, in the Church of S. Pietro in Vincoli in Rome. As we know, it was only a fragment of the gigantic tomb which the artist was to have erected for the powerful Pope Julius II.[1] It always delights me to read an appreciative sentence about this statue, such as that it is "the crown of modern sculpture"(Grimm).[2] For no piece of statuary has ever made a stronger impression on me than this. How often have I mounted the steep steps from the unlovely Corso Cavour to the lonely piazza where the deserted church stands, and have essayed to support the angry scorn of the hero's glance! Sometimes I have crept cautiously out of the half-gloom of the interior as though I myself belonged to the mob upon whom his eye is turned—the mob which can hold fast no conviction, which has neither faith nor patience, and which rejoices when it has regained its illusory idols.

But why do I call this statue inscrutable? There is not the slightest doubt that it represents Moses, the Law-giver of the Jews, holding the Tables of the Ten Commandments. That much is certain, but that is all. As recently as 1912 an art critic, Max Sauerlandt, has said, "No other work of art in the world has been judged so diversely as the Moses with the head of Pan. The mere interpretation of the figure has given rise to completely opposed views. . . ."

---

1. According to Henry Thode {*Michelangelo: kritische Untersuchungen über seine Werke,* vol. I (1908), 194} the statue was made between the years 1512 and 1516.

2. {*Leben Michelangelos,* 9th ed. (1900), 189.}

II

Long before I had any opportunity of hearing about psycho-analysis, I learnt that a Russian art-connoisseur, Ivan Lermolieff, had caused a revolution in the art galleries of Europe by question-ing the authorship of many pictures, showing how to distinguish copies from originals with certainty, and constructing hypothetical artists for those works whose former supposed authorship had been discredited. He achieved this by insisting that attention should be diverted from the general impression and main features of a pic-ture, and by laying stress on the significance of minor details, of things like the drawing of the fingernails, of the lobe of an ear, of halos and such unconsidered trifles which the copyist neglects to imitate and yet which every artist executes in his own characteris-tic way. I was then greatly interested to learn that the Russian pseu-donym concealed the identity of an Italian physician called Morelli, who died in 1891 with the rank of Senator of the Kingdom of Italy. It seems to me that his method of inquiry is closely related to the technique of psycho-analysis. It, too, is accustomed to divine secret and concealed things from despised or unnoticed features, from the rubbish-heap, as it were, of our observations.

Now in two places in the figure of Moses there are certain de-tails which have hitherto not only escaped notice but, in fact, have not even been properly described. These are the attitude of his right hand and the position of the two Tables of the Law. We may say that this hand forms a very singular, unnatural link, and one which calls for explanation, between the Tables and the wrathful hero's beard. He has been described as running his fingers through his beard and playing with its locks, while the outer edge of his hand rests on the Tables. But this is plainly not so. It is worth while examining more closely what those fingers of the right hand are doing, and describing more minutely the mighty beard with which they are in contact. . . .

We now quite clearly perceive the following things: the thumb of the hand is concealed and the index finger alone is in effective contact with the beard. It is pressed so deeply against the soft masses of hair that they bulge out beyond it both above and below, that is, both towards the head and towards the abdomen. The other three fingers are propped upon the wall of his chest and are bent at the upper joints; they are barely touched by the extreme right-hand lock of the beard which falls past them. They have, as it were, withdrawn from the beard. It is therefore not correct to say that the right hand is playing with the beard or plunged in it; the simple truth is that the index finger is laid over a part of the beard and makes a deep trough in it. It cannot be denied that to press one's beard with one finger is an extraordinary gesture and one not easy to understand.

The much-admired beard of Moses flows from his cheeks, chin and upper lip in a number of waving strands which are kept distinct from one another all the way down. One of the strands on his ex-treme right, growing from the cheek, falls down to the inward-pressing index finger, by which it is retained. We may assume that it resumes its course between that finger and the concealed thumb. The corresponding strand on his left side falls practically unim-peded far down over his breast. What has received the most un-usual treatment is the thick mass of hair on the inside of this latter strand, the part between it and the middle line. It is not suffered to follow the turn of the head to the left; it is forced to roll over loosely and form part of a kind of scroll which lies across and over the strands on the inner right side of the beard. This is because it is held fast by the pressure of the right index finger, although it grows from the left side of the face and is, in fact, the main portion of the whole left side of the beard. . . .

III

We may now, I believe, permit ourselves to reap the fruits of our endeavours. We have seen how many of those who have felt the in-fluence of this statue have been impelled to interpret it as repre-senting Moses agitated by the spectacle of his people fallen from grace and dancing round an idol. But this interpretation had to be given up, for it made us expect to see him spring up in the next moment, break the Tables and accomplish the work of vengeance. Such a conception, however, would fail to harmonize with the design of making this figure, together with three (or five) more seated figures; a part of the tomb of Julius II. We may now take up again the abandoned interpretation, for the Moses we have reconstructed will neither leap up nor cast the Tables from him. What we see before us is not the inception of a violent action but the remains of a movement that has already taken place. In his first transport of fury, Moses desired to act, to spring up and take vengeance and forget the Tables; but he has overcome the temptation, and he will now remain seated and still, in his frozen wrath and in his pain mingled with contempt. Nor will he throw away the Tables so that they will break on the stones, for it is on their especial account that he has controlled his anger; it was to preserve them that he kept his passion in check. In giving way to his rage and indignation, he had to neglect the Tables, and the hand which upheld them was withdrawn. They began to slide down and were in danger of being broken. This brought him to himself. He remembered his mission and for its sake renounced an indulgence of his feelings. His hand returned and saved the unsupported Tables before they had actually fallen to the ground. In this attitude he remained immobilized, and in this attitude Michelangelo has portrayed him as the guardian of the tomb.

As our eyes travel down it the figure exhibits three distinct emotional strata. The lines of the face reflect the feelings which have won the ascendancy; the middle of the figure shows the traces of suppressed movement; and the foot still retains the attitude of the projected action. It is as though the controlling influence had proceeded downwards from above. No mention has been made so far of the left arm, and it seems to claim a share in our interpretation. The hand is laid in the lap in a mild gesture and holds as though in a caress the end of the flowing beard. It seems as if it is meant to counteract the violence with which the other hand had misused the beard a few moments ago.

But here it will be objected that after all this is not the Moses of the Bible. For that Moses did actually fall into a fit of rage and did throw away the Tables and break them. This Moses must be a quite different man, a new Moses of the artist's conception; so that Michelangelo must have had the presumption to emend the sacred text and to falsify the character of that holy man. Can we think him capable of a boldness which might almost be said to approach an act of blasphemy?

The passage in the Holy Scriptures which describes Moses' action at the scene of the Golden Calf is as follows: (Exodus xxxii. 7) "And the Lord said unto Moses, Go, get thee down; for thy people, which thou broughtest out of the land of Egypt, have corrupted themselves: (8) They have turned aside quickly out of the way which I commanded them: they have made them a molten calf, and have worshipped it, and have sacrificed thereunto, and said, These be thy gods, O Israel, which brought thee up out of the land of Egypt. (9) And the Lord said unto Moses, I have seen this people, and, behold, it is a stiff-necked people: (10) Now therefore let me alone, that my wrath may wax hot against them, and that I may consume them; and I will make of thee a great nation. (11) And Moses besought the Lord his God, and said, Lord, why doth thy wrath wax hot against thy people, which thou hast brought forth out of the land of Egypt with great power, and with a mighty hand? . . .

"(14) And the Lord repented of the evil which he thought to do unto his people. (15) And Moses turned, and went down from the mount, and the two tables of the testimony were in his hand: the tables were written on both their sides; on the one side and on the other were they written. (16) And the tables were the work of God, and the writing was the writing of God, graven upon the tables. (17) And when Joshua heard the noise of the people as they shouted, he said unto Moses, There is a noise of war in the camp. (18) And he said, It is not the voice of them that shout for mastery, neither is it the voice of them that cry for being overcome; but the noise of them that sing do I hear. (19) And it came to pass, as soon as he came nigh unto the camp, that he saw the calf, and the dancing: and Moses' anger waxed hot, and he cast the tables out of his hands, and break them beneath the mount. (20) And he took the calf which they had made, and burnt it in the fire, and ground it to powder, and strawed it upon the water, and made the children of Israel drink of it. . . .

"(30) And it came to pass on the morrow, that Moses said unto the people, Ye have sinned a great sin: and now I will go up unto the Lord; peradventure I shall make an atonement for your sin. (31) And Moses returned unto the Lord, and said, Oh! this people have sinned a great sin, and have made them gods of gold! (32) Yet now, if thou wilt forgive their sin—; and if not, blot me, I pray thee, out of thy book which thou hast written. (33) And the Lord said unto Moses, Whosoever hath sinned against me, him will I blot out of my book. (34) Therefore now go, lead the people unto the place of which I have spoken unto thee. Behold, mine Angel shall go before thee: nevertheless, in the day when I visit, I will visit their sin upon them. (35) And the Lord plagued the people, because they made the calf which Aaron made."

It is impossible to read the above passage in the light of modern criticism of the Bible without finding evidence that it has been clumsily put together from various sources. In verse 8 the Lord Himself tells Moses that his people have fallen away and made themselves an idol; and Moses intercedes for the wrongdoers. And yet he speaks to Joshua as though he knew nothing of this (18), and is suddenly aroused to wrath as he sees the scene of the worshipping of the Golden Calf (19). In verse 14 he has already gained a pardon from God for his erring people, yet in verse 31 he returns into the mountains to implore this forgiveness, tells God about his people's sins and is assured of the postponement of the punishment. Verse 35 speaks of a visitation of his people by the Lord about which nothing more is told us; whereas the verses 20–30 describe the punishment which Moses himself dealt out. It is well known that the historical parts of the Bible, dealing with the Exodus, are crowded with still more glaring incongruities and contradictions.

The age of the Renaissance had naturally no such critical attitude towards the text of the Bible, but had to accept it as a consistent whole, with the result that the passage in question was not a very good subject for representation. According to the Scriptures Moses was already instructed about the idolatry of his people and had ranged himself on the side of mildness and forgiveness; nevertheless, when he saw the Golden Calf and the dancing crowd, he was overcome by a sudden frenzy of rage. It would therefore not surprise us to find that the artist, in depicting the reaction of his hero to that painful surprise, had deviated from the text from inner motives. Moreover, such deviations from the scriptural text on a much slighter pretext were by no means unusual or disallowed to artists. A celebrated picture by Parmigiano possessed by his native town depicts Moses sitting on the top of a mountain and dashing the Tables to the ground, although the Bible expressly says that he broke them "beneath the mount." Even the representation of a seated Moses finds no support in the text and seems rather to bear out those critics who maintain that Michelangelo's statue is not meant to record any particular moment in the prophet's life.

More important than his infidelity to the text of the Scriptures is the alteration which Michelangelo has, in our supposition, made in the character of Moses. The Moses of legend and tradition had a hasty temper and was subject to fits of passion. It was in a transport of divine wrath of this kind that he slew an Egyptian who was maltreating an Israelite, and had to flee out of the land into the wilderness; and it was in a similar passion that he broke the Tables of the Law, inscribed by God Himself. Tradition, in recording such a characteristic, is unbiased, and preserves the impression of a great personality who once lived. But Michelangelo has placed a different Moses on the tomb of the Pope, one superior to the historical or traditional Moses. He has modified the theme of the broken Tables; he does not let Moses break them in his wrath, but makes him be influenced by the danger that they will be broken and makes him calm that wrath, or at any rate prevent it from becoming an act. In this way he has added something new and more than human to the figure of Moses; so that the giant frame with its tremendous physical power becomes only a concrete expression of the highest mental achievement that is possible in a man, that of struggling successfully against an inward passion for the sake of a cause to which he has devoted himself.

We have now completed our interpretation of Michelangelo's statue, though it can still be asked what motives prompted the sculptor to select the figure of Moses, and a so greatly altered Moses, as an adornment for the tomb of Julius II. In the opinion of many these motives are to be found in the character of the Pope and in Michelangelo's relations with him. Julius II was akin to Michelangelo in this, that he attempted to realize great and mighty ends, and especially designs on a grand scale. He was a man of action and he had a definite purpose, which was to unite Italy under the Papal supremacy. He desired to bring about single-handed what was not to happen for several centuries, and then only through the conjunction of many alien forces; and he worked alone, with impatience, in the short span of sovereignty allowed him, and used violent means. He could appreciate Michelangelo as a man of his own kind, but he often made him smart under his sudden anger and his utter lack of consideration for others. The artist felt the same violent force of will in himself, and, as the more introspective thinker, may have had a premonition of the failure to which they were both doomed. And so he carved his Moses on the Pope's tomb, not without a reproach against the dead pontiff, as a warning to himself, thus, in self-criticism, rising superior to his own nature.

FOR THE LITERARY TRAVELER

According to Freud, the statue of Moses in the **Church of San Pietro in Vincoli**—St. Peter in Chains—on the Esquiline Hill (7–12:30; 3:30–6) captures the complex soul of the artist and "his"—Freud's—prophet. The horns appear because of a mistranslation by St. Jerome in the Latin Vulgate edition of the Bible: he thought "light coming out of the head" meant "horns." Throughout the Middle Ages, Moses was thought to have had horns. Michelangelo was aware of the error, but he kept the horns: in the ancient world they symbolized power and divinity. He gave Moses the body language of an anguished human being and a compassionate prophet, a man with the power and will to bring to light the hidden things of the world for the wayward many. Freud, as the father of psychoanalysis, identified with this mission, which he addressed in this essay, and later, the year before he died, in his book *Moses and Mono-theism.* Today, tourists stare at Moses in confusion—*horns?*—remarking on the amazing beard as they pop flashbulbs at the masterpiece that has just undergone a five-year cleaning. "The Moses encapsulates Michel-angelo's real courage and passion," says the chief restorer, Antonio For-cellino, corroborating Freud's view of it as the autobiography in stone of Michelangelo's psyche. A later work—like the "Last Judgment" in the Sistine Chapel—reflects some of the bewilderment and despair Michelangelo felt in the uncompromising atmosphere of the Protestant Reformation and the Catholic Counter-Reformation.

The fifth-century church is named for the chains which held St. Peter captive in the Mamertine Prison in the Forum.

(The approach to the Moses, up Via Cavour from the Fori Imperiale and then up an arched flight of steps to the right, is not scenic. Leaving the church, turn left, then left again and downhill, coming out at the entrance to Domus Aurea on the Oppian Hill across from the Colos-seum. On the heights of **Parco del Colle Oppio,** *there's a breeze in summer, fountains, flowers, and free music at night.)*

SUSAN VREELAND

1946–

Author of Girl in Hyacinth Blue, *Susan Vreeland gives her idea of historical fiction in the opening of* The Passion of Artemisia *(2002), the novel excerpted here.*

> Any work of fiction about history or a historical person is and must be a work of the imagination. . . . Using what evidence is known, . . . I have imagined . . . Artemisia Gentileschi. . . . However, the trial record . . . [is] documented in art histories.

It is. Artemisia Gentileschi *(1593–1653), "one of the seventeenth-century's most formidable painters, Italy's greatest woman painter ever," according to Caravaggio's biographer, "who did her first important picture at the precocious age of seventeen," comes wrapped in conflicting legends. She was a whore, a victim, a heroic survivor. But the most compelling part of her life story is factual. The three-hundred-page transcript of the trial in Rome, the opening scene of Vreeland's novel, has survived. The daughter of the painter Orazio Gentileschi, Artemisia was raped at the age of seventeen, at home in Rome, in the studio where she and her father worked. The rapist was Agostino Tassi, an artist colleague of her father's. He was eventually convicted. Artemisia left Rome, painted her famous "Judith and Holofernes,"* and sold her numerous works into royal courts and great houses all over Europe.*

❧

---

*Judith's story appears in the Catholic and Orthodox Bibles but is considered apocryphal by Jews and Protestants. The famous Hebrew murderess began as a respected and beautiful widow of the town of Bethulia who objects to the elders' decision to surrender to the invading army of the Assyrians. She promises to deliver the town from the enemy. Entering the enemy camp, she pretends to be on the side of the Assyrians'

From THE PASSION OF ARTEMISIA

1
The Sibille

My father walked beside me to give me courage, his palm touching gently the back laces of my bodice. In the low-angled glare already baking the paving stones of the piazza and the top of my head, the still shadow of the Inquisitor's noose hanging above the Tor di Nona, the papal court, stretched grotesquely down the wall, its shape the outline of a tear.

"A brief unpleasantness, Artemisia," my father said, looking straight ahead. "Just a little squeezing."

He meant the *sibille*.

If, while my hands were bound, I gave again the same testimony as I had the previous weeks, they would know it was the truth and the trial would be over. Not my trial. I kept telling myself that: I was not on trial. Agostino Tassi was on trial.

The words of the indictment my father had sent to Pope Paul V rang in my ears: *"Agostino Tassi deflowered my daughter Artemisia and did carnal actions by force many times, acts that brought grave and enormous damage to me, Orazio Gentileschi, painter and citizen of Rome, the poor plaintiff, so that I could not sell her painting talent for so high a price."*

I hadn't wanted anyone to know. I wasn't even going to tell *him*, but he heard me crying once and forced it out of me. There was that missing painting, too, one Agostino had admired, and so he charged him.

"How much squeezing?" I asked.

"It will be over quickly."

---

military leader, Holofernes, a cruel despot. The Jews, she tells him, have sinned against God; her people deserve whatever destruction he plans to inflict. Seduced by her beauty, Holofernes dines alone with Judith. After he drinks himself into a stupor, Judith cuts off his head and walks back to her town, his severed head stuffed into her bag. The Jews rout the Assyrians, who are panicked by the death of their leader. Brave Judith has saved her people.

I didn't look at any faces in the crowd gathering at the entrance to the Tor. I already knew what they'd show—lewd curiosity, accusation, contempt. Instead, I looked at the yellow honeysuckle blooming against stucco walls the color of Roman ochre. Each color made the other more vibrant. Papa had taught me that.

"Fragrant blossoms," beggars cried, offering them to women coming to hear the proceedings in the musty courtroom. Anything for a giulio. A cripple thrust into my hand a wilted bloom, rank with urine. He knew I was Artemisia Gentileschi. I dropped it on his misshapen knee.

My dry throat tightened as we entered the dark, humid Sala del Tribunale. Leaving Papa at the front row of benches, I stepped up two steps and took my usual seat opposite Agostino Tassi, my father's friend and collaborator. My rapist. Leaning on his elbow, he didn't move when I sat down. His black hair and beard were overgrown and wild. His face, more handsome than he deserved, had the color and hardness of a bronze sculpture.

Behind a table, the papal notary, a small man swathed in deep purple, was sharpening his quills with a knife, letting the shavings fall to the floor. A dusty beam of light from a high window fell on his hands and lightened the folds of his sleeve to lavender. "Fourteen, May, 1612," the notary muttered as he wrote. Two months, and this was the first day he didn't have a bored look on his face. The day I would be vindicated. I pressed my hands tight against my ribs.

The Illustrious Lord Hieronimo Felicio, Locumtenente of Rome, appointed as judge and interrogator by His Holiness, swept in and sat on a raised chair, arranging his scarlet robes to be more voluminous. Papal functionaries were always posturing in public. Under his silk skull cap, his jowls sagged like overripe fruit. He was followed by a huge man with a shaved head whose shoulders bulged out of his sleeveless leather tunic—the Assistente di Tortura. A hot wave of fear rushed through me. With a flick of a finger the Lord High Locumtenente ordered him to draw a sheer curtain across the room separating us from Papa and the rabble crowded on benches on the other side. The curtain hadn't been there before.

The Locumtenente scowled and his fierce black eyebrows joined, making a shadow. "You understand, Signorina Gentileschi, our purpose." His voice was slick as linseed oil. "The Delphic sibyls always told the truth."

I remembered the Delphic sibyl on the ceiling of the Sistine Chapel. Michelangelo portrayed her as a powerful woman alarmed by what she sees. Papa and I had stood under it in silent awe, squeezing each other's hands to contain our excitement. Maybe the *sibille* would only squeeze as hard as that.

"Likewise, the *sibille* is merely an instrument designed to bring truth to women's lips. We will see whether you persist in what you have testified." He squinted his goat's eyes. "I wonder what tightening the cords might do to a painter's ability to hold a brush—properly." My stomach cramped. The Locumtenente turned to Agostino. "You are a painter too, Signor Tassi. Do you know what the *sibille* can do to a young girl's fingers?"

Agostino didn't even blink.

My fingers curled into fists. "What can it do? Tell me."

The Assistente forced my hands flat and wound a long cord around the base of each finger, then tied my hands palm to palm at my wrists and ran the cord around each pair of fingers like a vine. He attached a monstrous wooden screw and turned it just enough for the cords to squeeze a little.

"What can it do?" I cried. I looked for Papa through the curtain. He was leaning forward pulling at his beard.

"Nothing," the Locumtenente said. "It can do nothing, if you tell the truth."

"It can't cut off my fingers, can it?"

"That, signorina, is up to you."

My fingers began to throb slightly. I looked at Papa. He gave me a reassuring nod.

"Tell us now, for I'm sure you see reason, have you had sexual relations with Geronimo the Modenese?"

"I don't know anyone by that name."

"With Pasquino Fiorentino?"

"I don't know him either."

"With Francesco Scarpellino?"

"The name means nothing to me."

"With the cleric Artigenio?"

"I tell you, no. I don't know these men."

"That's a lie. She lies. She wants to discredit me to take my commissions," Agostino said. "She's an insatiable whore."

I couldn't believe my ears.

"No," Papa bellowed. "He's trying to pass her off as a whore to avoid the *nozze di riparazione.* He wants to ruin the Gentileschi name. He's jealous."

The Locumtenente ignored Papa and curled back his lip. "Have you had sexual relations with your father, Orazio Gentileschi?"

"I would spit if you had said that outside this courtroom," I whispered.

"Tighten it!" the Locumtenente ordered.

The hideous screw creaked. I sucked in my breath. Rough cords scraped across the base of my fingers, burning. Murmurs beyond the curtain roared in my ears.

"Signorina Gentileschi, how old are you?"

"Eighteen."

"Eighteen. Not so young that you don't know you should not offend your interrogator. Let us resume. Have you had sexual relations with an orderly to Our Holy Father, the late Cosimo Quorli?"

"He . . . he tried, Your Excellency. Agostino Tassi brought him into the house. I fought him away. They had both been hounding me. Giving me lewd looks. Whispering suggestions."

"For how long?"

"Many months. A year. I was barely seventeen when it started."

"What kind of suggestions?"

"I don't like to say." The Locumtenente flashed a look at the Assistente, who moved toward me. "Suggestions of my hidden beauty. Cosimo Quorli threatened to boast about having me if I didn't submit."

"And did you submit?"

"No."

"This same Cosimo Quorli reported to other orderlies of the

Palazzo Apostolico that he was, in truth, your father, that your mother, Prudenzia Montone, had frequently encouraged him to visit her privately, whereupon she conceived." He paused and scrutinized my face. "You must admit you do have a resemblance. Has he, on any occasion, ever revealed this to you?"

"The claim is ludicrous. I must now defend my mother's honor as well as mine against this mockery?"

It seemed enough to him that he had planted the idea. He cleared his throat and pretended to read some document.

"Did you not, on repeated occasions, engage in sexual relations willingly with Agostino Tassi?"

The room closed in. I held my breath.

The Assistente turned the screw.

I tightened all my muscles against it. The cords bit into my flesh. Rings of fire. Blood oozed between them in two places, three, all over. How could Papa let them? He didn't tell me there would be blood. I sucked in air through my teeth. This was Agostino's trial, not mine. How to make it stop? The truth.

"Not willingly. Agostino Tassi dishonored me. He raped me and violated my virginity."

"When did this occur?"

"Last year. Just after Easter."

"If a woman is raped, she must have done something to invite it. What were you doing?"

"Painting! In my bedchamber." I squeezed shut my eyes to get out the words. "I was painting our housekeeper, Tuzia, and her baby as the Madonna and Child. She let him in. My father was away. She knew Agostino. He was my father's friend. My father hired him to teach me perspective."

"Why did you not cry out?"

"I couldn't. He held a handkerchief over my mouth."

"Did you not try to stop him?"

"I pulled his hair and scratched his face and . . . his member. I even threw a dagger at him."

"A virtuous woman keeps a dagger in her bedchamber?"

My head was about to split. "A threatened woman does."

"And after that occasion?"

"He came again, let in by Tuzia. He pushed himself on me . . . and in me." Sweat trickled between my breasts.

"Did you resist?"

"I scratched and pushed him."

"Did you always resist?"

I searched Agostino's face. Immovable as a painting. "Say something." Only two months ago he had said he loved me. "Agostino," I pleaded. "Don't let them do this."

He looked down and dug dirt from his fingernails.

The Locumtenente turned to Agostino. "Do you wish to amend your claim of innocence?"

Agostino's strong-featured face turned cold and ugly. I didn't want to beg. Not him. Santa Maria, I prayed, don't let me beg him.

"No," he said. "She's a whore just like her mother."

"She thought she was betrothed!" Papa bellowed from beyond the curtain. "It was understood. He would marry her. A proper *nozze di riparazione*."

The Locumtenente leaned toward me. "You haven't answered the question, signorina. The *sibille* can be made to cut off a finger."

"It's Agostino who's on trial, not I. Let him be subjected to the *sibille*."

"Tighten!"

Madre di Dio, let me faint before I scream. Blood streamed. My new white sleeve was soaked in red. Papa, make them stop. What was I to do? Tell them what they want? Lie? Say I'm a whore? That would only set Agostino free. Another turn. "Oh oh oh oh stop!" Was I screaming?

"For the love of God, stop!" Papa shouted and stood up.

The Locumtenente snapped his fingers to have him gagged. "God loves those, Signor Gentileschi, who tell the truth." He leered at me. "Now tell me, and tell me truthfully, signorina, after the first time did you always resist?"

The room blurred. The world swirled out of control. The

screw, my hands—there was nothing else. Pain so wicked I—I—
Che Dio mi salvi—would the cords touch bone?—*Che Santa Maria
mi salvi*—*Gesù*—*Madre di Dio*—make it stop. I had to tell.

"I tried to, but in the end, no. He promised he would marry me,
and I . . . I believed him." *Dio mi salvi,* stop it stop it stop it. "So I
allowed him . . . against my desires . . . so he would keep his
promise. What else could I do?"

My breath. I couldn't get my breath.

"Enough. Adjourned until tomorrow." He waved his hand in
disgust and triumph. "All parties to be present."

The *sibille* was loosened and removed.

Rage hissed through me. My hands trembled, and shook blood
onto my skirt. Agostino lurched toward me, but the guards grabbed
him to take him away. I wanted to wait until the crowd left, but a
guard pushed me out with everyone else and I had to walk through
hoots and jeers with bleeding hands. In the glare of the street, I felt
something thrown at my back. I didn't turn around to see what it
was. Beside me, Papa offered me his handkerchief.

"I'd rather bleed."

"Artemisia, take this."

"You didn't tell me what the *sibille* could do." I passed him, and
walked faster than he could. At home I shoved my clothing *cassa-
panca* behind my chamber door with my knees, and flung myself
onto my bed and cried.

How could he have let this happen? How could he be so selfish?
My dearest papa. All those happy times on the Via Appia—picnics
with Mama listening for doves and Papa gathering sage to scrub
into the floor. Papa wrapping his feet and mine in scrubbing cloths
soaked in sage water, sliding to the rhythm of his love songs, his
voice warbling on the high notes, waving his arms like a cypress in
the wind until I laughed. That was my papa.

Was.

And all his stories about great paintings—sitting on my bed, letting me snuggle in his arms, slipping me some candied orange rind.
Wonderful stories. Rebekah at the well at Nahor, her skin so clear
that when she raised her chin to drink, you could see the water flow-

ing down her throat. Cleopatra floating the Nile on a barge piled with fruit and flowers. Danaë and the golden shower, Bathsheba, Judith, sibyls, muses, saints—he made them all real. He had made me want to be a painter, let me trace the drawings in his great leatherbound *Iconologia,* taught me how to hold a brush when I was five, how to grind pigments and mix colors when I was ten. He gave me my very own grinding muller and marble slab. He gave me my life.

What if I could never paint again with these hands? What was the use in living then? The dagger was still under the bed. I didn't have to live if the world became too cruel.

But there was my Judith to paint—if I could. More than ever I wanted to do that now. . . .

2
Judith

A conversation at our neighborhood bakery shop ended abruptly with embarrassed looks when I came in with bound fingers. The baker's boys held up their hands with their fingers splayed in mockery. On my way home our tailor's wife leaning over her windowsill spat just as I walked by. Crossing the Via del Corso in the searing heat, I stopped to watch swallows careening among laundry strung from upper windows. *"Puttana!* Whore!" I heard. I looked down the street, but there was only an old woman selling fruit. *"Puttana!"* I heard again, a husky voice. I straightened my back and walked on, refusing to look around. From an upstairs window, a chamber pot splashed down not three steps ahead of me. . . .

I put on a shawl and tucked my hands inside, took side streets and crossed the large piazza to the church of Santa Maria del Popolo. Caravaggio's *Conversion of Saint Paul* hung in a small chapel there. I studied his chiaroscuro, how he used bright light right against darkness, and I yearned to try it myself. Saint Paul was lying on his back at the moment of his conversion, head and shoulders forward in the picture plane and his body foreshortened. I could do Holofernes like that, with his head practically bursting through the canvas toward the viewer, upside down, at an impossible angle if it were fully attached, but still living, taking his last horrific breath as he thrust his fist into Abra's chin.

I remembered being disappointed when Papa had shown me Caravaggio's Judith. She was completely passive while she was sawing through a man's neck. Caravaggio gave all the feeling to the man. Apparently, he couldn't imagine a woman to have a single thought. I wanted to paint her thoughts, if such a thing were possible— determination and concentration and belief in the absolute necessity of the act. The fate of her people resting on her shoulders. Not relishing the act, just getting it done. And his thoughts too. Confusion and terror. The world out of control. Yes, I knew about that. I could do that part.

But could I do Judith?

As I left, I pulled the hood over my head even though the heat shimmered up from the ground ahead of me. On the way down Via del Babuino to Piazza di Spagna, I kept my head down so our apothecary might not recognize me from the door of his shop. Going up the Pincian hill, I straddled the ruts and avoided loose stones as I made a wide arc around the shiftless men who always lounged on this steep course between city and church. They'd be the first to shout some epithet at me. Toward the top of the hill, I climbed more slowly, up to the twin bell towers of Santa Trinità dei Monti. Breathing heavily, I turned at the church and went up the long stairway next to it, which led to the convent. I pulled the bell rope. . . .

Sister Graziela was alone, sitting on a tall stool by the narrow window where a shaft of pale honey-colored light shone on her cheeks and the tip of her pointed nose. Dust motes floated around her in a golden swirl. Her black habit and white cowl framed her unlined, oval face, which glowed with contentment and absorption. Her downward gaze was fixed on painting the border of a page. She reminded me of Mary in Michelangelo's marble *Pietà* in St. Peter's. Like Mary, she was lost in peaceful thought, and, like Mary, she was beautiful to me.

She had placed the oyster shells I had given her years ago along the edge of her worktable. Each shell held pigments of the most glorious, pure, saturated colors—dark red madder, bright vermilion, the deep ultramarine blue of crushed lapis lazuli, the yellow of saffron, and a green as bright as spring parsley. It made me happy that she still used them.

She looked up. "Artemisia! Bless you for coming. I've longed to see you."

She motioned for me to bring over a low stool. She was illuminating a page with delicate vines and tendrils tied in intricate, loose knots and studded with bright red blossoms.

I could do that, sitting here with Graziela. If I lived here forever, I could do whole books. The convent would become famous for its illuminated manuscripts.

"It's lovely. I like the yellow bird."

"It's a Psalter for Cardinal Bellarmino, that hammer of the heretics who crushes anyone with an idea of his own. People don't make these books by hand much anymore, but this is a gift from the convent. We're hoping he'll take a moment from his Holy Inquisitions to pay attention to our request for roof repair. For years we've had buckets in our upstairs cells to catch the rain." . . .

"I have something to tell you."

She laid down the tiniest brush I had ever seen and placed her hand gently on my arm. "We have known it."

"The trial?"

"Even though we're cloistered, the convent walls would have to be thick indeed for such a tale not to find its way in. We have been greatly grieved."

"You know everything?"

"We know more than we need to. Are you all right?"

I brought my hands out from under the cape. They were still swollen and oozing under the stained bandages.

She gasped. "Poor lamb. Where was your father when this happened?"

"He let them. He said it would prove my innocence if I kept to my testimony while the cords were on. I don't know which was

worse, my hands or . . . today. Today they had two midwives examine me, you know where, with a notary watching. I know people could see through the curtain. They wanted to show me lying
that way."

"Dio ti salvi." She held me and I laid my head on her lap. "It's
just another way to break any woman who accuses a man. They are
without conscience."

"They're beasts, all of them," I wailed into her habit.

"They may be, but they cannot destroy you." She cradled me,
stroking the back of my head and my hair, letting me cry.

"My own papa let them."

"Cara mia," she crooned. "Fathers aren't always fatherly. They
may try, but many fail. They're only mortal."

I turned my head to one side, and saw that my dress was smeared
with the midwives' grease. I pulled it away from Graziela's black
wool. . . .

"There is no way in to the fortress of the soul," she murmured.
"Our Heavenly Father is the guard thereof. He does not betray us.
Remember that, Artemisia. Though they might make you a vic-
tim, they cannot make you a sinner."

I could only sob.

"Paint it out of you, *carissima*. Paint out the pain until there's
none left. Don't take on shame from their mockery. That's what
they want. They want you to shrivel up and die, and you know
why?"

I shook my head in her lap.

"Because your talent is a threat. Promise me—don't pray as a
penitent when you have no need to be one. Don't plead. Approach
the Lord with dignity, and affirm His goodness. No matter what."

"He abandoned me."

"Then love Him all the more. That will please Him most."

"But everybody thinks—"

"Don't care a fig for what they think. The world is larger than
Rome, Artemisia. Remember that. Think of your *Susanna and the
Elders*. When that painting becomes famous, the whole world will
know your innocence."

"How?"

"Because in that painting you showed her intimidation at the lewd looks of those two men, her vulnerability and fear. It shows you understood her struggle against forces beyond her control. Beyond her control, Artemisia."

"You remember all that?"

"I'll never forget it. Her face averted and her arms raised, fending off their menace? The night after you brought it here, her face was blazing in my dreams. By the way you had her turn from that leering elder shushing her so she wouldn't cry out and reveal them, I knew then that you were being threatened."

"I painted that before it happened."

"Yes, but I could tell you were suffering some menace just as Susanna was. That's the brilliance of your skill, to have a masterpiece reflect your own feelings and experience."

"I can't even hold a brush now."

"You will. Nothing can stop you from bringing your talent to fruition. You are young yet. Never forget that the world needs to know what you have to show them."

"The world. What does the world care? The world is full of cruelty." I touched the rough edge of one of the oyster shells. "If I stayed in here with you, the world wouldn't matter."

"Artemisia." The word rang with a tone of authority. "One doesn't live a cloistered life to get away from something. One lives here to serve God because one feels an undeniable voice calling. Any other reason is illegitimate."

"I might discover a calling."

"You already have. Your art."

The bell rang for vespers, which meant I had to go. . . .

FOR THE LITERARY TRAVELER

Torture and execution, used by the Inquisition to punish heretics, non-believers, and Jews, were well-established methods by the time the judge in *The Passion of Artemisia* used finger cords to bleed a confession out of Artemisia. The **Tor di Nona,** the court where the torture was performed, was also a prison with a terrifying reputation. Dominican philosopher-mathematician-astronomer Giordano Bruno, accused of heresy, was held here for seven years before he was burned alive in 1600. The Tor stood upstream of what is today Ponte Umberto, which leads to the ugly Palace of Justice on the west bank of the Tiber. A century later the Teatro di Tor di Nona replaced the prison, under the direction of the eccentric Queen Christina of Sweden who brought Scarlatti and Corelli to perform. Later its name changed to Teatro Apollo, where Verdi's *Il Trovatore* had its premiere. Today the Tor survives in the name of the "Lungotevere di Tor di Nona" and the neighborhood Tor ni Nona, site of a black market during the German occupation, between Ponte Sant'Angelo and Ponte Umberto.

Following her day in a sadistic papal court, Artemisia walks up the Corso to the church of **Santa Maria del Popolo,** on the Piazza del Popolo (see page 303), to look at the masterpieces of her teacher, Michelangelo di Caravaggio (1571–1612): the "Crucifixion of St. Peter" and the "Conversion of St. Paul." In 2002 at the exhibition of Gentileschi paintings at the Metropolitan Museum of Art in New York, the curator of European paintings pointed out the strong influence of Caravaggio on daughter and father: the master painted directly from models, which added a new and shockingly dramatic element to his—and their—paintings, one that you don't see in the idealized portraits of the Renaissance. Caravaggio's life in Rome, like Artemisia's, is cloaked in mystery. Also like her, the only hard facts that survive about him come from Roman judicial records, which tell of his many clashes with the law. You can see Caravaggio's "Judith Beheading Holofernes" in the **Palazzo Barberini.** In contrast to her teacher's passive Judith, the student painted a passionately transgressive heroine. (Her "Judith" is in the Galleria Palatini in the Pitti Palace in Florence. The Uffizi has other paintings by Artemisia.)

Other paintings by Artemisia's teacher can be seen in the **Galleria Borghese** (Caravaggio's "Madonna with the Snake" spent only two days in St. Peter's for which it had been commissioned; objecting to Mary's low-cut dress and the Child's nakedness, the cardinals, rabid with Counter-Reformation zeal, excommunicated it); the **Galleria Doria Pamphili** (the exquisite "Rest on the Flight into Egypt," 1598–99, was his first sacred painting); the church of **San Luigi Dei Francesi** (the "Calling of St. Matthew," a fine example of the dramatic effect Caravaggio achieves with painted light); the Vatican Picture Galleries; the **Galleria Corsini** (the revolutionary "Narcissus," and "St. John the Baptist in the Desert"); and finally, the church of **Sant'Agostino** (where Renaissance courtesans, the favorites of cardinals and Borgias, used to confess; the chapels and tombs they built for themselves were later removed). In the first chapel on the left, the "Madonna with Pilgrims" depicts a woman of the people inclining toward two poor pilgrims, one with dirty feet. Such bold realistic touches upset the ecclesiastical patrons who considered "sublimity" and "nobility" essential to a religious picture and suspected that Caravaggio's bohemian individuality bordered on the subjectivism of the Reformation spirit.

In **Palazzo Spada** (8:30–7:30, closed Mon, www.galleriaborghese.it), off the Piazza Farnese in the pretty Piazza Capodiferro, you'll find paintings by Caravaggio's disciples, the Gentileschi father and daughter, upstairs in the **Galleria,** Room IV. Artemisia's "Madonna and Child," (#166), a classic nursing mother-and-child pose, captures the exhaustion of motherhood rather than its idealization. In Vreeland's novel the model for this painting is the serving girl, Tuzia, who admits the rapist to the studio while Artemisia is working on it. The nursing couple is flanked by Artemisia's "Saint Cecilia" (#149), the well-modeled flesh and the concentration of her face evoking a musician devoted to her art rather than a spiritualized virgin martyr.

The sunny, spacious Spada galleries, restored by Borromini for his friend Cardinal Spada, invite you to spend time. From the tall windows you see beautiful views of the city. Outside there's a garden of orange trees, as well as Borromini's ingenious trompe l'oeil, the "Prospectiva."

Though the gift shop sells postcards of Orazio's paintings and none of Artemisia's, her cultural moment has arrived. There's Vreeland's novel, the Gentileschi exhibit at the Met, and in the last few years extensive art criticism, a few plays ("Lapis Blue Blood Red"), a movie, and a novel by French writer Alexandra Lapierre who lived in Rome while she researched it. Given the benighted society that confined women in Renaissance and Baroque Italy, Artemisia was not supposed to happen. But, as she is reminded by the kindly nun at **Trinità dei Monti** which still operates a convent school for girls, at the top of the Spanish Steps, beside the French church and the lovely cloister—she is a child of God, with an artistic vocation. "Establish yourself within yourself," said St. Thomas Aquinas, advice that some Catholic educators passed on through the centuries.

Leaving Palazzo Spada, walking east toward the Corso, the Tiber at your back, you'll come into the **Campo de' Fiori** (Field of Flowers), a colorful market scene during the day (see page 264), frantic on summer nights, tragic during the years of the Inquisition when Artemisia was a Roman resident. Dominating the piazza is a huge statue of Giordano Bruno (1548–1600), who, as James Joyce wrote in *Ulysses,* "was terribly burned" here. Bruno holds a book, an image of the ideas he refused to denounce as inspired by the devil: that the universe is infinite and in perpetual motion; that God is not outside the world but everywhere in Nature; and that people should be free to think as they choose. His statue faces the Vatican, a defiant positioning by the people of Rome who raised the statue after 1870 when Itraly became a secular republic. The names of other "heretics" are preserved as medallions around the base of the statue: the humanist Erasmus, the English John Wyclif, and Jan Hus; the statue commemorating his incineration is now in the center of Prague's Old Town Square.

(*Dining and the history of murder combine in two good restaurants off the southeast corner of the Campo. At the movie theater, walk in the direction of the Corso:* **Hostaria Costanza** [*Piazza del Paradiso 63 / 65, tel 06 68661717, closed Sun*]*; and* **Pancrazio** [*Piazza del Biscione 92— Via Grotta Pinta 20, closed Wed*] *are both built into the concrete vaults and walls of Rome's first theater, the splendidly decorated Theater of Pompey, built by Caesar's rival, here in the Campo Marzio, in 61 B.C. On March 15, 44 B.C., Caesar was murdered by Brutus and Cassius in the Theater's Curia, the arcade of one hundred columns in front of it.*)

SIMON SCHAMA

1945–

In Landscape and Memory, *the British art historian Simon Schama, addressing the subject of flowing water in his study of the role of Nature in the development of western civilization, takes a close look at the Baroque fountains of Rome, those magnificent creations for which one sculptor and architect, above all others, is responsible. What Michelangelo is to Renaissance Rome, Gianlorenzo Bernini (1598–1680) is to the Baroque. He started out in Naples, his mother a Neapolitan, his father a sculptor from Florence. One way to look at the theatricality of his art (not to mention his temper) is to see it as the triumph of Naples over the North, Mama Angelica over the conventional Papa Pietro. A deeply religious man—Bernini attended Vespers at the Jesuit Church of the Gesù every day, received communion twice a week—he also had a nasty streak. When he caught his brother and his married mistress Costanza cheating on him, he beat his brother senseless and paid a servant to slash Costanza's face. One of the eleven children he went on to have with his Roman wife would later describe him as "stern by nature, steady in his work, passionate in his wrath."*

"Bernini was made for Rome, and Rome was made for him," remarked his friend Urban VIII, the Barberini pope who commissioned the Trevi fountain.

❧

From BERNINI AND THE FOUR RIVERS

The fountains of Versailles were in their infancy when Bernini told his French minder, Fréart de Chantelou, that all his life he had been "un amico dell'acqua."* He might have added that

---

*A friend of water.

water was, as it were, in his blood, for in addition to a career as a mediocre sculptor, his father, Pietro, had been invested with the office of superintendent of the Acqua Vergine. From the outset, Bernini had wanted to liberate the kinetic qualities of light and water from the rather stolid forms in which the fountain sculptors of the High Renaissance had encased them. Where they had stressed the contrary properties of stone mass and running water, Bernini wanted to bring them together in one fluid, musical sequence. To succeed in dissolving these substances in a glorious run of light, sound, and motion seemed the great response to Michelangelo's challenge of *difficoltà*. . . .

Art historians sometimes seem reluctant to take Bernini's fountains as seriously, which is to say, as *playfully,* as they deserve. Of Bernini's masterpiece, the Fountain of the Four Rivers in the Piazza Navona, one of his biographers comments loftily that its overall effect is compromised by features "that belong more to a circus-act" than to a great monumental sculpture. But the Fountain of the Four Rivers *does,* after all, stand in a circus, for the Piazza Navona preserves in its oval shape the stadium of the Agonale Circus, where, during the reign of the emperor Domitian, games were regularly held. From the late fifteenth century, the piazza was the site of a thriving Wednesday market, where hawkers sold all kinds of food, wine, household wares, and tools. And as was often the case with such places, it rapidly developed into a kind of street fair, too, with jugglers and quacks, street singers and actors of the *commedia dell'arte* jostling for space amidst the throng. The Piazza Navona was also a marketplace of power where political ideas, gossip, and scandal could be traded between the stalls of fruit and cheese. And by the second half of the sixteenth century, palazzi of the Roman nobility looked onto the open space, so that important days in the holy calendar would be marked by the ostentatious presence of carriages and retinues of the Aldobrandini, Torres, Orsini, and Pamphili.

Though one part of Bernini's personality was passionately devout and high-minded, another had the quality of an exuberant showman: the writer of satires and comedies, the composer and dramaturge. His uniqueness in the world of the Catholic Baroque was precisely the seamlessness of these qualities—his innocence that devotion and theatricality could ever be considered incompatible. And for all the sheer ingenuity and sophistication of both the concept and execution of his works, it is this adamant refusal to divide play and veneration that accounts for the humanity of so much of his sculpture.

In other words, Bernini took comedy seriously, even in the dramatic pieces he wrote for the theater of the Palazzo Barberini, which combined light, music, and startling effects in a conscious attempt to negate the boundary between audience and performance. In one play called *The Flooding of the Tiber* he went so far as to have water gush from the back of the stage toward the front rows, only to be diverted at the last moment by a canal, hidden from the public sight line.

For Bernini, then, the flow of the rivers contained its own powerful drama. And to channel that drama into a fountain that would somehow both symbolize and embody the sacred myths of the rivers was an irresistible challenge. To say that he met that challenge theatrically is, in the terms of the Baroque (or for that matter our own), to bestow on his achievement the highest accolade. For the Fountain of the Four Rivers is a masterpiece in the same way that Bernini's other great works of sacred theater, like the Cornaro Chapel or the *braccia* of St. Peter's, are masterpieces: in demanding the suspension of the beholder's disbelief, the surrender to a vision of the world in which profound cosmic mysteries are given visible, sensuous expression. And it is also the place where all the currents of river mythology, Eastern and Western, Egyptian and Roman, pagan and Christian, flowed toward one great sacred stream. . . .

Even by his own standards of inventiveness, Bernini's master-concept was phenomenally bold. It seemed to defy the conventions of matter, with Domitian's obelisk set atop a rock that was itself pierced on both axes, almost as if the column had erupted from the stone, cracking its mass as it emerged, but then, like a jet of water, leaving the realm of the crag altogether. At its tip, the obelisk was surmounted by a dove holding an olive branch that was simultaneously the emblem of the Pamphili dynasty and the Holy Ghost. Thus the column of the sun, at once light and matter, began in exploding rock and ended in the heavens, with its corporeal substance dissolved into the mystery of Christian triumph.

As if this were not enough, Bernini turned conventional fountain design upside down, both conceptually and structurally. Where fountains were assumed to situate mass in a solid-block base with jets of water rising above it, Bernini concentrates all the kinetic energy in the elemental world of animals, plants, and water in his Edenic rock pool. Above it lie his allegorical rivers, continuing the motion in titanic twists and turns, gesticulations, and muscular exertions, like the great motions of the rivers they personify. And, as always with Bernini, the body language is not a mere dumb show. It is an act of a sacred mystery, a response to *something,* and that something is the fixed, unyielding point in the whole tumultuous composition, the immutable obelisk; the ray of the sun, *Sol Invictus,* the godhead of Amun-Ra, the father of Osiris, the fountainhead of the whole Egypto-Romano-Christian tradition.

No other artist of the Baroque approached Bernini's intensely Catholic yearning for unity. Just as he was forever inventing new ways in which the unification of matter and spirit, body and soul, could be visualized and physically experienced, so, as Irving Lavin has memorably demonstrated, he orchestrated his many skills in a unified performance; the nearest the Baroque came to a sacred *Gesamtkunstwerk.** In his fountain in the Piazza Navona, the four rivers of paradise that divided the world are brought back to their single mysterious source: the rock of Creation. . . .

The construction of the Fountain of the Four Rivers continued through the Holy Year of 1650, with workmen busy not only carving but gilding the papal arms, coloring the palm tree and lilies. Shortly before its completion, the pope made an inspection along with a large retinue and asked Bernini if he would turn on the

---

*Masterpiece.

water supply. Typically, the artist refused, claiming he had not been given enough notice, but as Innocent was about to leave, according to Baldinucci, "he heard a loud sound of water" and, turning round, saw it "gushing out in great abundance."

At that time it was surely the greatest water spectacle in any urban space in Europe: the ultimate consummation, not merely of papal Rome's hydraulic revival but of the entire tradition of fluvial vitality. Perhaps it was in the spirit of paternal refreshment that a year later, in 1652, Innocent inaugurated the custom of the *piazza allagata,* by opening the sluices at the base of the fountain in the burning, dusty month of August and allowing the waters of the Acqua Vergine to flood the square. It was, in the first place, a boon to the parched throats and bodies of the citizenry, but before long (and for two centuries) a ritual had been created by which the most splendid carriages of the Roman nobility would process through the waters, the horses splashing about the ancient stadium to the cheers of the crowds.

But when Innocent bid the waters rise in the long oval of the Piazza Navona, he was, in effect, finally baptizing the pagan Circo Agonale, creating a sacred river in the heart of Rome, a stone's throw from the Tiber bend. . . .

FOR THE LITERARY TRAVELER

Piazza Navona. The name stirs exaltation in those who know it. Off the Corso Vittorio Emanuele II, along the narrow streets of the medieval quarter—the shops and sights so tempting you could take days to find it—Navona's dramatic center is Bernini's **Fontana del Quattro Fiumi**— the Fountain of the Four Rivers. He designed the whole but carved only the horse. The elliptical shape of the piazza indicates its original function as the Circus or Stadium built by the Emperor Domitian in 86 A.D. and used for horse racing and games. The name, *Navona,* recalls the old custom of flooding the piazza for the staging of mock naval battles. To this day Romans enjoy themselves here. Christmas is a month-long carnival. The Feast of Epiphany, on the eve and day of January 6th, has its own festival called Befana, the name of the witch who brings sugar to good little children, coal to the rest. (Her name, "Befana," is a corruption of "Epiphany.") On New Year's Day, young mothers wear mink to noon Mass in the church of **Sant'Agnese in Agone,** opposite the great Fountain; behind the women in the pews, young fathers watch over toddlers in strollers or the escapees who have the run of the aisles and no one blinks. The church was built by Bernini's rival, Borromini, over the ruins of the ancient Stadium of Domitian where St. Agnes is said to have been beheaded by the Emperor Diocletian. (See pages 91–92)

In all seasons Navona's energy sparks the crowds, who linger and stroll, people and place seeming to embody simultaneously the very spirit of Baroque art: an enthusiasm of feeling, expressing an affirmative and impetuous attitude toward life. Summertime Navona is best around midnight, when it's cool and calmer, and you can sit marvelling at one of the many outdoor cafes. (That *paradiso di dolci,* **Tre Scalini,** is famous for *tartufo*—a baroque dessert! You're free to sit until the shutters go down and *buona notte* fills the air.)

Other jewels of the Baroque enrich the neighborhood surrounding Navona. Borromini's exquisite church of **Sant'Ivo alla Sapienza,** its spiraled dome a landmark from Rome's hills, two minutes away in Rinascimento, No. 40; the cortile, or courtyard, home of the University of Rome from the fifteenth century until 1935, is a pretty setting for the lively concerts performed in summer at 9 P.M. (Tickets at the door, all day the date of the concert.)

Farther east, beyond the Pantheon, along Via Del Seminario (toward the other Corso, Via del Corso), is the church of **Sant'Ignazio,** with a wild Baroque ceiling to celebrate the founder of the Jesuits. "The tiny piazza it commands," said Elizabeth Bowen, "is architected in elegant unity with the church's frontage; here is Rome's most perfect little outdoor 'drawing room'—as distinct from ballroom." Enjoy it in the restaurant, **Le Cave di Sant'Ignazio Da Sabatini,** Piazza Sant'Ignazio 169, tel 06 686 5308.

Returning to the Corso Vittorio Emanuele, in the **Chiesa Nuova**— the New Church of the beloved Counter-Reformation priest, St. Philip Neri—there are paintings by Bernini's contemporary, Peter Paul Rubens (1577–1640). (Across from it, at number 246, **Bella Napoli** is famous for its *sfogliatelle,* a delectably baroque pastry from Naples, considered the best in Rome.) A ten-minute walk south, to Via Del Plebiscito, the **Gesù,** the first Jesuit church built in Rome (1568–1584), epitomizes over-the-top Counter-Reformation architecture and decoration. Bernini's painting of St. Robert Bellarmine, a theologian and stalwart of the Inquisition—he interrogated Bruno—hangs in a side chapel.

In the seventeenth century, Rome was not only the capital of Catholic Christianity but the artistic center of the whole of Western Europe. Bernini was regarded as its master artist, and the works that made his reputation are all over the city, far beyond Navona. Here's a small selection.

In the **Galleria Borghese** (www.galleriaborghese.it), **Daphne and Apollo.** In the **Cornaro Chapel** in the church of **Santa Maria della Vittoria,** the sculptured group of **St. Teresa in Ecstasy.** Bernini and other Baroque artists represent religion as a sensual experience, body and soul bursting and overflowing with the longing for infinity. In the church of **San Francesco a Ripa** in Trastevere (which preserves the cell of St. Francis of Assisi who came to Rome in 1219 to ask the pope's permission to start his new order) Bernini's amazing sculpture of **Blessed Ludovica Albertoni** has been variously interpreted as a woman on her deathbed and as a woman surrendered to sensual pleasure. Both Teresa and Ludovica have much in common with the period's language of religious emotionalism, evident in exaggerated hymns, litanies, official prayers, and devotions. In the church of **Sant'Andrea della Fratte,** two of the angels that Bernini sculpted for the Ponte Sant'Angelo stand near the main altar. (Bernini lived across from the church's piazza, in the palazzo at Via della Mercede 11.) In the colossal ellipse of **Piazza San Pietro,** the wide embrace of Bernini's semicircular colonnades expresses his version of Catholicism: expansive, generous, a giant hug to the thousands of pilgrims who gather in front of the basilica.

But Bernini, the lifelong *amico dell'acqua*—friend of water—seems his most magnificent in Rome's fountains. Some of the Grand Tourists who arrived en masse in the next century said they were more enraptured by the fountains of Rome, that profusion of rushing water, than all the other wonders of the city. There are fountains of all sizes everywhere, but Bernini's "greats" include: the **Triton** and the small **Fountain of the Bees** in Piazza Barberini; the **Barcaccia** in Piazza di Spagna;

Fontana delle Tartarughe, or the Turtle Fountain, in Piazza Mattei to which Bernini added the turtles; possibly **Fontana di Trevi**—the Trevi Fountain—which he worked on for the Barberini Pope Urban VIII; the fountain in Piazza San Pietro; and his masterpiece, Navona's Four Rivers of the world.

When British writer Dorothy Sayers read Dante's *Paradiso,* she rejoiced:

> This is what he thought reality was like, when you get to the *eterna fontana* at the center of it: this laughter, this inebriation, this riot of charity and hilarity.

The riot of Navona comes to mind, Bernini's wild fountain at the inebriate heart of Rome.

ROME OF THE GRAND TOUR(ISTS)

Eighteenth Century to the Present

The Farnesina ❧ The Botanical Gardens ❧ Villa Doria Pamphili
St. Prassede ❧ The Capitoline Hill ❧ The Monkey Tower
Church of the Capuchins ❧ The Catacombs ❧ The Pincian Hill
The Esquiline Hill ❧ The Campagna ❧ The Corso
Villa d'Este, Tivoli ❧ The Borghese Gardens ❧ Villa Borghese
Piazza dell'Esedra ❧ The Baths of Diocletian ❧ Palazzo Altemps
Octagonal Hall ❧ Piazza Venezia ❧ St. Maria in Aracoeli
Via Nazionale ❧ The Protestant Cemetery ❧ Keats's House
Via Coronari ❧ Palazzo Taverna ❧ Lake Nemi
The Spanish Steps ❧ Piazza di Spagna ❧ Via del Babuino
Caffé Greco ❧ St. Maria Sopra Minerva ❧ Piazza Campitelli

❧

*Goethe ❧ Robert Browning ❧ Nathaniel Hawthorne
Henry James ❧ Edith Wharton ❧ William Carlos Williams
John Updike ❧ Eleanor Clark ❧ Muriel Spark ❧ Alice Steinbach
William Murray ❧ André Aciman*

*In Rome you learn to "See with an eye that can feel, feel with a
hand that can see."*

—GOETHE

JOHANN WOLFGANG GOETHE

1749–1832

Famous as the author of The Sorrows of Young Werther, *Goethe abruptly quit his job with the Weimar government in 1786 and left for Italy.* Italian Journey, *excerpted here, recounts his two years in Rome, Naples, and Sicily in the form of journal entries and letters. We meet a young man who is seeing everything, walking everywhere, meeting everyone, all the while working on* Iphigenia *and* Faust *and* Egmont. *He took drawing lessons in Rome because he thought drawing was the best way to train himself to pay attention to the external world, a sure defense against the writer's tempation to excessive subjectivity. He's the best kind of travel writer, affectionate, energetic, specific, his intelligent outsider's eye catching the subtleties of Roman life. "To read about a man who is so enjoying himself is enormous fun," wrote Auden, who translated* Italian Journey. *Goethe was one of the best-known of the artists who, from the eighteenth century into the twentieth, came south on their "Grand Tour" to Rome: Tobias Smollett, James Boswell, Casanova, Bizet, Berlioz, Gogol, Wagner, Liszt, Stendhal, Balzac, Byron, the Shelleys, the Brownings, Margaret Fuller, Thackeray, Mark Twain, Ibsen, Chekhov, Dickens, James Fenimore Cooper, Emerson, Longfellow, Melville, Harriet Hosmer, Louisa May Alcott, Constance Fenimore Woolson, Henry Adams, Virginia Woolf, and the Americans who appear in this book, Henry James, Nathaniel Hawthorne, Edith Wharton, William Carlos Williams, John Updike, Eleanor Clark, William Murray. Any one of them might have echoed the words of one French traveler: "Rome is beautiful—so beautiful that all the rest of Italy seems to me little in comparison."*

From ITALIAN JOURNEY
[1786–1788]

10 November

I am now in a state of clarity and calm such as I had not known for a long time. My habit of looking at and accepting things as they are without pretension is standing me in good stead and makes me secretly very happy. Each day brings me some new remarkable object, some new great picture, and a whole city which the imagination will never encompass, however long one thinks and dreams.

Today I went to the pyramid of Cestius and in the evening climbed to the top of the Palatine, where the ruins of the imperial palaces stand like rocks. It is impossible to convey a proper idea of such things. Nothing here is mediocre, and if, here and there, something is in poor taste, it, too, shares in the general grandeur.

When I indulge in self-reflection, as I like to do occasionally, I discover in myself a feeling which gives me great joy. Let me put it like this. In this place, whoever looks seriously about him and has eyes to see is bound to become a stronger character: he acquires a sense of strength hitherto unknown to him.

His soul receives the seal of a soundness, a seriousness without pedantry, and a joyous composure. At least, I can say that I have never been so sensitive to the things of this world as I am here. The blessed consequences will, I believe, affect my whole future life.

So let me seize things one by one as they come; they will sort themselves out later. I am not here simply to have a good time, but to devote myself to the noble objects about me, to educate myself before I reach forty.

Rome, 17 November

Here we are back again! Tonight there was a tremendous downpour with thunder and lightning. It still goes on raining, but remains warm. Today I saw the frescoes by Domenichino in Sant'Andrea della Valle and the Carracci in the Farnese Gallery. Too much for months, let alone for a single day.

18 November

The weather has been fine and clear. In the Farnesina I saw the story of Psyche, colour reproductions of which have for so long brightened my rooms. Later I saw Raphael's *Transfiguration* in San Pietro in Montorio. These paintings are like friends with whom one has long been acquainted through correspondence and now sees face to face for the first time. The difference when one lives with them is that one's sympathies and antipathies are soon revealed.

In every corner there are magnificent things which are almost never mentioned and have not been disseminated over the world in etchings and reproductions. I shall bring some with me, done by excellent young artists.

22 November
On the Feast of St Cecilia

I must write a few lines to keep alive the memory of this happy day or, at least, make a historical report of what I have been enjoying. The day was cloudless and warm. I went with Tischbein to the square in front of St Peter's. We walked up and down until we felt too hot, when we sat in the shadow of the great obelisk—it was just wide enough for two—and ate some grapes we had bought nearby. Then we went into the Sistine Chapel, where the light on the frescoes was at its best. Looking at these marvellous works of Michelangelo's, our admiration was divided between the Last Judgement and the various paintings on the ceiling. The self-assurance, the virility, the grandeur of conception of this master defy expression. After we had looked at everything over and over again, we left the chapel and entered St Peter's. Thanks to the brilliant sunshine outside, every part of the church was visible. Since we were determined to enjoy its magnitude and splendour, we did not, this time, allow our overfastidious taste to put us off and abstained from carping criticism. We enjoyed everything that was enjoyable.

Then we climbed up on to the roof, where one finds a miniature copy of a well-built town with houses, shops, fountains, churches (at least they looked like churches from the outside) and a large temple—everything in the open air with beautiful walks between. We went into the Cupola and looked out at the Apennines, Mount Soracte, the volcanic hills behind Tivoli, Frascati, Castel Gandolfo, the plain and the sea beyond it. Below us lay the city of Rome in all its length and breadth with its hill-perched palaces, domes, etc. Not a breath of air was stirring, and it was as hot as a greenhouse inside the copper ball. After taking in everything, we descended again and asked to have the doors opened which lead to the cornices of the dome, the tambour and the nave. One can walk all the way round and look down from the height on the whole church. As we were standing on the cornice of the tambour, far below us we could see the Pope walking to make his afternoon devotions. St Peter's had not failed us. Then we climbed all the way down, went out into the square and had a frugal but cheerful meal at an inn nearby, after which we went on to the church of St Cecilia. . . .

2 December

To have beautiful warm weather, with only an occasional rainy day, at the end of November is a new experience for me. We spend the fine days out of doors, the wet ones in our room, and always find something to enjoy, to study or to do. . . .

The sun was almost too warm as we dragged ourselves to the Villa Pamfili and stayed in its lovely gardens until evening. A large meadow, bordered with evergreen oaks and tall stone-pines, was dotted with daisies which all had their little heads turned to the sun. This set me off again on botanical speculations, which I resumed the next day during a walk to Monte Mario, Villa Mellini and Villa Madama. It is fascinating to observe how a vegetation behaves when its lively growth is never interrupted by severe cold. One sees no buds here and realizes for the first time what a bud is. The arbutus is again in bloom while its last fruits are still ripening. The orange trees also show blossoms, as well as half- and fully-ripe fruits, but these, unless they stand between buildings, are covered at this time of year. There is room for speculation about the cypress, which, when it is very old and full-grown, is the most dignified of all trees. Soon I shall pay a visit to the Botanical Garden, where I hope to learn a good deal. Nothing, above all, is comparable to the new life that a reflective person experiences when he observes a new country. Though I am still always myself, I believe I have been changed to the very marrow of my bones.

For The Literary Traveler

Goethe's almost two years in Rome was a time of conversion for him, as a writer and a man. Were you to follow in his footsteps, you'd see every ancient monument and ruin, the Christian basilicas, the Renaissance palazzos converted into museums, the paintings in the galleries, the gardens. (If you dove into the Tiber during a heat wave, as he did, one gulp would kill you.) He loved taking long strolls at night, sitting late in the piazza. "The moonlit nights here are like those in dreams or fairytales."

He found many of his pleasures on the Trastevere side of the river: Raphael's masterpieces (1483–1520)—though Michelangelo would remain Goethe's favorite—at the **Villa Farnesina** (Via della Lungara

230; bus 280 to Lungotevere, Farnesina, or walk south from St. Peter's. Open 9–1, Tues–Sat). "One of the high-water marks of the Renaissance," Keith Christiansen calls the vault of the ceiling, the **Loggia of Cupid and Psyche:** "The story of Cupid and his beloved Psyche, who, after various tasks, is finally admitted to the company of the gods. . . . The pagan joy and wit of these scenes no less than their sheer beauty provide endless delight . . . don't miss the phallic cucumber fertilizing a fig above the hand of Mercury—just in case you didn't get the erotic subtext of the story!" The Villa was built as a suburban retreat by Raphael's patron, the surreally rich Sienese banker, Agostino Chigi, "Agostino the Magnificent" as he was called. No Grand Tourist would miss this splendor of architecture and painting. In the **Sala di Galatea** the fresco of **Galatea,** the beautiful sea nymph, framed by scenes in the lunettes from Ovid's *Metamorphoses,* are gorgeous. At the time he was working here, Raphael's lover was "La Fornarina," the daughter of a baker, from the nearby parish of Santa Dorotea (the church is left, then right, of Porta Settimiana), who, according to legend, lived in what is now the restaurant next to Porta Settimiana, **Romolo della Fornarina.** (12–3; 7:30–12, Tues–Sun; in summer ask for a table in the candle-lit outdoor garden). When Raphael seemed to be taking too long to complete the commission—he took time off to visit "La Fornarina" (Margherita Luta)—Chigi moved her into the Villa for the sake of a more productive work schedule for his artist-in-residence. Raphael's supposed portrait of his lover, which scandalized Hawthorne (that "trollop," he snapped, disowning with one word his transgressive Hester Prynne), hangs in Palazzo Barberini. According to Auden, Goethe, after a ten-year platonic relationship with an older woman in Germany, experienced sexual satisfaction for the first time in Italy; it shows in the portraits that were made of him while he was living in Rome. (He once considered *Erotica Romana* as a title for one of his books about Rome.)

Off Via Lungara, two minutes away from Villa Farnesina, Via Corsini leads into the **Botanical Gardens,** which Goethe, lover of nature, student of plant biology, and author of *The Metamorphosis of Plants* (1790), came to know well (9–6:30, closed Sun). The shady unvisited gardens—orchids, palm trees, sequoias, seven thousand plant species from all over the world, drizzling fountains, and ponds—belong to the

University of Rome, whose students will answer your questions. Goethe, the inspired naturalist, also roamed the parkland of the Villa Doria Pamphili on the Janiculum, and, on the other side of the Tiber, the Borghese Gardens; Rome placed a monument to his memory on the Via Goethe near the Porta Pinciana. A lover of music, he attended the sung liturgies in honor of the patron saint of music, St. Cecilia, in the ancient church in southern Trastevere that was originally her home in the third century and is named after her. Musical services are still held in her honor on her feast day.

Nearby, across the piazza from the church, is the popular restaurant **Da Meo Patacca,** Piazza di Mercanti 30, which also accompanies the fare with music. Tel 06 581 6198.

Walking north along the Tiber to St. Peter's, which Goethe visited frequently, you'll find the **Vatican Gardens** on the north and west slopes of Vatican Hill, another site for botanical research and stunning views of St. Peter's dome framed by palm trees. To visit this 109-acred sanctuary of gushing fountains, a sixteenth-century Casina—garden house—and jasmine arches, you must book a guided tour (10 A.M., every day except Wed and Sun; reserve at least a day in advance at the entrance to the Vatican Museums; tel 06 698 84676).

On occasion, Goethe stayed home. His residence, now the **Casa di Goethe** in Via del Corso 18, saw the early days of the Corso as a popular site of promenade and carriage rides for the wealthy Grand Tourists. (In the Middle Ages it served as a race course for horses during Carnivale, from Piazza del Popolo to Piazza Venezia.) The shops along the streets that cross it, Ferragamo, Armani, Prada, Gucci, are still thronged with well-heeled foreign visitors, who began their patronage in the eighteenth century. Goethe's house, now a museum, exhibits his sketches of Rome (10–6, closed Tues). The **Goethe Institute** (Via Savoia 15, www.goethe.de/rom) is a contemporary film and cultural center.

Whether writing indoors or exploring on foot, Goethe said he was happier in Rome than he had ever been in his life. "No one who has not been here can have any conception of what an education Rome is. One is, so to speak, reborn. . . ." And then in four words, he put his finger on why this city stirs such happiness: "Nothing here is mediocre," he wrote.

ROBERT BROWNING

1812–1889

"Open my heart and on it see / Graved inside it, Italy!" It was after his
second encounter with the country where he felt most at home that Browning began corresponding with Elizabeth Barrett. After their elopement,
they moved to Italy in 1846, and stayed until Elizabeth's death in 1861.
Florence was their main residence, but they made long trips to Rome, their
house in the neighborhood near the Spanish Steps favored by the English
community of artists and Grand Tourists, at the intersection of the lovely
Via Bocca di Leone and Vicolo del Lupo. Rome provided Browning with
a rich source of material for his dramatic monologues— "The Bishop Orders His Tomb at Saint Praxed's Church," "My Last Duchess," and
"Porphyria's Lover"—about the corruption and evil he saw in the lives of
Renaissance nobles and churchmen. At first, his most enthusiastic readers
were Americans, who were attracted to his unchurched vigorous Protestantism and who used his poems as cultural Baedekers. American travel
agencies used them to advertise steamship voyages to Europe. Ezra Pound
considered Browning the greatest writer of Victorian English and the ances-
tor of modern poetry.

❧

The Bishop Orders His Tomb at Saint Praxed's Church

Rome, 15—

> Vanity, saith the preacher, vanity!
> Draw round my bed: is Anselm keeping back?
> Nephews—sons mine . . . ah God, I know not! Well—
> She, men would have to be your mother once,

Old Gandolf envied me, so fair she was!
What's done is done, and she is dead beside,
Dead long ago, and I am Bishop since,
And as she died so must we die ourselves,
And thence ye may perceive the world's a dream.
Life, how and what is it? As here I lie
In this state-chamber, dying by degrees,
Hours and long hours in the dead night, I ask
"Do I live, am I dead?" Peace, peace seems all.
Saint Praxed's ever was the church for peace;
And so, about this tomb of mine. I fought
With tooth and nail to save my niche, ye know:
—Old Gandolf cozened me, despite my care;
Shrewd was that snatch from out the corner South
He graced his carion with, God curse the same!
Yet still my niche is not so cramped but thence
One sees the pulpit o' the epistle-side,
And somewhat of the choir, those silent seats,
And up into the aery dome where live
The angels, and a sunbeam's sure to lurk:
And I shall fill my slab of basalt there,
And 'neath my tabernacle take my rest,
With those nine columns round me, two and two,
The odd one at my feet where Anselm stands:
Peach-blossom marble all, the rare, the ripe
As fresh-poured red wine of a mighty pulse.
—Old Gandolf with his paltry onion-stone,
Put me where I may look at him! True peach,
Rosy and flawless: how I earned the prize!
Draw close: that conflagration of my church
—What then? So much was saved if aught were missed!
My sons, ye would not be my death? Go dig
The white-grape vineyard where the oil-press stood,
Drop water gently till the surface sink,
And if ye find . . . Ah God, I know not, I! . . .
Bedded in store of rotten fig-leaves soft,

And corded up in a tight olive-frail,
Some lump, ah God, of *lapis lazuli,*
Big as a Jew's head cut off at the nape,
Blue as a vein o'er the Madonna's breast . . .
Sons, all have I bequeathed you, villas, all,
That brave Frascati villa with its bath,
So, let the blue lump poise between my knees,
Like God the Father's globe on both his hands
Ye worship in the Jesu Church so gay,
For Gandolf shall not choose but see and burst!
Swift as a weaver's shuttle fleet our years:
Man goeth to the grave, and where is he?
Did I say basalt for my slab, sons? Black—
'Twas ever antique-black I meant! How else
Shall ye contrast my frieze to come beneath?
The bas-relief in bronze ye promised me,
Those Pans and Nymphs ye wot of, and perchance
Some tripod, thyrsus, with a vase or so,
The Saviour at his sermon on the mount,
Saint Praxed in a glory, and one Pan
Ready to twitch the Nymph's last garment off,
And Moses with the tables . . . but I know
Ye mark me not! What do they whisper thee,
Child of my bowels, Anselm? Ah, ye hope
To revel down my villas while I gasp
Bricked o'er with beggar's mouldy travertine
Which Gandolf from his tomb-top chuckles at!
Nay, boys, ye love me—all of jasper, then!
'Tis jasper ye stand pledged to, lest I grieve.
My bath must needs be left behind, alas!
One block, pure green as a pistachio-nut,
There's plenty jasper somewhere in the world—
And have I not Saint Praxed's ear to pray
Horses for ye, and brown Greek manuscripts,
And mistresses with great smooth marbly limbs?
—That's if ye carve my epitaph aright,

Choice Latin, picked phrase, Tully's every word,
No gaudy ware like Gandolf's second line—
Tully, my masters? Ulpian serves his need!
And then how I shall lie through centuries,
And hear the blessed mutter of the mass,
And see God made and eaten all day long,
And feel the steady candle-flame, and taste
Good strong thick stupefying incense-smoke!
For as I lie here, hours of the dead night,
Dying in state and by such slow degrees,
I fold my arms as if they clasped a crook,
And stretch my feet forth straight as stone can point,
And let the bedclothes, for a mortcloth, drop
Into great laps and folds of sculptor's-work:
And as yon tapers dwindle, and strange thoughts
Grow, with a certain humming in my ears,
About the life before I lived this life,
And this life too, popes, cardinals and priests,
Saint Praxed at his sermon on the mount,
Your tall pale mother with her talking eyes,
And new-found agate urns as fresh as day,
And marble's language, Latin pure, discreet,
—Aha, ELUCESCEBAT[1] quoth our friend?
No Tully, said I, Ulpian at the best!
Evil and brief hath been my pilgrimage.
All *lapis*, all, sons! Else I give the Pope
My villas! Will ye ever eat my heart?
Ever your eyes were as a lizard's quick,
They glitter like your mother's for my soul,
Or ye would heighten my impoverished frieze,
Piece out its starved design, and fill my vase
With grapes, and add a vizor and a Term,[2]
And to the tripod ye would tie a lynx

1 "He was famous."—Wrongly formed from the Latin verb.

2 A bust on a square pillar, named for the Roman god of boundaries, Terminus.

That in his struggle throws the thyrsus down,
To comfort me on my entablature
Whereon I am to lie till I must ask
"Do I live, am I dead?" There, leave me, there!
For ye have stabbed me with ingratitude
To death—ye wish it—God, ye wish it! Stone—
Gritstone, a-crumble! Clammy squares which sweat
As if the corpse they keep were oozing through—
And no more *lapis* to delight the world!
Well go! I bless ye. Fewer tapers there,
But in a row: and, going, turn your backs
—Ay, like departing altar-ministrants,
And leave me in my church, the church for peace,
That I may watch at leisure if he leers—
Old Gandolf, at me, from his onion-stone,
As still he envied me, so fair she was!

FOR THE LITERARY TRAVELER

The voice of the poem is cold and cynical but its setting, **Santa Prassede,** is one of the loveliest churches in Rome. "Saint Praxed's ever was the church for peace," says the dying old fraud of a bishop, the narrator of Browning's dramatic monologue. You might visit Santa Prassede on the same walk that takes you to Santa Pudenziana (see page 77): it's just up the Viminale hill and across the piazza from Santa Maria Maggiore. Enter through a side door into the right aisle, and there, immediately to your right, is a chapel laid with bishops' tombs.

Prassede and Pudenziana were sisters, daughters of Pudens, and according to early Christian stories, St. Peter's converts. The apse mosaic shows them being introduced to Christ by Peter and Paul. The apostles' friendly gesture—their hands fall on the sisters' shoulders—recalls the easygoing warmth of Paul's salute to his Roman friends in the Letter to the Romans (see pages 86–87). The humanity of the apse image and its bright colors, the friends of Christ happy in their blue heaven, amidst poppies and the palm trees of paradise, the effect makes later Christian history—the centuries of "papal sin" that interested Browning—seem unreal. Supposedly the church, a second-century oratory, was built above the house where Prassede hid persecuted Christians. After twenty-three of them were slaughtered in front of her, she sponged up their blood and put it in a well where she was later buried: a circle of porphyry marks the spot on the cosmatesque floor in the center of the nave. In the famous **Chapel of St. Zeno**—"the most exquisite little mosaic-decorated chapel in Rome," in the words of Georgina Masson— you see on the left wall a mosaic of Theodora "Episcopa," crowned with the white square nimbus, an image Karen Jo Torjesen in her book *When Women Were Priests* claims as evidence that women acted as bishops in the early church, long before Browning's bishop of the 1500s has his moment of deathbed self-perception: "Evil and brief hath been my pilgrimage." His ruminations on the precious stones that might be used on his tomb may have been inspired by the beautiful stones that decorate this church, including a broken column of jasper against which Christ was said to have been scourged (against a wall to the right of the Chapel of St. Zeno).

Another ancient Roman church figures in Browning's verse novel *The Ring and the Book:* **San Lorenzo in Lucina,** to the west/left off Via del Corso (walking north), and near the poet's neighborhood (right off the Corso). Despite many restorations, the antiquity of this pretty piazza and the church is striking, as well as the gloom of the church interior. Built to commemorate the martyrdom of St. Lorenzo (a chapel preserves a part of the gridiron on which he was roasted alive), the church figures in Browning's story of Pompilia, a young woman who loses her life, a victim of collusion among evil people, including the officiating priest at her marriage in San Lorenzo to a hideous old man when she was a child of thirteen:

> I am just seventeen years and five months old,
> And, if I lived one day more, three full weeks;
> 'Tis writ so in the church's register,
> Lorenzo in Lucina, all my names
> At length, so many names for one poor child,
> —Francesca Camilla Vittoria Angela
> Pompilia Comparini,—laughable!

Also 'tis writ that I was married there
Four years ago

        All these few things
I know are true,—will you remember them?
Because time flies. The surgeon cared for me,
To count my wounds,—Twenty-two dagger-wounds,
Five deadly, but I do not suffer much—
Or too much pain,—and am to die to-night. . . .

The Ring and the Book is long, but reads like a gothic novel. Its multiple points of view and psychological subtlety show why Ezra Pound called Browning an early modern writer.

(***Caffè Teichner,*** *in the pretty Piazza San Lorenzo in Lucina 17, has excellent coffee and sandwiches, and a place to sit if you want to continue with Pompilia's awful story.*)

Browning's street, **Via Bocca di Leone,** on the other side of the Corso and intersecting **Via Condotti,** is a pedestrian walkway through the nineteenth-century English ghetto, its fashionable prosperity worlds away, it would seem, from the cruelty of Browning's religious hypocrites. The **Hotel Inghilterra,** number 14, welcomed Lizst, Henry James, Hemingway, William Murray (who praises the bar's perfect martini), and Elizabeth Bowen, while she worked on *A Time in Rome;* the lounges still breathe with the luxury required by the Grand Tourists, though their character has changed since the visitations of artists and writers.

A few blocks south, the **Anglo-American Bookstore** in Via della Vite 102 (Mon–Fri 9–1, 4–8, Sat 9–7:30; tel 06 6795222; www.aab.it) stocks the literary Grand Tourists and contemporary writers: Browning's *Ring,* James's novels, the poetry of Keats and Shelley and Byron, all the Penguins. Italian writers who've been translated into English are also available, including *Ragazzi,* the hard-to-find novel of Pier Paolo Pasolini. The owners, a Roman family of three generations, are knowledgeable and gracious.

NATHANIEL HAWTHORNE

1804–1864

Hawthorne was the celebrated author of The Scarlet Letter *when he arrived in Rome in January 1858. The mercurial and handsome New Englander couldn't shake the cold he picked up in the drafty palazzo he rented. "How I dislike the place," he griped. But some months later, he changed his tune: "Rome certainly does draw into itself my heart." The city he loved and hated became the core of his next and last novel* The Marble Faun *(1860). To this day, readers and travelers use it as a guide to Rome. The man whom his friend Herman Melville called "deep as Dante" had once written in "The Custom-House" what descendants of Puritan Salem knew in their marrow bone: "The past was not dead." Rome was radical proof.*

From THE MARBLE FAUN: OR, THE ROMANCE OF MONTE BENI

I
Miriam, Hilda, Kenyon, Donatello

Four individuals, in whose fortunes we should be glad to interest the reader, happened to be standing in one of the saloons of the sculpture-gallery, in the Capitol, at Rome. It was that room (the first, after ascending the staircase) in the centre of which reclines the noble and most pathetic figure of the Dying Gladiator, just sinking into his death-swoon. Around the walls stand the Antinous, the Amazon, the Lycian Apollo, the Juno; all famous productions of antique sculpture, and still shining in the undiminished majesty and beauty of their ideal life, although the marble, that embodies them, is yellow with time, and perhaps corroded by the damp earth in which they lay buried for centuries. Here, likewise, is seen a symbol (as apt, at this moment, as it was two thousand years ago) of the Human Soul, with its choice of Innocence or Evil close at hand, in the pretty figure of a child, clasping a dove to her bosom, but assaulted by a snake.

From one of the windows of this saloon, we may see a flight of broad stone steps, descending alongside the antique and massive foundation of the Capitol, towards the battered triumphal arch of Septimius Severus, right below. Farther on, the eye skirts along the edge of the desolate Forum, (where Roman washerwomen hang out their linen to the sun,) passing over a shapeless confusion of modern edifices, piled rudely up with ancient brick and stone, and over the domes of Christian churches, built on the old pavements of heathen temples, and supported by the very pillars that once up-held them. At a distance beyond—yet but a little way, considering how much history is heaped into the intervening space—rises the great sweep of the Coliseum, with the blue sky brightening through its upper tier of arches. Far off, the view is shut in by the Alban mountains, looking just the same, amid all this decay and change, as when Romulus gazed thitherward over his half-finished wall.

We glance hastily at these things—at this bright sky, and those blue, distant mountains, and at the ruins, Etruscan, Roman, Christian, venerable with a threefold antiquity, and at the company of world-famous statues in the saloon—in the hope of putting the reader into that state of feeling which is experienced oftenest at Rome. It is a vague sense of ponderous remembrances; a perception of such weight and density in a by-gone life, of which this spot was the centre, that the present moment is pressed down or crowded out, and our individual affairs and interests are but half as real, here, as elsewhere. Viewed through this medium, our narrative—into which are woven some airy and unsubstantial threads, intermixed with others, twisted out of the commonest stuff of human existence—may seem not widely different from the texture of all our lives. Side by side with the massiveness of the Roman Past, all matters, that we handle or dream of, now-a-days, look evanescent and visionary alike.

It might be, that the four persons, whom we are seeking to introduce, were conscious of this dreamy character of the present, as compared with the square blocks of granite wherewith the Romans built their lives. Perhaps it even contributed to the fanciful merriment which was just now their mood. When we find ourselves fading into shadows and unrealities, it seems hardly worth while to be sad, but rather to laugh as gaily as we may, and ask little reason wherefore.

Of these four friends of ours, three were artists, or connected with Art; and, at this moment, they had been simultaneously struck by a resemblance between one of the antique statues, a well-known master-piece of Grecian sculpture, and a young Italian, the fourth member of their party.

"You must needs confess, Kenyon," said a dark-eyed young woman, whom her friends called Miriam, "that you never chiselled out of marble, nor wrought in clay, a more vivid likeness than this, cunning a bust-maker as you think yourself. The portraiture is perfect in character, sentiment, and feature. If it were a picture, the resemblance might be half-illusive and imaginary; but here, in this Pentelic marble, it is a substantial fact, and may be tested by absolute touch and measurement. Our friend Donatello is the very Faun of Praxiteles. Is it not true, Hilda?"

"Not quite—almost—yes, I really think so," replied Hilda, a slender, brown-haired, New England girl, whose perceptions of form and expression were wonderfully clear and delicate.—"If there is any difference between the two faces, the reason may be, I suppose, that the Faun dwelt in woods and fields, and consorted with his like; whereas, Donatello has known cities a little, and such people as ourselves. But the resemblance is very close, and very strange."

"Not so strange," whispered Miriam mischievously; "for no Faun in Arcadia was ever a greater simpleton than Donatello. He has hardly a man's share of wit, small as that may be. It is a pity there are no longer any of this congenial race of rustic creatures, for our friend to consort with!"

"Hush, naughty one!" returned Hilda. "You are very ungrateful, for you well know he has wit enough to worship you, at all events."

"Then the greater fool he!" said Miriam so bitterly that Hilda's quiet eyes were somewhat startled.

"Donatello, my dear friend," said Kenyon, in Italian, "pray gratify us all by taking the exact attitude of this statue."

The young man laughed, and threw himself into the position in which the statue has been standing for two or three thousand years. In truth, allowing for the difference of costume, and if a lion's skin could have been substituted for his modern Talma, and a rustic pipe for his stick, Donatello might have figured perfectly as the marble Faun, miraculously softened into flesh and blood.

"Yes; the resemblance is wonderful," observed Kenyon, after examining the marble and the man with the accuracy of a sculptor's eye.—"There is one point, however—or, rather, two points—in respect to which our friend Donatello's abundant curls will not permit us to say whether the likeness is carried into minute detail."

And the sculptor directed the attention of the party to the ears of the beautiful statue which they were contemplating.

But we must do more than merely refer to this exquisite work of art; it must be described, however inadequate may be the effort to express its magic peculiarity in words.

The Faun is the marble image of a young man, leaning his right arm on the trunk or stump of a tree; one hand hangs carelessly by his side; in the other, he holds the fragment of a pipe, or some such sylvan instrument of music. His only garment—a lion's skin, with the claw upon his shoulder—falls half-way down his back, leaving the limbs and entire front of the figure nude. The form, thus displayed, is marvellously graceful, but has a fuller and more rounded outline, more flesh, and less of heroic muscle, than the old sculptors were wont to assign to their types of masculine beauty. The character of the face corresponds with the figure; it is most agree-

able in outline and feature, but rounded, and somewhat volup-
tuously developed, especially about the throat and chin; the nose is
almost straight, but very slightly curves inward, thereby acquiring
an indescribable charm of geniality and humour. The mouth, with
its full, yet delicate lips, seems so nearly to smile outright, that it
calls forth a responsive smile. The whole statue—unlike anything
else that ever was wrought in that severe material of marble—
conveys the idea of an amiable and sensual creature, easy, mirthful,
apt for jollity, yet not incapable of being touched by pathos. It is
impossible to gaze long at this stone image without conceiving a
kindly sentiment towards it, as if its substance were warm to the
touch, and imbued with actual life. It comes very close to some of
our pleasantest sympathies.

Perhaps it is the very lack of moral severity, of any high and
heroic ingredient in the character of the Faun, that makes it so delightful an object to the human eye and to the frailty of the human
heart. The being, here represented, is endowed with no principle
of virtue, and would be incapable of comprehending such. But he
would be true and honest, by dint of his simplicity. We should expect from him no sacrifice nor effort for an abstract cause; there is
not an atom of martyr's stuff in all that softened marble; but he has
a capacity for strong and warm attachment, and might act devot-
edly through its impulse, and even die for it at need. It is possible,
too, that the Faun might be educated through the medium of his
emotions; so that the coarser, animal portion of his nature might
eventually be thrown into the back-ground, though never utterly
expelled.

The animal nature, indeed, is a most essential part of the Faun's
composition; for the characteristics of the brute creation meet and
combine with those of humanity, in this strange, yet true and natural conception of antique poetry and art. Praxiteles has subtly dif-
fused, throughout his work, that mute mystery which so hopelessly
perplexes us, whenever we attempt to gain an intellectual or sym-
pathetic knowledge of the lower orders of creation. The riddle is
indicated, however, only by two definite signs; these are the two
ears of the Faun, which are leaf-shaped, terminating in little peaks,

like those of some species of animals. Though not so seen in the marble, they are probably to be considered as clothed in fine, downy fur. In the coarser representations of this class of mythological creatures, there is another token of brute kindred—a certain caudal appendage—which, if the Faun of Praxiteles must be supposed to possess it at all, is hidden by the lion's skin that forms his garment. The pointed and furry ears, therefore, are the sole indications of his wild, forest nature.

Only a sculptor of the finest imagination, the most delicate taste, the sweetest feeling, and the rarest artistic skill—in a word, a sculptor and a poet too—could have first dreamed of a Faun in this guise, and then have succeeded in imprisoning the sportive and frisky thing, in marble. Neither man nor animal, and yet no monster, but a being in whom both races meet, on friendly ground! The idea grows coarse, as we handle it, and hardens in our grasp. But, if the spectator broods long over the statue, he will be conscious of its spell; all the pleasantness of sylvan life, all the genial and happy characteristics of creatures that dwell in woods and fields, will seem to be mingled and kneaded into one substance, along with the kindred qualities in the human soul. Trees, grass, flowers, woodland streamlets, cattle, deer, and unsophisticated man! The essence of all these was compressed long ago, and still exists, within that discoloured marble surface of the Faun of Praxiteles.

And, after all, the idea may have been no dream, but rather a poet's reminiscence of a period when man's affinity with Nature was more strict, and his fellowship with every living thing more intimate and dear. . . .

VI
The Virgin's Shrine

After Donatello had left the studio, Miriam herself came forth, and taking her way through some of the intricacies of the city, entered what might be called either a widening of a street, or a small piazza. The neighborhood comprised a baker's oven, emitting the usual fragrance of sour bread; a shoe-shop; a linen-draper's shop; a pipe and cigar-shop; a lottery-office; a station for French soldiers, with a sentinel pacing in front; and a fruit-stand, at which a Roman matron was selling the dried kernels of chestnuts, wretched little figs, and some bouquets of yesterday. A church, of course, was near at hand, the façade of which ascended into lofty pinnacles, whereon were perched two or three winged figures of stone, either angelic or allegorical, blowing stone trumpets in close vicinity to the upper windows of an old and shabby palace. This palace was distinguished by a feature not very common in the architecture of Roman edifices; that is to say, a mediæval tower, square, massive, lofty, and battlemented and machicolated at the summit.

At one of the angles of the battlements stood a shrine of the Virgin, such as we see everywhere at the street-corners of Rome, but seldom or never, except in this solitary instance, at a height above the ordinary level of men's views and aspirations. Connected with this old tower and its lofty shrine, there is a legend which we cannot here pause to tell; but, for centuries, a lamp has been burning before the Virgin's image, at noon, at midnight, and at all hours of the twenty-four, and must be kept burning forever, as long as the tower shall stand; or else the tower itself, the palace, and whatever estate belongs to it, shall pass from its hereditary possessor, in accordance with an ancient vow, and become the property of the Church.

As Miriam approached, she looked upward, and saw—not, indeed, the flame of the never-dying lamp, which was swallowed up in the broad sunlight that brightened the shrine—but a flock of white doves, skimming, fluttering, and wheeling about the topmost height of the tower, their silver wings flashing in the pure transparency of the air. Several of them sat on the ledge of the upper window, pushing one another off by their eager struggle for this favourite station, and all tapping their beaks and flapping their wings tumultuously against the panes; some had alighted in the street, far below, but flew hastily upward, at the sound of the window being thrust ajar, and opening in the middle, on rusty hinges, as Roman windows do.

A fair young girl, dressed in white, showed herself at the aperture, for a single instant, and threw forth as much as her two small hands could hold of some kind of food, for the flock of eleemosynary doves. It seemed greatly to the taste of the feathered people; for they tried to snatch beaksful of it from her grasp, caught it in the air, and rustled downward after it upon the pavement.

"What a pretty scene this is!" thought Miriam, with a kindly smile. "And how like a dove she is herself, the fair, pure creature! The other doves know her for a sister, I am sure."

Miriam passed beneath the deep portal of the palace, and turning to the left, began to mount flight after flight of a staircase, which, for the loftiness of its aspiration, was worthy to be Jacob's ladder, or, at all events, the staircase of the Tower of Babel. The city-bustle, which is heard even in Rome, the rumble of wheels over the uncomfortable paving-stones, the hard, harsh cries, re-echoing in the high and narrow streets, grew faint and died away; as the turmoil of the world will always die, if we set our faces to climb heavenward. Higher, and higher still; and now, glancing through the successive windows that threw in their narrow light upon the stairs, her view stretched across the roofs of the city, unimpeded even by the stateliest palaces. Only the domes of churches ascend into this airy region, and hold up their golden crosses on a level with her eye; except that, out of the very heart of Rome, the column of Antoninus thrusts itself upward, with Saint Paul upon its summit, the sole human form that seems to have kept her company.

Finally, the staircase came to an end; save that, on one side of the little entry where it terminated, a flight of a dozen steps gave access to the roof of the tower and the legendary shrine. On the other side was a door, at which Miriam knocked, but rather as a friendly announcement of her presence than with any doubt of hospitable welcome; for, awaiting no response, she lifted the latch and entered.

"What a hermitage you have found for yourself, dear Hilda!" she exclaimed. "You breathe sweet air, above all the evil scents of Rome; and even so, in your maiden elevation, you dwell above our vanities and passions, our moral dust and mud, with the doves and the angels for your nearest neighbors. I should not wonder if the Catholics were to make a Saint of you, like your namesake of old; especially as you have almost avowed yourself of their religion, by undertaking to keep the lamp a-light before the Virgin's shrine."

"No, no, Miriam!" said Hilda, who had come joyfully forward to greet her friend. "You must not call me a Catholic. A Christian girl—even a daughter of the Puritans—may surely pay honour to the idea of Divine Womanhood, without giving up the faith of her forefathers. But how kind you are to climb into my dove-cote!"

"It is no trifling proof of friendship, indeed," answered Miriam. "I should think there were three hundred stairs, at least."

"But it will do you good," continued Hilda. "A height of some fifty feet above the roofs of Rome gives me all the advantages that I could get from fifty miles of distance. The air so exhilarates my spirits, that sometimes I feel half-inclined to attempt a flight from the top of my tower, in the faith that I should float upward!"

"Oh, pray don't try it!" said Miriam laughing. "If it should turn out that you are less than an angel, you would find the stones of the Roman pavement very hard; and if an angel indeed, I am afraid you would never come down among us again."

This young American girl was an example of the freedom of life which it is possible for a female artist to enjoy at Rome. She dwelt in her tower, as free to descend into the corrupted atmosphere of the city beneath, as one of her companion-doves to fly downward into the street;—all alone, perfectly independent, under her own sole guardianship, unless watched over by the Virgin, whose shrine she tended;—doing what she liked, without a suspicion or a shadow upon the snowy whiteness of her fame. The customs of artist-life bestow such liberty upon the sex, which is elsewhere restricted within so much narrower limits; and it is perhaps an indication that, whenever we admit woman to a wider scope of pursuits and professions, we must also remove the shackles of our present con-ventional rules, which would then become an insufferable restraint on either maid or wife. The system seems to work unexceptionably in Rome; and in many other cases, as in Hilda's, purity of heart and life are allowed to assert themselves, and to be their own proof and security, to a degree unknown in the society of other cities. . . .

XXXVI
Hilda's Tower

When we have once known Rome, and left her where she lies, like a long decaying corpse, retaining a trace of the noble shape it was, but with accumulated dust and a fungous growth overspreading all its more admirable features;—left her in utter weariness, no doubt, of her narrow, crooked, intricate streets, so uncomfortably paved with little squares of lava that to tread over them is a penitential pilgrimage, so indescribably ugly, moreover, so cold, so alley-like, into which the sun never falls, and where a chill wind forces its deadly breath into our lungs;—left her, tired of the sight of those immense, seven-storied, yellow-washed hovels, or call them palaces, where all that is dreary in domestic life seems magnified and multiplied, and weary of climbing those staircases, which ascend from a ground-floor of cook-shops, coblers' stalls, stables, and regiments of cavalry, to a middle region of princes, cardinals, and ambassadours, and an upper tier of artists, just beneath the unattainable sky;—left her, worn out with shivering at the cheerless and smoky fireside, by day, and feasting with our own substance the ravenous little populace of a Roman bed, at night;—left her, sick at heart of Italian trickery, which has uprooted whatever faith in man's integrity had endured till now, and sick at stomach of sour bread, sour wine, rancid butter, and bad cookery, needlessly bestowed on evil meats;— left her, disgusted with the pretence of Holiness and the reality of Nastiness, each equally omnipresent;—left her, half-lifeless from the languid atmosphere, the vital principle of which has been used up, long ago, or corrupted by myriads of slaughters;—left her, crushed down in spirit with the desolation of her ruin, and the hopelessness of her future;—left her, in short, hating her with all our might, and adding our individual curse to the Infinite Anathema which her old crimes have unmistakeably brought down;—

when we have left Rome in such mood as this, we are astonished by the discovery, by-and-by, that our heart-strings have mysteriously attached themselves to the Eternal City, and are drawing us thitherward again, as if it were more familiar, more intimately our home, than even the spot where we were born!

It is with a kindred sentiment, that we now follow the course of our story back through the Flaminian Gate,* and threading our way to the Via Portoghese, climb the staircase to the upper chamber of the tower, where we last saw Hilda.

Hilda all along intended to pass the summer in Rome; for she had laid out many high and delightful tasks, which she could the better complete while her favourite haunts were deserted by the multitude that thronged them, throughout the winter and early spring. Nor did she dread the summer-atmosphere, although generally held to be so pestilential. She had already made trial of it, two years before, and found no worse effect than a kind of dreamy languor, which was dissipated by the first cool breezes that came with Autumn. The thickly populated centre of the city, indeed, is never affected by the feverish influence that lies in wait in the Campagna, like a besieging foe, and nightly haunts those beautiful lawns and woodlands, around the suburban villas, just at the season when they most resemble Paradise. What the flaming sword was to the first Eden, such is the malaria to these sweet gardens and groves. We may wander through them, of an afternoon, it is true; but they cannot be made a home and a reality, and to sleep among them is death. They are but illusions, therefore, like the show of gleaming waters and shadowy foliage, in a desert.

But Rome, within the walls, at this dreaded season, enjoys its festal days, and makes itself merry with characteristic and hereditary pastimes, for which its broad piazzas afford abundant room. It leads its own life with a freer spirit, now that the artists and foreign visitors are scattered abroad. No bloom, perhaps, would be visible in a cheek that should be unvisited, throughout the summer, by more invigorating winds than any within fifty miles of the city; no

---

*At Piazza del Popolo.

bloom, but yet (if the mind kept its healthy energy) a subdued and colourless well-being. There was consequently little risk in Hilda's purpose to pass the summer-days in the galleries of Roman palaces, and her nights in that aërial chamber, whither the heavy breath of the city and its suburbs could not aspire. It would probably harm her no more than it did the white doves, who sought the same high atmosphere at sunset, and, when morning came, flew down into the narrow streets, about their daily business, as Hilda likewise did.

With the Virgin's aid and blessing, (which might be hoped for even by a heretic, who so religiously lit the lamp before her shrine,) the New England girl would sleep securely in her old Roman tower, and go forth on her pictorial pilgrimages without dread or peril. In view of such a summer, Hilda had anticipated many months of lonely, but unalloyed enjoyment. Not that she had a churlish disinclination to society, or needed to be told that we taste one intellectual pleasure twice, and with double the result, when we taste it with a friend. But, keeping a maiden heart within her bosom, she rejoiced in the freedom that enabled her still to choose her own sphere, and dwell in it, if she pleased, without another inmate. . . .

For The Literary Traveler

Hawthorne was delighted the first time he saw the statue of the Faun in the **Palazzo Nuovo** of the **Capitoline Museum** (www.museicapitolini. org). "I looked at the Faun of Praxiteles," he wrote, "and was sensible of a peculiar charm in it; a sylvan beauty and homeliness, friendly and wild at once. The lengthened, but not preposterous ears, and the little tail, which we infer, have an exquisite effect, and make the spectator smile in his very heart. . . . It seems to me that a story . . . might be contrived on the idea of their species having become intermingled with the human race. . . ." And so he conceived *The Marble Faun,* his "moonshiny romance" about Donatello, the free-spirited sensualist who loves Miriam, a woman with a dark secret, and an opposite couple, the stolid Kenyon who loves Hilda, the Protestant American saint. The drama centers on the moral transformation of these four as they interact with

Rome, which, for Hawthorne, mirrors the psyche's conflicted capacity for evil and virtue. ("Man's conscience was his theme," said Henry James.) A realist, Hawthorne neither sweetens nor resolves the psychic split. It's up to the reader to decide which of the four characters enjoying the Faun on that giddy day in the Capitoline turns into the most pathetic ruin at the end.

Hawthorne's red marble image of innocence and impulse stands on the second (it's called the first) floor of the Capitoline's Palazzo Nuovo museum, the building to your left as you climb the **Cordonata**—the great staircase—and enter the **Piazza del Campidoglio,** the entire astonishing space, the first planned piazza in Rome, designed by Michelangelo (1536). From the windows of the Palazzo Nuovo's galleries, the views of Rome are the same now as what Hawthorne describes (though no laundry hangs in the Forum). The prospect is especially beautiful from the windows of the **Sala degli Imperatori (IV)** in which the Roman imperial busts—so many individualized portraits and expressions!—make you think the history of fiction begins here.

To your right is the other Capitoline Museum, the **Palazzo dei Conservatori.** In its splendid courtyard, nighttime concerts (Rossini, Donizetti, Vivaldi) are held in July and August as part of the "Summer in Rome" festival. The (literal) high point of the Conservatori—and perhaps, in good company, the most delightful place of repose in Rome—is the rooftop cafeteria and terrace restaurant. The domed city is spread out in front of you, and in the clay-colored distance the Tiber cuts beneath the Janiculum's dark green.

Down on the ground, to the right, behind the **Palazzo Senatorio,** the piazza's middle building, through an arch, you'll find the best vantage point for looking down at the Forum, and where the Via del Campidoglio joins the Via di Monte Tarpeio, you can follow the path around the backside of the Capitoline Hill to the site beneath the Palazzo Caffarelli, the best place to see the **Tarpeian Rock,** named after Tarpeia, who betrayed Rome to the Sabines and paid with her life. In ancient Rome, traitors were hurled to their death from this precipice. Hawthorne makes it the setting of the murder that turns *The Marble Faun* into a kind of weird funeral procession. Follow the Via delle Tre

Pile, which climbs left from the balustrade overlooking the Forum, to the **Belvedere di Monte Tarpeio,** a pleasant park planted with trees and open to the public.

The priggish Hilda, Hawthorne's high-toned young Christian woman, holds on to her innocence, high in her virgin Tower, the **Torre della Scimmia,** or Tower of the Monkey. You'll find it where Miriam does: east of Piazza Navona, at the end of Rinascimento, then right, under an arch, then an immediate left (the church of Sant'Agostino is on your right). Tucked into the oblique angle where **Via di Pianellari** and **Via dei Portoghesi** (off Via della Scrofa) meet, above the "Barbiere" sign, you'll see, on top of the Tower, the shrine to the Virgin, the votive lamp still lit in front of it. It shone first in the seventeenth century when a child, snatched by the pet monkey of the resident Scapucci family, was carried to the roof; the father prayed to the Virgin for help as he whistled up at the monkey, who then climbed down the water pipe, the child in its arms, and returned him to his parents. Ever since, the Virgin's shrine with its eternal flame (it's now electric) has borne witness to this miracle of the baby and the ape and the father's promise to honor the Virgin forever if she saved the child. Hilda, whose Protestantism opposes her to the cult of the Virgin, shows her independence by keeping Mary's lamp lit. She's an angel, like the gold ones with trumpets flying above the church of **Sant'Antonio dei Portoghesi** (on your right as you stand looking up at the Tower), a small gem of the Catholic Baroque with a richly colored marble interior and virgin saints high on the ceiling.

Hilda's Tower is inspired by one of the sunnier historical anecdotes Hawthorne weaves into the novel. And he indulges Hilda, sketching with affection her interest in painting, and her living on her own in a city as sinister and pagan as Rome. Nineteenth-century Rome had numerous American women artists in residence who were friends of the Hawthornes, Harriet Hosmer the best-known.

Mostly, though, Hawthorne's love of the macabre drives his plot. In Chapter IV, the foursome visits the **Catacomb of San Callisto** off the **Via Appia Antica,** the largest of the tombs. Miriam gets lost in the six-mile-long tunnels, finally turning up shadowed by death in the form of a ghost. In Hawthorne's time, a young French lieutenant was lost in "the wide and dreary precincts of the catacombs" for days, and only by a stroke of luck did he manage to find his way out. (*To follow Haw-thorne's pilgrims, take bus 660 from the Metro station Colli Albani, on linea A; get off at the Appia Antica terminus, a trip of forty-five minutes. This route allows for a walk along the Via Appia, with its long vistas of the tomb of Cecilia Metella and of the Campagna, a carpet of wildflow-ers in spring (see page 192). Or take bus 218 across from St. John Lat-eran; get off at Fosse Ardeatine, and walk, watching your back. (Vespas enjoy terrorizing tourists.) There are multilingual guides with flashlights available at each of the catacombs: San Callisto; San Sebastiano; San Domitilla. (Open 8:30–12; 2:30–5, closed Wed, www.s.calisto@catacombe. roma.it*).

The plot twists of *The Marble Faun* are comically improbable, yet they unfold to the pleasure of literary pilgrims as Hawthorne moves his char-acters along his favorite walks. They stroll through the great gardens— the Borghese, Villa Sciarra in Trastevere, the Medici—and in the museums they track down his favorite art. In **Palazzo Barberini** (9–7, closed Mon; www.galleria borghese.it), they climb the Bernini staircase to see the portrait of Beatrice Cenci (Reni's "The Portrait of a Lady," on the second floor), the innocent teenaged girl beheaded in 1599 by order of the pope for allegedly having collaborated in the murder of her incestuous and brutal father; she never confessed, even under torture. Her severed head was displayed on the Ponte Sant'Angelo where the exe-cution was done. Shelley dramatized her story in a verse drama, *The Cenci,* and Stendhal, Dickens, and Alberto Moravia fictionalized her. The girl's sadness—the portrait's authenticity is now a question mark—upset the novelist from Salem, where the corpses of innocent victims of a witch hunt had swung from the village gibbet, haunting generations of guilt-ridden Puritans. Continuing the mournful mood, Hawthorne marches his foursome into one of the creepiest—*the* creepiest—cavern of Roman Catholicism: the church of **the Cappuccini**—Capuchins— and the Crypt of the Capuchins (also called the church of the Immacu-late Conception), at the bottom of the Via Veneto (closed Thurs). For a fee you may gaze upon stacks of bones of four thousand dead monks, which are used to decorate the church (to save space); finger bones make up the numbers on a clock framed with vertebrae. Whole walls are covered with skulls and skeletons (displays that impressed the Marquis de Sade). Other churches featuring "bone art" include the church of Our Lady of Prayer and Death, in the Via Giulia, its lamps made out of bones; a chapel in the church of the Stigmata in Largo Argentina, decorated with bones, with a mosaic made out of teeth. All over Rome the death-obsessed Hawthorne found images of sin and punishment, ancient proof of ruin and waste as the alpha and omega of human existence. He is, as he says in "Hilda's Tower," at once repelled and attracted by the Eternal City, his dark soul's true home.

*(There are creature comforts along the pessimistic trail of Hawthorne's subconscious. Opposite Hilda's Tower, in Via della Scrofa 32, **Volpetti's** is the best gourmet deli-rosticcerie in Rome. You can eat here or order take-out. There's a larger Volpetti's in Testaccio—see page 312. To the right of the Tower, and a bit farther on, **Il Convivio** serves a more luxurious repast [Vicolo dei Soldati 31, tel 06 6869432, reservations required, closed Sun]. A five-minute walk north from Volpetti's, toward Piazza del Popolo, at Via di Ripetta 36, the **Buca di Ripetta** restaurant is very good. [Reservations required; tel 06 3219391]. In the same direction, bearing right, the stalls of the **Outdoor Print Market** at Largo Fontanella Borghese are packed with maps, old opera scores, books, and prints of Rome in the time of Hawthorne and everyone else before and since [closed Mon].)*

HENRY JAMES

1843–1916

His letter to his brother William describing his first day in Rome was utter ecstasy:

> At last—for the time—I live! It beats everything: it leaves the Rome of your fancy—your education—nowhere. It makes Venice—Florence—Oxford—London—seem like little cities of pasteboard. I went reeling and moaning thro' the streets, in a fever of enjoyment. In the course of four or five hours I traversed almost the whole of Rome and got a glimpse of everything—the Forum, the Coliseum (stupendissimo!) . . . I've seen the Tiber hurrying along, as swift and dirty as history! . . . In fine I've seen Rome, and I shall go to bed a wiser man than I last rose—yesterday morning.

Henry James was twenty-six when he first arrived and had published only travel articles and reviews. In his lifetime he would write nineteen novels, twelve volumes of short stories, five volumes of literary essays, five plays, several travel books, two autobiographies, notebooks, and forty thousand letters. A confirmed expatriate, he traveled widely, made and lost many friends, but his feelings for Rome never changed. "No one who has ever loved Rome as Rome could be loved in youth wants to stop loving her," he wrote, almost fifty years later.

From ITALIAN HOURS

E ven if you are on your way to the Lateran you won't grudge
the twenty minutes it will take you, on leaving the Colosseum, to turn away under the Arch of Constantine, whose noble
battered bas-reliefs, with the chain of tragic statues—fettered,
drooping barbarians—round its summit, I assume you to have profoundly admired, toward the piazzetta of the church of San Giovanni e Paolo, on the slope of Cælian. No spot in Rome can show
a cluster of more charming accidents. The ancient brick apse of
the church peeps down into the trees of the little wooded walk before the neighbouring church of San Gregorio, intensely venerable
beneath its excessive modernisation; and a series of heavy brick
buttresses, flying across to an opposite wall, overarches the short,
steep, paved passage which leads into the small square. This is
flanked on one side by the long mediæval portico of the church of
the two saints, sustained by eight time-blackened columns of granite and marble. On another rise the great scarce-windowed walls of
a Passionist convent, and on the third the portals of a grand villa,
whose tall porter, with his cockade and silver-topped staff, standing sublime behind his grating, seems a kind of mundane St. Peter,
I suppose, to the beggars who sit at the church door or lie in the
sun along the farther slope which leads to the gate of the convent.
The place always seems to me the perfection of an out-of-the-
way corner—a place you would think twice before telling people
about, lest you should find them there the next time you were to
go. It is such a group of objects, singly and in their happy combi-
nation, as one must come to Rome to find at one's house door; but
what makes it peculiarly a picture is the beautiful dark red campanile of the church, which stands embedded in the mass of the
convent. It begins, as so many things in Rome begin, with a stout
foundation of antique travertine, and rises high, in delicately quaint
mediæval brickwork—little tiers and apertures sustained on miniature columns and adorned with small cracked slabs of green and
yellow marble, inserted almost at random.

When there are three or four brown-breasted contadini* sleeping in the sun before the convent doors, and a departing monk leading his shadow down over them, I think you will not find anything in Rome more *sketchable*. . . .

If St. John Lateran disappoints you internally, you have an easy compensation in pacing the long lane which connects it with Santa Maria Maggiore and entering the singularly perfect nave of that most delightful of churches. The first day of my stay in Rome under the old dispensation I spent in wandering at random through the city, with accident for my *valet-de-place*. It served me to perfection and introduced me to the best things; among others to an immediate happy relation with Santa Maria Maggiore. First impressions, memorable impressions, are generally irrecoverable; they often leave one the wiser, but they rarely return in the same form. I remember, of my coming uninformed and unprepared into the place of worship and of curiosity that I have named, only that I sat for half an hour on the edge of the base of one of the marble columns of the beautiful nave and enjoyed a perfect revel of—what shall I call it?—taste, intelligence, fancy, perceptive emotion? The place proved so endlessly suggestive that perception became a throbbing confusion of images, and I departed with a sense of knowing a good deal that is not set down in Murray. I have seated myself more than once again at the base of the same column; but you live your life only once, the parts as well as the whole. The obvious charm of the church is the elegant grandeur of the nave—its perfect shapeliness and its rich simplicity, its long double row of white marble columns and its high flat roof, embossed with intricate gildings and mouldings. It opens into a choir of an extraordinary splendour of effect, which I recommend you to look out for of a fine afternoon. At such a time the glowing western light, entering the high windows of the tribune, kindles the scattered masses of colour into sombre brightness, scintillates on the great solemn mosaic of the vault, touches the porphyry columns of the superb bal-

*Peasants.

dachino with ruby lights, and buries its shining shafts in the deep-toned shadows that hang about frescoes and sculptures and mould-ings. The deeper charm even than in such things, however, is the social or historic note or tone or atmosphere of the church—I fumble, you see, for my right expression; the sense it gives you, in common with most of the Roman churches, and more than any of them, of having been prayed in for several centuries by an endlessly curious and complex society. It takes no great attention to let it come to you that the authority of Italian Catholicism has lapsed not a little in these days; not less also perhaps than to feel that, as they stand, these deserted temples were the fruit of a society leav-ened through and through by ecclesiastical manners, and that they formed for ages the constant background of the human drama. They are, as one may say, the *churchiest* churches in Europe—the fullest of gathered memories, of the experience of their office. There's not a figure one has read of in old-world annals that isn't to be imagined on proper occasion kneeling before the lamp-decked Confession beneath the altar of Santa Maria Maggiore. One sees after all, however, even among the most palpable realities, very much what the play of one's imagination projects there; and I pre-sent my remarks simply as a reminder that one's constant excursions into these places are not the least interesting episodes of one's walks in Rome.

January 21st.—The last three or four days I have regularly spent a couple of hours from noon baking myself in the sun of the Pincio to get rid of a cold. The weather perfect and the crowd (especially today) amazing. Such a staring, lounging, dandified, amiable crowd! Who does the vulgar stay-at-home work of Rome? All the grandees and half the foreigners are there in their carriages, the bourgeoisie on foot staring at them and the beggars lining all the approaches. The great difference between public places in America and Europe is in the number of unoccupied people of every age and condition sitting about early and late on benches and gazing at you, from your hat to your boots, as you pass. Europe is certainly the conti-nent of the practised stare. The ladies on the Pincio have to run the gauntlet; but they seem to do so complacently enough. The European woman is brought up to the sense of having a definite part in the way of manners or manner to play in public. To lie back in a barouche alone, balancing a parasol and seeming to ignore the extremely immediate gaze of two serried ranks of male creatures on each side of her path, save here and there to recognise one of them with an imperceptible nod, is one of her daily duties. The number of young men here who, like the cœnobites of old, lead the purely contemplative life is enormous. They muster in especial force on the Pincio, but the Corso all day is thronged with them. They are well-dressed, good-humoured, good-looking, polite; but they seem never to do a harder stroke of work than to stroll from the Piazza Colonna to the Hôtel de Rome or *vice versâ*. Some of them don't even stroll, but stand leaning by the hour against the doorways, sucking the knobs of their canes, feeling their back hair and settling their shirt-cuffs. . . .

The Pincio continues to beguile; it's a great resource. I am forever being reminded of the "æsthetic luxury," as I called it above, of living in Rome. To be able to choose of an afternoon for a lounge (respectfully speaking) between St. Peter's and the high precinct you approach by the gate just beyond Villa Medici—counting nothing else—is a proof that if in Rome you may suffer from ennui, at least your ennui has a throbbing soul in it. It is something to say for the Pincio that you don't always choose St. Peter's. Sometimes I lose patience with its parade of eternal idleness, but at others this very idleness is balm to one's conscience. Life on just these terms seems so easy, so monotonously sweet, that you feel it would be unwise, would be really unsafe, to change. The Roman air is charged with an elixir. . . .

May 17th.—It was wonderful yesterday at St. John Lateran. The spring now has turned to perfect summer; there are cascades of verdure over all the walls; the early flowers are a fading memory, and the new grass knee-deep in the Villa Borghese. The winter aspect of the region about the Lateran is one of the best things in Rome; the sunshine is nowhere so golden and the lean shadows nowhere so purple as on the long grassy walk to Santa Croce. But yesterday I seemed to see nothing but green and blue . . . and the Alban Hills, which in January and February keep shifting and melt-ing along the whole scale of azure, were almost monotonously fresh, and had lost some of their finer modelling. But the sky was ultramarine and everything radiant with light and warmth—warmth which a soft steady breeze kept from excess. . . . The charm of charms at St. John Lateran is the admirable twelfth-century cloister, which was never more charming than yesterday. The shrubs and flowers about the ancient well were blooming away in the in-tense light, and the twisted pillars and chiselled capitals of the per-fect little colonnade seemed to enclose them like the sculptured rim of a precious vase. Standing out among the flowers you may look up and see a section of the summit of the great façade of the church. The robed and mitred apostles, bleached and rain-washed by the ages, rose into the blue air like huge snow figures. . . . I was in the loving mood of one's last days in Rome. . . .

Farewell, packing, the sharp pang of going. One would like to be able after five months in Rome to sum up, for tribute and homage, one's experience, one's gains, the whole adventure of one's sensi-bility. But one has really vibrated too much—the addition of so many items isn't easy. What is simply clear is the sense of an ac-quired passion for the place and of an incalculable number of gath-ered impressions. Many of these have been intense and momentous, but one has trodden on the other—there are always the big fish that swallow up the little—and one can hardly say what has become of them. They store themselves noiselessly away, I suppose, in the dim but safe places of memory and "taste," and we live in a quiet faith that they will emerge into vivid relief if life or art should demand them. As for the passion we needn't perhaps trouble ourselves about that. Fifty swallowed palmfuls of the Fountain of Trevi couldn't make us more ardently sure that we shall at any cost come back.

1873.

FOR THE LITERARY TRAVELER

Henry James walked his way into a lifelong intimacy with Rome. Back streets, main streets, every piazza, church, palazzo, the public gardens, Seven Hills, the cafes. ("The great thing," he said, "is to be *saturated* with something—that is, in one way or another, with life. . . .") To see his city, you must follow him on foot. His point of view on this church or that ritual may strike you as intolerant, but abroad in Rome, he excluded nothing. His is a Catholic taste in a Protestant soul. He preferred the statue of Marcus Aurelius astride his splendid horse in the Campidoglio to the sight of "that poor sexless old Pope"—Pius IX—officiating in St. Peter's. But while in Rome he named the religious passion "the strongest of man's heart."

From the hotels he stayed at, on and off **the Corso** (Hotel de Rome, the Inghilterra), he set out on his daily explorations, climbing the Spanish Steps, proceeding along Via Sistina and up and over the **Esquiline,** stopping in **Santa Maria Maggiore** before continuing along Via Gregoriana (Merulana) to the beautiful **Lateran** cloister. Or he might wind through back streets from the Corso to the Capitol, through the Forum to the Colosseum (where his Daisy Miller breathed in death), followed by a stroll over the Palatine or a detour up Via Claudia to the loveliness of **San Giovanni e Paolo** on the Caelian Hill (see page 98). In the travel articles he wrote for *The Nation*—later collected in the volume excerpted here, *Italian Hours*—he repeats the names of certain places, like a musical leitmotif, the darlings of his heart. ("You care for *places*?" Oscar Wilde exclaimed, finding James's local affections provincial. "The *world* is my home," said Oscar.) James's favorites include the **Pincio** or the **Pincian Hill,** an elegant setting in *Daisy Miller*, and the terrace of the **Piazzale Napoleone** where the carriages stopped to watch the sun set over the dome of St. Peter's (and small-minded idlers observed Daisy Miller's every glance and twitch). Walking along the Pincian Hill, in the direction of the Spanish Steps, you'll pass a terrace where the **Casina Valadier** (1813–1817), commemorating Giuseppe Valadier who designed the Pincian Gardens, is now a cafe. From the terrace, a romantic out-of-the-way spot on a summer afternoon, you see rooftop gar-

dens, their greenery bright patches on the crazy quilt of red-tiled palazzos, apartments, convents.

Further along, the **Villa Medici,** now the French Academy, exhibits
art, its huge interiors perfect for the sculpture of Rodin in 2003 (Viale
Trinità dei Monti 1, closed Tues); in James's Roman Notebook he calls
the Medici Gardens "perhaps the most enchanting place in Rome."
(*Guided tours Feb–May, Sat, Sun at 10:30 and 11:30; times subject to
change. Tel 06 67611.*)

The **Campagna,** along the **Via Appia Antica,** James saw as a
pedestrian and on horseback: "The golden atmosphere, the violet
mountains, the flower-strewn grass, the lonely arches crowned with
wild weeds and crumbling in the sunshine." (James's Isabel Archer, for
whom the Campagna was "almost a daily habit," and George Eliot's
Dorothea Brooke both enjoyed their solo carriage rides out here, their
desiccated mates left behind.) It's dangerous to walk along its edge
now, on that narrow road, mad with Vespas and Fiats. But access by
public transportation is easy (see page 183), and looking out a bus window, you do see pilgrims making the trip along the Via Appia on foot.
Once you're out there, walking south, beyond the entrance to the Catacomb of St. Sebastian, you see, on top of those wide undulating plains,
a landmark of the Campagna, the **Tomb of Cecilia Metella** (open
Tues–Sat 9–4, in winter, 6 in summer; Sun–Mon 9–1), shaped like Hadrian's tomb on the Tiber (see page 55) and built for a well-connected
Roman matron, the daughter-in-law of Marcus Crassus, who aroused
Byron's curiosity:

> But who was she, the lady of the dead,
> Tomb'd in a palace? Was she chaste and fair?
> Worthy a king's—or more—a Roman's bed?

To travelers as different as Henry Adams and Virginia Woolf, the
Campagna was one of the most beautiful landscapes in Europe, as Virginia told Vanessa: "We rambled over the Campagna on Sunday. I suppose France is all right, and England is all right, but I have never seen
anything as beautiful as this is. . . . The campagna, blue and green, with
an almond-coloured farm, with oxen and sheep, and more ruined

arches, and blocks of marble fallen on the grass, . . . and lovers curled up among the broken pots." As the site of malarial marshes in James's time, this idyllic plain was also the source of the disease that killed Daisy Miller.

(*In the nineteenth century they picnicked in the shadow of Cecilia Metella's Tomb. Today, there's the terrace of the* **Cecilia Metella,** *entrance on the Via Appia Antica 125, serving Roman cuisine [closed Mon]; in a farmhouse just beyond the Catacombs,* **L'Archeologia,** *Via Appia Antica 139 [closed Thurs], resembles the taverns Henry James describes stopping in at the end of a visit to the Campagna.*)

Back inside the city walls, James frequently visited friends who lived in palazzos (Palazzo Barberini and the Palazzo Odescalchi in the Piazza dei Santi Apostoli), so he's on familiar ground when he writes the architecture and decoration of opulent Roman apartments into his Roman novels, *Roderick Hudson* (1875), *Daisy Miller* (1878), and *The Portrait of a Lady* (1881).

As James grew older, more and more he stayed at home in England, deploring "the swarming democracy of your fellow-tourists," condemning Italy's flourishing tourist industry as the ruination of a sophisticated visitor's pleasure. American tourists were "the barbarians of the Roman Empire." On his last trip to Rome, in 1907, he visited the grave of his close friend Constance Fenimore Woolson, an American writer who committed suicide in Venice and was buried in the **Protestant Cemetery** in Rome (see page 228), near Shelley's grave. In a letter to "Fenimore's" relatives, he called the place of her burial "the most beautiful thing in Italy, . . . that particular spot below the great grey wall, the cypresses and the time-silvered pyramid. It is tremendously, inexhaustibly touching—its effect never fails to overwhelm." He realized after her death that "Fenimore" had loved him; she had also perceived and rued the emotional distance he maintained between himself and other human beings. His recognition of the wisdom of her insights—after she was dead and buried—inspired one of the most powerful of his late works, "The Beast in the Jungle," which beats with the troubling pulse of Jamesian ambiguity. He feels both the bitterness of death—when life has been wasted for a lack of love—and the heartbreaking beauty of the place of burial. He allows no false consolation. "Everything's terrible, *cara,* in the heart of man," says the Roman Prince Amerigo in *The Golden Bowl.*

Though he shared a sense of sin with fellow New Englander Nathaniel Hawthorne, Henry James enjoyed himself in Rome, dining and drinking in places where travelers can still spend a pleasant interlude before returning to the long Jamesian walks. At the bottom of the Spanish Steps is **Babington's English Tea Rooms** (a replacement in 1894 of the former English Coffee House, at Piazza di Spagna 85). **Caffè Greco,** in the fashionable Via Condotti 86 (see page 311), was the meeting place of many *stranieri,* the foreigners who wintered in Rome. Goethe, Stendhal, Keats and Shelley, Ibsen, Liszt, Mendelssohn, Thackeray, Leopardi, Mark Twain all gathered here, and though it's now a national monument, more popular with tourists than artists, Caffè Greco's small sitting rooms clustered with round marble tables, the walls covered with the artists' pictures, recall the past. Might that be the ghost of Mark Twain whispering the wisdom of *Innocents Abroad:* "Travel is fatal to prejudice, bigotry and narrow-mindedness and many of our people need it sorely on these accounts . . ." But not to linger inside old haunts. As James often remarked in his Roman Notebook, life in this "inexhaustible" city "goes on in the streets."

EDITH WHARTON

1862–1937

Italy was Edith Wharton's first European love, her annual visit there the happiest time of the year. In 1903 the Century magazine asked her to write travel articles about Italian villas and their gardens. With her indefatigable energy—Henry James called her "The Angel of Devastation"—she visited about eighty villas, no detail escaping her critical eye. As the following piece shows, she could be as blunt about a garden's shortcomings as she was charmed by its beauty. On the basis of Italian Villas and Their Gardens *(1904), excerpted here, and* Italian Backgrounds *(1905), biographer R. W. B. Lewis ranks Wharton as one of the most accomplished practitioners of travel writing in American literary history. The famous novels that followed the Italian books* (The House of Mirth, Ethan Frome, The Custom of the Country, The Age of Innocence) *have, as part of their power, Wharton's evocations of place, which makes the setting of a story as real as human character.*

❧

From Italian Villas and Their Gardens

VILLA D'ESTE

O f the three great villas built by cardinals beyond the immediate outskirts of Rome, the third and the most famous is the Villa d'Este at Tivoli.

Begun before 1540 by the Cardinal Bishop of Cordova, the villa became the property of Cardinal Ippolito d'Este, son of Alfonso I of Ferrara, who carried on its embellishment at the cost of over a million Roman scudi. Thence it passed successively to two other cardinals of the house of Este, who continued its adornment, and finally, in the seventeenth century, was inherited by the ducal house of Modena.

The villa, an unfinished barrack-like building, stands on a piazza at one end of the town of Tivoli, above gardens which descend the steep hillside to the gorge of the Anio.* These gardens have excited so much admiration that little thought has been given to the house, though it is sufficiently interesting to merit attention. It is said to have been built by Pirro Ligorio,** and surprising as it seems that this huge featureless pile should have been designed by the creator of the Casino del Papa, yet one observes that the rooms are decorated with the same fantastic pebble-work used in such profusion at the Villa Pia. In extenuation of the ugliness of the Villa d'Este it should, moreover, be remembered that its long facade is incomplete, save for the splendid central portico; and also that, while the Villa Pia was intended as shelter for a summer afternoon, the great palace at Tivoli was planned to house a cardinal and his guests, including, it is said, "a suite of two hundred and fifty gentlemen of the noblest blood of Italy." When one pictures such a throng, with their innumerable retainers, it is easy to understand why the Villa d'Este had to be expanded out of all likeness to an ordinary country house.

The plan is ingenious and interesting. From the village square only a high blank wall is visible. Through a door in this wall one passes into a frescoed corridor which leads to a court enclosed in an open arcade, with fountains in rusticated niches. From a corner of the court a fine intramural stairway descends to what is, on the garden side, the *piano nobile* of the villa. On this side, looking over the gardens, is a long enfilade of rooms, gaily frescoed by the Zuccari and their school; and behind the rooms runs a vaulted corridor built against the side of the hill, and lighted by bull's-eyes in its roof. This corridor has lost its frescoes, but preserves a line of niches decorated in coloured pebbles and stucco-work, with gaily painted

---

*The River Anio, below Tivoli.

**Pirro Ligorio (1493–1580) of Naples, an architect, made additions to the Vatican and designed the Villa d'Este.

stucco caryatids supporting the arches; and as each niche contains a semicircular fountain, the whole length of the corridor must once have rippled with running water.

The central room opens on the great two-storied portico or loggia, whence one descends by an outer stairway to a terrace running the length of the building, and terminated at one end by an ornamental wall, at the other by an open loggia overlooking the Campagna.* From this upper terrace, with its dense wall of box and laurel, one looks down on the towering cypresses and ilexes of the lower gardens. The grounds are not large, but the impression produced is full of a tragic grandeur. The villa towers above so high and bare, the descent from terrace to terrace is so long and steep, there are such depths of mystery in the infinite green distances and in the cypress-shaded pools of the lower garden, that one has a sense of awe rather than of pleasure in descending from one level to another of darkly rustling green. But it is the omnipresent rush of water which gives the Este gardens their peculiar character. From the Anio, drawn up the hillside at incalculable cost and labour, a thousand rills gush downward, terrace by terrace, channelling the stone rails of the balusters, leaping from step to step, dripping into mossy conchs, flashing in spray from the horns of sea-gods and the jaws of mythical monsters, or forcing themselves in irrepressible overflow down the ivy-matted banks. The whole length of the second terrace is edged by a deep stone channel, into which the stream drips by countless outlets over a quivering fringe of maidenhair. Every side path or flight of steps is accompanied by its sparkling rill, every niche in the retaining-walls has its water-pouring nymph or gushing urn; the solemn depths of green reverberate with the tumult of innumerable streams. "The Anio," as Herr Tuckermann says, "throbs through the whole organism of the garden like its inmost vital principle."

The gardens of the Villa d'Este were probably begun by Pirro

---

*The Campagna di Roma is a plain, the territory of Old Latium, surrounding Rome. Flocks of grazing sheep and the ruins of Roman aqueducts and tombs give the landscape a particular charm that appealed to Wharton, Henry James, and other writers.

Ligorio, and, as Herr Gurlitt thinks,* continued later by Giacomo della Porta. It will doubtless never be known how much Ligorio owed to the taste of Orazio Olivieri, the famous hydraulic engineer, who raised the Anio to the hilltop and organized its distribution through the grounds. But it is apparent that the whole composition was planned about the central fact of the rushing Anio: that the gardens were to be, as it were, an organ on which the water played. The result is extraordinarily romantic and beautiful, and the versatility with which the stream is used, the varying effects won from it, bear witness to the imaginative feeling of the designer.

When all has been said in praise of the poetry and charm of the Este gardens, it must be owned that from the architect's standpoint they are less satisfying than those of the other great cinque-cento villas. The plan is worthy of all praise, but the details are too complicated, and the ornament is either trivial or cumbrous. So inferior is the architecture to that of the Lante gardens and Caprarola that Burckhardt was probably right in attributing much of it to the seventeenth century. Here for the first time one feels the heavy touch of the baroque. The fantastic mosaic and stucco temple containing the water-organ above the great cascade, the arches of triumph, the celebrated "grotto of Arethusa," the often-sketched fountain on the second terrace, all seem pitiably tawdry when compared with the garden-architecture of Raphael or Vignola. Some of the details of the composition are absolutely puerile—such as the toy model of an ancient city, thought to be old Rome, . . . and there are endless complications of detail, where the earlier masters would have felt the need of breadth and simplicity. Above all, there is a want of harmony between the landscape and its treatment. The baroque garden-architecture of Italy is not without charm, and even a touch of the grotesque has its attraction . . . but the cypress-groves of the Villa d'Este are too solemn, and the Roman landscape is too august, to suffer the nearness of the trivial.

---

*Cornelius Gurlitt was a German art historian whose *Geschichte des Barockstils in Italien* (1887) influenced Wharton's appreciation of the art and architecture of the Baroque.

FOR THE LITERARY TRAVELER

Villa d'Este in Tivoli, twenty miles east of Rome, can be reached by several coach tours (see page 56), or by taking the Metro, *linea* B, to the last stop, Rebibbia, and transferring to the Cotral bus, which leaves every twenty minutes. In less than an hour you'll be in this city of flowing water, the delight of Horace, Catullus, and other ancient writers who retreated to villas built into the sides of rocky slopes overhanging the misty valley of the River Anio. The wildly Baroque garden behind the Villa d'Este gushes with amazing fountains, the mythological statues surprising you at every step you take down the steep and beautifully cultivated paths. The sculpture and the garden have been cleaned up and restored recently: The fountain-powered organ plays again, for five minutes every two hours; likewise the fountain that imitates bird calls. The Fountain of the Ephesian Goddess shoots curved streams of water all day long from her eighteen breasts. Wharton finds these performances of "water theater" too "complicated." The villa towering above the garden was originally a Benedictine convent, but Cardinal d'Este, son of Lucrezia Borgia, supposedly inspired by Hadrian's Villa, which he plundered, accomplished a radical renovation. It's easy to imagine the powers of Renaissance society in this sumptuous setting. The cardinals—d'Este and his brother cardinals—and their attendant "nephews," the courtesans, all making their silken entrances, whispering intrigues along the **Passeggiata del Cardinale,** the balconied terrace along the front of the palace. Wharton saves the daydreams for her novels. (Open daily, 8:30–an hour before sunset.)

There are many wonderful day trips south of Rome to Wharton's villas and gardens, but you need a car to reach them. There are coach trips to the Colle Albani—the Alban Hills—and the Castelli Romani.* Some pass through the pretty hill town of **Frascati.** "The most famous group of villas in the Roman country-side lies on the hill above Frascati," writes Wharton, but the famous Villa Aldobrandini that dominates the town is

---

*A group of more than a dozen towns scattered over the Alban Hills, once the sites of castles of popes and the Roman aristocracy. They include Castel Gandolfo, Nemi, Albano, and Frascati.

no longer open to the public. A glass of chilled Frascati wine is served to coach visitors in the museum, just below the Villa in the main square, and the town, cool in summer, is a pleasure to explore. The panoramic view from the restaurant **Cacciare** (Via A. Diaz 13; tel 06 942 0378) makes sunset dining a delight.

In Rome, Wharton's interest in the **Borghese Gardens** and the **Villa Borghese** was an informed passion. She had every niche down cold. With her mentally challenged husband, Teddy (they divorced after almost thirty years of a celibate marriage), she took daily walks and carriage rides within the four-mile circumference of the park surrounding the Villa, which is now the property of the Italian government. (*A pleasant place to relax and eat in the Borghese Gardens is the indoor and outdoor cafeteria of the National Gallery of Modern Art:* **Delle Arti,** *Via Gramsci 73; tel 06 326 51326.*) You can enter the Gardens from the Piazzale Flaminio, a short walk from Piazza del Popolo; or at Porta Pinciana, at the end of the Via Veneto; and from the Pincian Hill where Henry James liked to walk. Wharton and he met in 1903, and biographer Lewis calls their friendship "a main source of comfort" to her. The Villa Borghese displays a generous portion of the sculpture of Bernini (and others) in the Museo, and the upstairs Galleria Borghese or Pinacoteca displays paintings. There are seven Caravaggios, and Titian's "Sacred and Profane Love." (*Open 9–7, closed Mon, reservations required. Tel 06 199757510; www.ticketeria.it.*)

In the Gardens, you can take rowboats out on the artificial Giardino del Lago, studded with temples and statues. The human scene plays as uninterrupted Roman theater. Strolling grandmothers and daughters, fathers teaching sons to ride bikes, romping dogs, red-hot lovers, friends arm-in-arm, it makes no sense to walk away in search of a statue of Byron or Goethe. In his novel *Ragazzi,* Pier Paolo Pasolini describes nighttime bench life in the Borghese, along hidden paths not trafficked by tourists.

Edith Wharton's passion for great Italian houses did correspond to her novelist's interest in human character. As novelist, travel writer, and lonely woman she made a connection between the domestic interior and a woman's psyche:

I have sometimes thought that a woman's nature is like a great house full of rooms: there is the hall, through which everyone passes in going in and out; the drawing room, where one receives formal visits; the sitting room, where the members of the family come and go as they list; but beyond that, far beyond, are other rooms, the handles of whose doors are never turned; no one knows the way to them, no one knows whither they lead; and in the innermost room, the holy of holies, the soul sits alone and waits for a footstep that never comes.

Someone, Morton Fullerton, did arrive when she was in her forties, and for three years they had a passionate love affair. Then, for the rest of her life she lived in France, in a beautiful villa of her own creation, where she died, alone.

WILLIAM CARLOS WILLIAMS

1883–1963

Williams was a medical student and Ezra Pound was studying Romance languages when they met at the University of Pennsylvania and became friends. Pound settled in Europe, and Williams practiced medicine in Rutherford, New Jersey (the Paterson *of his masterpiece), writing poetry and fiction after hours. For years Pound badgered him to put his medical career on hold and "come across and broaden your mind." In 1923, Williams took up the challenge and sailed off for a "magnificent year," which he turned into the travel novel* A Voyage to Pagany *(excerpted here). Dr. "Dev" Evans is the protagonist, a traveler in Pagany, the name Williams chose for all Europe. "Pagans," in the words of Harry Levin's introduction, "had originally been dwellers in rural villages; the early Christians used the term at Rome for those who still practiced idolatry; more neutrally, a* paganus *was a person who did not share the prevailing beliefs." Williams—and his alter ego, Evans—fits the definition. Nonconformist, anti-puritan, he walks Rome and has a few idolatrous apparitions: Venus, the primal force of Pagany, incarnated in stone; and the young German girl staying at his pensione. The fictional Dr. Evans's experience of the city shows his passion for the beautiful particulars, like the artist who went back home to carve some of the most concrete images in American literature into the corpus of modern poetry.* So much depends upon a red wheel barrow . . .

❧

From A VOYAGE TO PAGANY

Chapter XVII
To Rome

Two days later he was on his way to Rome leaving the Arno and its vivid relics gladly behind. He had closed his eyes sharply to, at the height of his enjoyment, at the peak of his understanding. Enough. . . .

Rome! he could see St. Peter's in the distance. Rome! for an hour the fields had richened, farms, vineyards, orchards, planted fields—the servitors of that city they remained now as then. The Roman Campagna made him aware at once of how the ancient city lived, far from the rocks, surrounded by this great fertile oasis—yet limited. A taste of plenty these fields had offered them in this nook caught in a wild Apennine. River and field, grove and pool, and in the center, by the river, there was a rise in the ground, oaks, elms and a cave or two for shepherds or emperors; a house, a temple and the burning sun. All else came after.

Crossing from the Terminal at the *Piazza delle Terme,* he saw the ruins of Diocletian's baths and the brimming Fountain of the Mermaids squirting its stream of purity and plenty into the evening air. At once he felt the modern capital living upon the ancient like barnacles on rock, the old rock coming through,—and the wash of instinct over it all. Evans was possessed with Rome on the instant of landing there. . . .

His room at the Pension Octavia was paved with red baked tiles. There were two iron beds in it; a table by the window with a red-figured cheap tablecloth on it. Outside, the new German Lutheran church shone in the finely grained Italian sun. . . .

The host was a German, married to an Italian wife who had been recently delivered of her third infant and so was seldom to be seen. The man kept a decent table, fair wine and served broccoli—not too often. At breakfast next A.M. at the table back of Evans there was seated a German girl, too shy for talk but shining like some heavenly ornament. She had, when he looked at her, the brightest, fairest hair he had ever seen on a girl, and skin and eyes as if newly come into blossom, the inconceivable freshness of a spring flower still remembered in the clarity of her whole being. But he was sullen toward such things now. He saw her looking but he made no reply. He went out to walk. . . .

Chapter XVIII
In Rome

The next day he changed his seat at the little table in the pension dining-room, where they had put dried figs and raisins wrapped in grape leaves on a flat dish for him; he changed his place so that he could more easily observe the little German girl whom the day before he had noticed. She also had changed her place, no doubt the better to see him, so that now they looked directly at each other over the two tables.

With wide blue eyes she looked full into his own as if amazed to recognize him, which she seemed to do; a curious wonder. Evans wished he might speak to her but instead kept rigid his unrecognizing face. Perhaps she knew English. His German was atrocious. French? He could not talk Italian. What did he care? There was an older woman with her.

So he looked into her eyes. Clear pools they were certainly; the metaphor was never more apt. It was a Botticellian loveliness—it was *She** standing upon the shell; the hair, the eyes, the flesh that Botticelli had striven to imitate, though this thought did not occur thus fully to Evans at that time. And she was attracted, beyond a doubt by his darkness, his eyes—his age maybe. He turned to his raisins, unwrapping them from the dried leaves.

Later, it being Sunday, he went out for a walk, a long walk, turning into the Via Veneto, to the Piazza Barberini, past the dripping green-stained fountain of the Tritoni—as if raised newly from

---

*Venus.

the sea—and so on and on to the river and the Castel St. Angelo. Coming back, he stopped on the bridge. The Tiber was swollen with recent rains. The muddy water was whirling under the bridge arches, great twists of it holding a constant shape where the stone split the current so that the water seemed unmoving, the bridge to be rushing upstream.

Wood of all sorts was coming down in the current; roots, branches, bits of finished timbers, logs, boxes—all that could float; and on the left bank, where a turn in the river carried the stuff inshore, men were casting for it, stray bits of firewood, with forked weighted sticks on a line which they threw over the floating débris, snaring the wood and bringing it to the shore—if they could. It was a fine game requiring considerable skill.

Rome filled Evans with thought. It was to him a public place to which all the people of the world would come for an answer. All that his mind contained seemed pressing for review upon this day especially. As he walked, witnessing the streets, the trams, noting that here the men kept their shoes always highly polished and not dull as in Paris; feeling the vivacity, the carefree youthfulness of the life against the ruins of a grandiose antiquity; seeing the many horse-drawn cabs whose surefooted and well-driven animals were scampering about in every street—it was like a stream loosening the very dregs of his semi-northern dreaming. Rome! Over and over again he said it. It seemed to him to be full of a motion, a motion of crumbling monuments, himself crumbling, loosened at the base, the motion of the sun itself, a stream of light, insuppressible among the ruins. He felt a quiet happiness beginning far off. He felt a loosening throughout his own stalled sinews; his whole body seemed to relax, as if it might fall apart. He thought perhaps he might be going to be ill, and among flower venders, dogs, the muddy back entrance to the Queen Mother's palace, the Facisti boys, the wood in the river—through it all, he saw the Cypriari in her awkward German clothes and by her side the other, not her mother, not her equal surely, no relative—an attendant she was, but under her control. Evans had to confess, good or ill, he had never fully admired a girl or woman yet, but there was more or less of German in her.

It was still very early spring about the city. . . .

Names came up as he walked back from the Tiber—old names of football players, school-boy friends dead and enucleated by their desperation, breath-taking daring which took life like a cherry from which it spit the stone laughing.

Yes, yes, that is life, a grass sandwich.—Eagerly he always listened to men who had lived that way, avidly, avidly without thought of anything. And always he had had the same feeling in himself. They eat so as to be blind. . . .

And the names of . . . reckless Roman emperors came to his mind; their unchecked voluptuousness, headlong humor, which understood rightly, is the fullness of life, the obverse of that virtue among the saints which they fathered.—The same is the best of modern Paris. Eyes wide open will discover nothing till the man go on to the end as they do there. Frightened after the emperors the next age turned back to save what it could—and got into a maze of sophistry. Science should salute the Imperial Roman debauchés. We should adore their fullness of abandon. These then—who live desperately—are the salt of the world. The emperors, in manners, were one with the modern genius in chemistry, but larger, whose way with life, more mapped—falls down. Check not the children. The whole confused mass of modern thought oppressed him.

Rome! city of churches. Coming back along the Corso, Evans walked into that gloom. He did not know the name, it was near the Palazzo Strozzi. And there he saw "the church," created by excesses, calling the lambs, a shepherd with its shepherd's pipes, to come and drink of its pure spring. Pure! in view of all of life that it ignores.

Science! he thought again, coming once more into the street from the church. Anyone can bemuse himself with labor toward "discovery," but few can stay upon the point of the difficulty long. The difficulty is to keep on, not to stop. That was their honor, when they had it—the emperors. They exceed philosophy and science.—Evans had been berated in that he gave up hope of academic distinction as a boy, gave up a promising career in the city to go home to sit down at the place of his birth—to think and to see if there were any way—to do anything. Paris he could see, yes, for some it was a way. Not for him. . . .

But now he was in Rome, in Rome while passing back to the point of his departure, the place of his birth. What is the place of my birth? The place of my birth is the place where the word begins. Evans had not gotten further, nor had he detected any wise enough to instruct him. He laughed at his own egotism.—Which is at least well checked, and will destroy nothing—if it do not achieve clarity, if it do not create.

To create—it sounded hollow as his footsteps on the stones of the Via Pilotta into which he had turned. To create was no longer to be an emperor; this is futile. But to create is to shoot a clarity through the oppressing, obsessing murk of the world; *that* would be a reward. But not the church which lays waste nine parts of the light, the major part of morals, to have its penny's worth of clammy candle-promise of eternity. There must be in Rome a greater thing, inclusive of the world of love and of delight; unoppressive— loosing the mind so that men shall again occupy that center from which they have been avulsed by their own sordidness—and failure of imagination.

He felt somehow relieved, scarcely knowing how he had come around again. Mounting the Spanish steps, up to the Villa Medici, he came to the Pincio once more. . . .

In the afternoon it came on to rain. Restless, hating the narrowness of his room, tired of writing, this would be the moment for the *Museo Nazionale.* Thither he went and in under the great ruined dome of Diocletian's *tepidarium,* his heart fearfully throbbing, to face those ancient wonders gathered there.

Instantly his slightly held new peace had left him. His knees shook, he could not calmly breathe. For he knew that marble certainty which he must see and the defeat which he must somehow steel himself to suffer.

He went from piece to piece, not yielding easily but half surlily, looking the exhibits up and down. Yet he was afraid.

It was that this reality that had once inspired these marbles, but now outside of experience, seemed more living than the living all about him, that unhorsed his wits. Before the two wings of the altar to Aphrodite, the seated figures of the women, he almost choked, between their beauty and anger at the world, so that he did not know where to rest, but depressed by the marble he had to go driven, driven—as before.

Between these feelings, the stonelike reality of ancient excellence and the pulpy worthlessness of every day, he wandered lost; or coming out of the worst of it, striving to find a footing and walking about from piece to piece,—about the old cloister built by the monks in the vast ruins of the ancient baths—he was bewildered, yet felt himself rescued at a turn in the wall by some new wonder of that old assertion—the Mercury's forward thrust leg of a fine dancer; and then he fell, it might be said, by chance, upon that white and perfect girl, the Venus Anadyomene of Cyrene— dug from that sea-loosened bank of Africa.

Coming alone into the narrow chamber where this solitary, bit of marble stood, it seemed to him perfection, actually, which had survived the endless defamations of the world. Actually alive she seemed, that perfect girl, in quiet pose, pure white—her fringed robe hanging from a dolphin's sculptured flukes. He looked and looked at those perfections of the breasts, the torso, the thighs— forgetting the stone, seeing a woman—young and tranquil standing by the sea—and nothing of stone, just quietness and fulfillment.

He felt in this no defeat,—he was amazed, filled up. In this shameful room he stood looking long and excitedly at the marble knees of Venus. Then he returned to the Pension for supper. Fräulein whatever-her-name was, was there as before. She glanced up at him. But his eyes filled with the Venus, he paid no heed.

Yet he was not wholly pacified. Rome frightened him. He could not sleep that night until he had made up his mind to get out of the city next day for a while at least.

So lying there in the dark after the first distracting glimpse of it, he decided to leave Rome for a southern tour—to be back again in a week. Having tested the character of the place, seen a few of the strong features, he would start south for Naples in the morning.

FOR THE LITERARY TRAVELER

The Rome chapters of *A Voyage to Pagany* focus on the beauty of women and the phenomenon of rushing water, an erotic current that moves Evans through the city, and, in the end, into the presence of the marble perfection of Venus.

Arriving from Florence, he disembarks at the main railroad station—**Stazione Termini** (one of the largest train stations in Europe)—across from and named after the Baths (Terme) of Diocletian. These ruins face the **Piazza dell'Esedra,** the name still used by Romans for a piazza that's long been called **Piazza della Repubblica** on maps. The "brimming Fountain of the Mermaids" in the center of Esedra catches Evans's eye. The sexy stone naiads cavorting with sea monsters under high jets of water created a furor, even in Pagany, when the fountain was unveiled in 1901. The *pensiones* in the semicircular palazzos surrounding Esedra look out on the exuberant sea girls, the battle of the sexes depicted as water play.

This is a hectic part of the city, but there are air-conditioned oases of bookstores a few minutes away from the fast-food joints and hotels inside Esedra's bordering colonnades: **Libreria Feltrinelli International,** open daily 9–7:30, Via Orlando 84 / 86 (you can sit as long as you like downstairs next to the shelves of Henry James, Muriel Spark, Don DeLillo, Hemingway, Joyce, Mary Gordon, each having Rome in their biography); the excellent **MEL Bookstore,** open 9–8, Sun 10–1, 4–7:30, Via Nazionale 254–55. In the other direction, across Via Nazionale in Via Torino 136, near the Opera House, the gloomy **Economy Book and Video Center** has a decent used book section.

Visiting bookstores is entirely in the spirit of Williams's Roman pilgrimage since what his protagonist wants above all is to write, to "shoot a clarity through the oppressing murk of the world." And as Saul Bellow put it, "A writer is a reader moved to emulation."

Along Williams's/Evans's meandering route is the **Baths of Dioclet-**

ian, the entrance to the newly restored Baths across from the railway station where he began his visit (and where Bernard Malamud's powerful Roman story "The Last Mohican" begins). The interior of Rome's largest baths, built in 299 A.D. serving three thousand people at a time—(visiting the Baths was like going to your health club)—now provides cool high-vaulted spaces for the display of the archaeological finds of the **Museo Nazionale Romano.** This is the collective name for the State collections of ancient Roman art which are housed in four museums in the city.

First: The Baths of Diocletian.

Second: The most important part of the collection is displayed on the south side of the nearby busy Piazza dei Cinquecento in the newly restored **Palazzo Massimo alle Terme** on Viale Einaudi (open 9–7:45, closed Mon). On the second floor there's a room from the Villa of Livia, the wife of the Emperor Augustus, from her country retreat at Prima Porta, which delighted Elizabeth Bowen in *A Time in Rome.*

Third Before the **Altar to Aphrodite** Evans, overwhelmed by its beauty, "almost choked." The altar is in the magnificent **Palazzo Altemps,** 46 Piazza Sant'Apollinaire, north of Piazza Navona (open 9–7:45, Sun 10–2, closed Mon). This newly restored sixteenth-century palace, a jewel of the Roman Renaissance, houses the famous Ludovisi collection of ancient Roman sculptures. The Altar—in Room XV, number 189A—depicts the birth of Aphrodite as she rises out of the sea. The goddess of love comes into the world with a smile, welcomed by a female flute player on one end of the altar and a veiled priestess on the other. For many travelers, including this writer, the fifth-century B.C. Greek sculpture is the most beautiful in Rome, "never," according to Georgina Masson, "to be forgotten." The lighting and the generous space surrounding it intensify the effect, which you can contemplate, since Palazzo Altemps is not a stop on the usual tourist trail. (The Ludovisi Juno that Goethe loved is here, too: number 190A.)

Fourth: Evans, a pilgrim in search of the non-religious sacred, hurries, without a glance, through **Michelangelo's Cloister,** behind the Baths of Diocletian, missing the attached church of Santa Maria degli Angeli, originally the frigidarium of the Baths, and still nicely cool in summer. His pilgrimage reaches its climax in a building just to the left of the Baths, in the **Octagonal Hall,** or **Aula Ottagonale,** on the corner of Via Parigi and Via Romita 8 (open 9–2, closed Mon, tel 06 487 0690). Some of the Roman sculptures displayed around the hall were found in the Baths of Caracalla, an older and more splendid facility than Diocletian's. (Opera is once again performed at Caracalla in summer, with the hulking sun-baked ruins as backdrop, one of the most splendid experiences in night-time Rome. Via delle Terme di Caracalla, Tues–Sat, 9–dusk, Mon 9–1, closed Sun, tel 06 575 8626.)

In the last niche of the Ottagonale, on a pedestal to your right, Evans finds a marble image, the **Venus of Cyrene,** "that white and perfect girl" his beatific vision before which he stands transfixed. (*In restauro,* 2003.) If the Octagonal Hall is not open when the sign says it should be, you can gain admission if you dare. The friendly tourist office around the corner in Via Parigi 11 couldn't explain why the *Ottagonale* was closed when it was supposed to be open so this visitor was told to just stand outside the locked building and shout. The shouts—*Aiute! Per favore, Aiuto!*—"Help, please help!"—did bring the guards, who unlocked the door and let me in. They didn't explain why the doors had been locked. They were amused by how desperately this shrieking traveler wanted to see the Venus of Cyrene. Williams's hymn to her—he has found the meaning of life, the fountain of truth—recalls the Emperor Hadrian acknowledging Venus as the Mother of Love in the *Memoirs:* "my heavenly counsellor." Great pagans think alike. And admission to the Octagonal Hall is worth shouting for. Even if the object of your quest is *in restauro,* the hall is beautiful.

JOHN UPDIKE

1932–

"By dint of both quality and quantity he is American literature's greatest short-story writer, and arguably our greatest writer without a single great novel," according to Lorrie Moore. The following story about the Maples in Rome is taken from The Early Stories, 1953–1975. *Updike has also written thousands of essays, reviews, and travel pieces. In "Mea Culpa, a Travel Note" he remembers the time he climbed to the Lantern of St. Peter's dome and instead of ecstasy felt only sheer terror. Unpersuaded by Rome's mystique (like Martin Luther), he has said that he distrusts the spectacular, the extraordinary. "Let literature concern itself, as the Gospels do, with the inner lives of hidden men."*

❧

TWIN BEDS IN ROME

The Maples had talked and thought about separation so long it seemed it would never come. For their conversations, increasingly ambivalent and ruthless as accusation, retraction, blow, and caress alternated and cancelled, had the final effect of knitting them ever tighter together in a painful, helpless, degrading intimacy. And their lovemaking, like a perversely healthy child whose growth defies every deficiency of nutrition, continued; when their tongues at last fell silent, their bodies collapsed together as two mute armies might gratefully mingle, released from the absurd hostilities decreed by two mad kings. Bleeding, mangled, reverently laid in its tomb a dozen times, their marriage could not die. Burning to leave one another, they left, out of marital habit, together. They took a trip to Rome.

They arrived at night. The plane was late, the airport grand. They had left hastily, without plans; and yet, as if forewarned of their arrival, nimble Italians, speaking perfect English, took their luggage in hand, reserved a hotel room for them by telephone from the airport, and ushered them into a bus. The bus, surprisingly, plunged into a dark rural landscape. A few windows hung lantern-like in the distance; a river abruptly bared its silver breast beneath them; the silhouettes of olive trees and Italian pines flicked past like shadowy illustrations in an old Latin primer. "I could ride this bus forever," Joan said aloud, and Richard was pained, remembering, from the days when they had been content together, how she had once confessed to feeling a sexual stir when the young man at the gas station, wiping the windshield with a vigorous, circular motion, had made the body of the car, containing her, rock slightly. Of all the things she had ever told him, this remained in his mind the most revealing, the deepest glimpse she had ever permitted into the secret woman he could never reach and had at last wearied of trying to reach.

Yet it pleased him to have her happy. This was his weakness. He wished her to be happy, and the certainty that, away from her, he could not know if she were happy or not formed the final, unexpected door barring his way when all others had been opened. So he dried the very tears he had whipped from her eyes, withdrew each protestation of hopelessness at the very point when she seemed willing to give up hope, and their agony continued. "Nothing lasts forever," he said now.

"You can't let me relax a minute, can you?"

"I'm sorry. Do relax."

She stared through the window a while, then turned and told him, "It doesn't feel as if we're going to Rome at all."

"Where are we going?" He honestly wanted to know, honestly hoped she could tell him.

"Back to the way things were?"

"No. I don't want to go back to that. I feel we've come very far and have only a little way more to go."

She looked out at the quiet landscape a long while before he realized she was crying. He fought the impulse to comfort her, inwardly shouted it down as cowardly and cruel, but his hand, as if robbed of restraint by a force as powerful as lust, crept onto her arm. She rested her head on his shoulder. The shawled woman across the aisle took them for lovers and politely glanced away.

The bus slipped from the country dark. Factories and residential rows narrowed the highway. A sudden monument, a massive white pyramid stricken with light and inscribed with Latin, loomed beside them. Soon they were pressing their faces together to the window to follow the Colosseum itself as, shaped like a shattered wedding cake, it slowly pivoted and silently floated from the harbor of their vision. At the terminal, another lively chain of hands and voices rejoined them to their baggage, settled them in a taxi, and carried them to the hotel. As Richard dropped six hundred-lira pieces into the driver's hand, they seemed the smoothest, roundest, most tactfully weighted coins he had ever bestowed. The hotel desk was one flight up. The clerk was young and playful. He pronounced their name several times, and wondered why they had not gone to Naples. The halls of the hotel, which had been described to them at the airport as second-class, were nevertheless of rose marble. The marble floor carried into their room. This and the amplitude of the bathroom and the imperial purple of the curtains blinded Richard to a serious imperfection until the clerk, his heels clicking in satisfaction with the perhaps miscalculated tip he had received, was far down the hall.

"Twin beds," he said. They had always had a double bed.

Joan asked, "Do you want to call the desk?"

"How important is it to you?"

"I don't think it matters. Can you sleep alone?"

"I guess. But—" It was delicate. He felt they had been insulted. Until they finally parted, it seemed impertinent for anything, even a slice of space, to come between them. If the trip were to kill or cure (and this was, for the tenth time, their slogan), then the attempt at a cure should have a certain technical purity, even though—or, rather, all the more because—in his heart he had already doomed it to fail. And also there was the material question of whether he could sleep without a warm proximate body to give his sleep shape.

"But what?" Joan prompted.

"But it seems sort of sad."

"Richard, don't be sad. You've been sad enough. You're supposed to relax. This isn't a honeymoon or anything, it's just a little rest we're trying to give each other. You can come visit me in my bed if you can't sleep."

"You're such a nice woman," he said. "I can't understand why I'm so miserable with you."

He had said this, or something like it, so often before that she, sickened by simultaneous doses of honey and gall, ignored the entire remark, and unpacked with a deliberate serenity. On her suggestion, they walked into the city, though it was ten o'clock. Their hotel was on a shopping street that at this hour was lined with lowered steel shutters. At the far end, an illuminated fountain played. His feet, which had never given him trouble, began to hurt. In the soft, damp air of the Roman winter, his shoes seemed to have developed hot inward convexities that gnashed his flesh at every stride. He could not imagine why this should be, unless he was allergic to marble. For the sake of his feet, they found an American bar, entered, and ordered coffee. Off in a corner, a drunken male American voice droned through the grooves of an unintelligible but distinctly feminine circuit of complaints; the voice, indeed, seemed not so much a man's as a woman's deepened by being played at a slower speed on the phonograph. Hoping to cure the growing dizzy emptiness within him, Richard ordered a "hamburger" that proved to be more tomato sauce than meat. Outside, on the street, he bought a paper cone of hot chestnuts from a sidewalk vender. This man, whose thumbs and fingertips were charred black, agitated his hand until three hundred lira were placed in it. In a way, Richard welcomed being cheated; it gave him a place in the Roman economy. The Maples returned to the hotel, and side by side on their twin beds fell into a deep sleep.

———

That is, Richard assumed, in the cavernous accounting rooms of his subconscious, that Joan also slept well. But when they awoke in the morning, she told him, "You were terribly funny last night. I couldn't go to sleep, and every time I reached over to give you a little pat, to make you think you were in a double bed, you'd say 'Go away' and shake me off."

He laughed in delight. "Did I really? In my sleep?"

"It must have been. Once you shouted 'Leave me alone!' so loud I thought you must be awake, but when I tried to talk to you, you were snoring."

"Isn't that funny? I hope I didn't hurt your feelings."

"No. It was refreshing not to have you contradict yourself."

He brushed his teeth and ate a few of the cold chestnuts left over from the night before. The Maples breakfasted on hard rolls and bitter coffee in the hotel and walked again into Rome. His shoes resumed their inexplicable torture. With its strange, almost mocking attentiveness to their unseen needs, the city thrust a shoe store under their eyes; they entered, and Richard bought, from a gracefully reptilian young salesman, a pair of black alligator loafers. They were too tight, being smartly shaped, but they were dead—they did not pinch with the vital, outraged vehemence of the others. Then the Maples, she carrying the Hachette guidebook and he his American shoes in a box, walked down the Via Nazionale to the Victor Emmanuel Monument, a titanic flight of stairs leading nowhere. "What was so great about him?" Richard asked. "Did he unify Italy? Or was that Cavour?"

"Is he the funny little king in *A Farewell to Arms*?"

"I don't know. But nobody could be *that* great."

"You can see now why the Italians don't have an inferiority complex. Everything is so huge."

They stood looking at the Palazzo Venezia until they imagined Mussolini frowning from a window, climbed the many steps to the Piazza del Campidoglio, and came to the equestrian statue of Marcus Aurelius on the pedestal by Michelangelo. Joan remarked how like a Marino Marini it was, and it was. She was so intelligent. Perhaps this was what made leaving her, as a gesture, exquisite in conception and difficult in execution. They circled the square. The portals and doors all around them seemed closed forever, like the doors in a drawing. They entered, because it was open, the side door of the church of Santa Maria in Aracoeli. They discovered themselves to be walking on sleeping people, life-sized tomb-reliefs worn nearly featureless by footsteps. The fingers of the hands folded on the stone breasts had been smoothed to finger-shaped shadows. One face, sheltered from wear behind a pillar, seemed a vivid soul trying to rise from the all-but-erased body.

Only the Maples examined these reliefs, cut into a floor that once must have been a glittering lake of mosaic; the other tourists clustered around a chapel that preserved, in slippers and vestments, behind glass, the child-sized greenish remains of a pope. Joan and Richard left by the same side door and descended steps and paid admission to the ruins of the Roman Forum. The Renaissance had used it as a quarry; broken columns lay everywhere, loaded with perspective, like a de Chirico. Joan was charmed by the way birds and weeds lived in the crevices of this exploded civic dream. A delicate rain began to fall. At the end of one path, they peeked in glass doors, and a small uniformed man with a broom limped forward and admitted them, as if to a speakeasy, to the abandoned church of Santa Maria Antiqua. The pale vaulted air felt innocent of worship; the seventh-century frescoes seemed recently, nervously executed. As they left, Richard read the question in the broom man's smile and pressed a tactful coin into his hand. The soft rain continued. Joan took Richard's arm, as if for shelter. His stomach began to hurt—a light, chafing ache at first, scarcely enough to distract him from the pain in his feet. They walked along the Via Sacra, through roofless pagan temples carpeted in grass. The ache in his stomach intensified. Uniformed guards, old men standing this way and that in the rain like hungry gulls, beckoned them toward further ruins, further churches, but the pain now had blinded Richard to everything but the extremity of his distance from anything that might give him support. He refused admittance to the Basilica of Constantine, and asked instead for the *uscita,* mispronouncing it. He did not feel capable of retracing his steps. The guard, seeing a source of tips escaping, dourly pointed toward a small gate in a nearby wire fence. The Maples lifted the latch, stepped through, and stood on the paved rise overlooking the Colosseum. Richard walked a little distance and leaned on a low wall.

"Is it so bad?" Joan asked.

"Oddly bad," he said. "I'm sorry. It's funny."

"Do you want to throw up?"

"No. It's not like that." His sentences came jerkily. "It's just a . . . sort of gripe."

"High or low?"

"In the middle."

"What could have caused it? The chestnuts?"

"No. It's just, I think, being here, so far from anywhere, with you, and not knowing . . . why."

"Shall we go back to the hotel?"

"Yes. I think if I could lie down."

"Shall we get a taxi?"

"They'll cheat me."

"That doesn't matter."

"I don't know . . . our address."

"We know sort of. It's near that big fountain. I'll look up the Italian for 'fountain.' "

"Rome is . . . full of . . . fountains."

"Richard. You aren't doing this just for my benefit?"

He had to laugh, she was so intelligent. "Not consciously. It has something to do . . . with having to hand out tips . . . all the time. It's really an ache. It's incredible."

"Can you walk?"

"Sure. Hold my arm."

"Shall I carry your shoebox?"

"No. Don't worry, sweetie. It's just a nervous ache. I used to get them . . . when I was little. But I was . . . braver then."

They descended steps to a thoroughfare thick with speeding traffic. The taxis they hailed carried heads in the rear and did not stop. They crossed the Via dei Fori Imperiali and tried to work their way back, against the sideways tug of interweaving streets, to the familiar territory containing the fountain, the American Bar, the shoe store, and the hotel. They passed through a market of bright food. Garlands of sausages hung from striped canopies. Heaps of lettuce lay in the street. He walked stiffly, as if the pain he carried were precious and fragile; holding one arm across his abdomen seemed to ease it slightly. The rain and Joan, having been in some way the pressures that had caused it, now became the pressures that enabled him to bear it. Joan kept him walking. The rain masked him, made his figure less distinct to passersby, and thus less distinct to himself, and so dimmed his pain. The blocks seemed cruelly uphill and downhill. They climbed a long slope of narrow pavement beside the Banca d'Italia. The rain lifted. The pain, having expanded into every corner of the chamber beneath his ribs, had armed itself with a knife and now began to slash the walls in hope of escape. They reached the Via Nazionale, blocks below the hotel. The shops were unshuttered, the distant fountain was dry. He felt as if he were leaning backward, and his mind seemed a kind of twig, a twig that had deviated from the trunk and chosen to be this branch instead of that one, and chosen again and again, becoming finer with each choice, until, finally, there was nothing left for it but to vanish into air. In the hotel room he lay down on his twin bed, settled his overcoat over him, curled up, and fell asleep.

When he awoke an hour later, everything was different. The pain was gone. Joan was lying in her bed reading the Hachette guide. He saw her, as he rolled over, as if freshly, in the kind of cool library light in which he had first seen her; only he knew, calmly, that since then she had come to share his room. "It's gone," he told her.

"You're kidding. I was all set to call up a doctor and have you taken to a hospital."

"No, it wasn't anything like that. I knew it wasn't. It was nervous."

"You were dead white."

"It was too many different things focusing on the same spot. I think the Forum must have depressed me. The past here is so . . . much. So complicated. Also, my shoes hurting bothered me."

"Darley, it's Rome. You're supposed to be happy."

"I am now. Come on. You must be starving. Let's get some lunch."

"Really? You feel up to it?"

"Quite. It's gone." And, except for a comfortable reminiscent soreness that the first swallow of Milanese salami healed, it was. The Maples embarked again upon Rome, and, in this city of steps, of sliding, unfolding perspectives, of many-windowed surfaces of sepia and rose ochre, of buildings so vast one seemed to be out-doors in them, the couple parted. Not physically—they rarely left each other's sight. But they had at last been parted. Both knew it. They became with each other, as in the days of courtship, courte-ous, gay, and reserved. Their marriage let go like an overgrown vine whose half-hidden stem has been slashed in the dawn by an ancient gardener. They walked arm in arm through seemingly solid blocks of buildings that separated, under examination, into widely different slices of style and time. At one point she turned to him and said, "Darley, I know what was wrong with us. I'm classic, and you're baroque." They shopped, and saw, and slept, and ate. Sitting across from her in the last of the restaurants that like oases of linen and wine had sustained these level elegiac days, Richard saw that Joan was happy. Her face, released from the tension of hope, had grown smooth; her gestures had taken on the flirting irony of the young; she had become ecstatically attentive to everything about her; and her voice, as she bent forward to whisper a remark about a woman and a handsome man at another table, was rapid, as if the very air of her breathing had turned thin and free. She was happy, and, jealous of her happiness, he again grew reluctant to leave her.

FOR THE LITERARY TRAVELER

To the jet-lagged Maples, the **Colosseum** at first sight appears "shaped like a shattered wedding cake." With that image, we enter the torpor of their disaffection. They arrive in winter, once the glittering season when the nineteenth-century Grand Tourists wore themselves out sightseeing, socializing, and pontificating about the glories and grandeur of the epicenter of western civilization. But the Maples' Rome is imagined by a contemporary realist who refuses idealization, just as his Lutheran ancestors refused the idolatry of Rome's official religion.

Joan and Richard walk dutifully from their hotel down the hill of **Via Nazionale** (depressing on Sundays when the stores are closed and there's no one around). Then they climb steps: up to the arrogant **Victor Emmanuel Monument** from which they look down on the battlemented **Palazzo Venezia,** where (they remember) Mussolini used to address the idolatrous fascist mob from the balcony. The first great Renaissance palace in the city, the Venezia is used now for art exhibits, their subjects displayed on colorful buntings draped across the front of the loggia where *Il Duce* rallied the citizenry round, first, to a pre-emptive strike against Ethiopia in 1935—*Duce! Duce! Duce!* they shouted—and three years later, to welcoming the visiting Hitler.

They next ascend Michelangelo's Cordonata to the **Campidoglio,** where the statue of Marcus Aurelius on his horse rouses Mrs. Maple to a bit of pedantry. To their tired eyes, the piazza, one of the most harmonious spaces in Rome, "seemed closed forever." They don't climb the 124 steps leading to the austere red-brown facade of the fifth-century church next to the Capitol, **Santa Maria in Aracoeli.** They enter through a side door and walk over the tombstones of cardinals.

Outside, the **Forum,** too, is a torment, the husband's indigestion and aching feet manifesting the pain of a marriage in ruins. The ironies are not lost on Updike's prototypical couple. In this city of triumphal and ruined monuments, they are two who have broken faith, failed to live up to their monumental promise: "For better or worse . . . till death us do part." The proud city has also suffered chaos, invasions, plagues; it's a wise setting for a story of emotional devastation. Updike, like the other New England literary pilgrims in Rome, Hawthorne and Henry James, insists that shadows, like the theology of sin, originate in something real. The false comfort of a temporary tourist happiness—the couple's reconciliation—is not in the Protestant cards.

At the top of the long stairway leading up to Santa Maria in

Aracoeli—you feel as if you've climbed a mountainside—the prospect below, in certain lights, has a strange poignancy. The Aracoeli, built over the ancient temple of Juno, is filled with treasure and thick with myths. But the Maples can't feel themselves part of any history beyond their own, a hardening that recalls Elizabeth Bowen's observation about the tragedies of Roman history: "There can be a saturation point with regard to feeling, an instinctive reaction against memory. . . . there is a stone-coldness about great Roman thought. . . ."

(*The Maples do enjoy the food in Rome. To dine in the neighborhood of their discontent, descend the long Aracoeli stairway and head across the mad four-laned Via dell Teatro di Marcello—another of Mussolini's wide efficient thoroughfares cut through the city center. On the other side, assuming you get there, follow the narrow alleys curving around the palazzos and bear left. Beneath the vine-covered tower in* **Piazza Margana** *is* **La Taverna degli Amici A Tormargana** *[Piazza Margana 36/37, tel 06 692 00493, closed Mon]. Couples or solo travelers can occupy a (preferably outdoor) table in this pretty spot—stronger on ambience than cuisine—for as long as you like. For simpler fare, there's the* **Antico Caffè del Teatro Marcello** *in the treacherous Via del Teatro Marcello 42.*)

Back in the direction of the Maples' hotel, across Piazza Venezia (where there's a busy taxi stand), bearing right and ascending **Via Nazionale,** you'll pass, at the beginning, the **Largo Magnanapoll,** with an oasis of palm trees in the center, then, behind the markets, the brick medieval tower **Torre delle Milizie,** conspicuous on the Roman skyline from any overlook. (Off Via Nazionale in Via Genova 32, **Da Ricci** is said to be Rome's oldest pizzeria, and some say the best.) On the right side of the street, high walls border the gardens of Villa Aldobrandini which gave its name to a famous fresco of a marriage scene, the **"Aldobrandini Marriage,"** now in the Vatican. Part of the gardens are now a small park with good views (entrance on Via Mazzarino), where traveling couples of any disposition may rest their weary feet. There's also good shopping along Nazionale.

ELEANOR CLARK

1913–1996

Years after she published Rome and a Villa, *a classic of the literature of place, Eleanor Clark wondered where it all began. "What is Rome? What is Rome to me? What* was *Rome to me? How did I, how could anybody, have the nerve to take on this subject?"*

In 1947, as a novelist and winner of a Guggenheim, she settled in at the American Academy on top of the Janiculum to work on her second novel. But the city beyond the Academy gates seduced her—like all Rome lovers, she was a tireless walker—and, finally, as she put it, "good-bye novel." The sketches she wrote of Roman places became the book Rome and a Villa. *The final chapter, written for an updated edition in 1974 and excerpted here, is a portrait of the Protestant cemetery where Keats is buried.*

❧

From ROME AND A VILLA

BESIDE THE PYRAMID

A nd still they were the same bright, patient stars. . . . And plunged all noiseless into the deep night." "Saturn, sleep on! while at thy feet I weep."

It is no small part of the beauty of the so-called Protestant Cemetery in Rome that Keats is buried there. The word *felicity* comes to mind around that fact, because it is of that order of experience to be brought up against all the tough intellectual rigor, the nearly impossible demands of vision and fitness of thought, that went into his sense of "beauty" and could make it equate with "truth"—the very opposite of wallowing in facile landscape. Yet of course there is another fitness in the place having remained as beautiful as it has in the ordinary meaning, and still another in his having some rather good company there, though mostly of later times and on the whole of something less than the genius often vaguely associated with it. The charm, taking that word too as deeply as we can manage, of this piece of ground next to Rome's one pyramid, while enhanced by thoughts of the "truly great," is both more and less than the titillation of looking at tombstones of famous people. Less because there are not so many there, far fewer than of their and other people's infant children. More because the charm is of Rome itself, in its hold on the mind of the world outside Italy.

It is a foreign enclave, of non-Catholics—Germans, Scandinavians, English, Americans, Greeks, Russians—administered by diplomatic representatives of the countries chiefly involved; an exception may have been made now and then but the rule is that Italian Protestants, or agnostics or atheists, are not allowed to be buried there unless married or related to a foreigner. So one might expect a feeling of double alienation, from life and from home, unless with Shelley one were inclined to be "half in love with death, at the thought that one should be buried in so sweet a place," which is taking the matter beyond nationality with rather a vengeance, understandably in his case. But no, although he was right about the quality of the place and would be still by some strange mercy today, it is not like any of that, or need not be. It would be too callow to call the cemetery festive, but gloomless it certainly is, and homeless its dead are not. One might even speak of it as having, as a community shared also by its lovely vegetation and the large colony of cats at the base of the adjacent pyramid, a rare sense of humor. At least it serves as sufficient comment on the outbreak of Thanatology courses and other vulgarities on the subject in our country nowadays, of the Facing the Facts and How to Be Bereaved and Like It categories, rather more horrid than the inhibitions they replace; and yes, toward those embarrassments as in other ways, surely we can imagine this little plot in Rome, unique in the world as it is, as wearing something in the nature of a smile.

Not the "infant's smile" Shelley gave it in *Adonais,* nor quite "the light of laughing flowers" he saw there over the dead. It would be a gentle and generous one, though so many battles have swirled around the spot and the names can't all be of people who were generous and peaceable in life. This quiet garden keeps the dignity of human grief. For the non-Catholic and non-Latin mind it does so far more than the enormous Campo Verano, the regular cemetery of Rome since 1837, out by San Lorenzo Fuori le Mura, quite beautiful too in its setting and planting but where pathos is crushed by the bella figura: the expense, the show, the need to outdo in pomposity of monuments, along with the sorry custom of trying to immortalize the deceased with portraits and photographs, down to the cheapest snapshots of the poor in their little boxes tier on tier in the walls. No bella figura there and there must be many who cannot afford even that. By the Pyramid, there are relatively few pretentious monuments, and probably not many of very poor people either, aside from some of the artists and students and political refugees. By and large the foreign colonies in Rome over the past two hundred years have been something short of indigent.

At the time of Keats's death, in the still sorrowful and resonant little room over Piazza di Spagna, in 1821, there were not many stones or names of any kind in the cemetery. There was no wall around any part of it, then or for another half a century, except the Pyramid and the adjoining section of the Aurelian wall at the top of the slope. It was part of what was called the Agro, the "fields of the Roman people," and looks very rural indeed in engravings of the time, with its small sprinkling of tombstones close to the Pyramid as though for protection from its age and bulk, and ox-cart tracks between the clusters. The trees around appear to be live oaks; the pines and cypresses were planted much later. Protection was needed, and Caius Cestius, he of the Pyramid, dead in 12 B.C., was not always up to the job. Monte Testaccio, down at what is now the other end of the block, the hill formed from debris of ancient potsherds, was a site of all sorts of rowdy goings-on, with drinking places in its caverns. Tombs were sometimes vandalized and funeral groups were apt to be attacked, perhaps less out of

Catholic devotion than proprietary feeling about the fields. This is given as the reason for the prohibition of daytime funerals; one burial scene by torchlight, in an etching by Pinelli of 1811, looks more like a witches' Sabbat. Another prohibition may or may not have had to do with a fear of stirring up popular outrage; more likely it reflects the motto of ruling Church circles—*Extra ecclesiam nulla salus.** Until 1870 crosses were forbidden over the graves, as were the word God, quotations from Scripture, or any hint of eternal salvation.

That would have been a plus to Shelley, and no worry to Keats, who in the atrocious misery of his last months, the only months of his life in Rome, yet knew of what kind his salvation would be if any were in the cards: "I think I shall be among the English poets after my death." What pleased him was Joseph Severn's report of the wildflowers, especially violets and daisies, that grew in profusion around the ground. Severn, in his heroic efforts to soothe a mind already close to cracking, from loss and hopelessness and the particular torments of that long dying, would not have mentioned the possible violences at the cemetery, if he knew of them. No other plan was possible in any case.

Keats is rare, though not alone, in having had next to no firsthand experience of Rome or even acquaintance with it. The voice, the air, the common language of the cemetery—and there is one, beyond all the linguistic divisions commemorated there; the flowers and rambling vines and crooked little paths have their say in it—has for one element a curious reciprocity between people and city, of a kind that occurs nowhere else. With all its cruelties, perhaps in part because of them, it has in its depths welcome to spare for whatever fragments of humanity are drawn to it.

This is to speak of an overall charity and grace that everyone feels in the cemetery, no matter how they express it or fail to. It is true of all graveyards that visitors, sightseers, wander more slowly

---

*Outside the church, there is no salvation.

than they are accustomed to, "repressing haste, as too unholy there," but from this one it would be hard to find a person so stupefied as to come away without a mellower sense of life. "Lovely," "moving," "beautiful," "nice," even Shelley's now bygone "sweet" are the common adjectives—all referring to a charmed relaxation of strain around the fact of death and toward those psychologists and others, who would beat our brains out groping for ultimate answers in the absence of religion. Not that groping isn't in order, but the all-day question mark seems a little less useful than the hair shirt, or than Shelley's game of Demogorgon—now you get it, now you don't—as a guide to living. Keats in his genius of sympathy with all that makes up the flow of life, a reason among others for his being so profoundly at home with Shakespeare, said it very well in the famous letter to his brothers on "*Negative Capability,* that is when man is capable of being in uncertainties, Mysteries, doubts, without any irritable reaching after fact and reason. . . ." A sentence liable to be mistaken as crudely antiphilosophical if taken out of the whole context of his work and letters. All it means is that he had Shakespeare's generic *kind* of intelligence, as against the isolated, frameless—therefore un-Miltonic, un-Dantesque—overreaching after the Reason For It All, sure poison to poetry. The key word is *irritable.* In that sense his grave could not be more appropriate. . . .

FOR THE LITERARY TRAVELER

The American Academy in Rome marked the starting point of Clark's long rambles through the city. On top of the Janiculum (Via Angelo Masina 5), the Academy houses winners of the Rome Prize, and writers working on projects connected with Italy. John Guare's comedy *Chaucer in Rome* is set here, an insider's look at the hilarious eccentricities of a place that to a stranger seems as subdued as a monastery. (Guare's wife, Adele Chatfield-Taylor, is the Academy's current director.) The eleven acres of gardens are lovely, and there are annual art exhibits, the black-and-white photography of Georgina Masson's Rome a highlight of

2003. Some former Academy residents have contributed their personal favorites in Rome to a small guidebook, *City Secrets: Rome.*

Eleanor Clark's observations are similarly subjective and original. Following her to the **Protestant Cemetery,** you can map several routes from the top of the Janiculum: Cross the Tiber on any one of the bridges out of Trastevere, and follow Ovid's route on the way to Ostia (see page 45). If you cross at the Ponte Sublicio on a Sunday morning, just before the bridge you'll see the open-air flea market at the Porta Portese and maybe recall a scene from Vittorio de Sica's movie *The Bicycle Thief.* Once across the bridge, walk straight along Via Marmorata, through **Testaccio,** toward the Pyramid of Cestius and the Porta San Paolo. At the Pyramid, turn right into Via Caio Cestio, an empty silent street, hugging the cemetery wall. Approaching the entrance gate at number 6, you pass a narrow slit in the wall through which you can see the grave of John Keats (1796–1821), in the shelter of cypresses and pines.

Keats's grave, in the spare Old Cemetery, is to the left of the entrance, in the direction of the Pyramid. The crowded New Cemetery (opened in 1822) rises on a slope opposite the entrance and spreads out to the right, up steps, beneath trees that shade the monuments and wild-flowered paths. The most visited grave in this section—there's always a pile of notes and mementos on top of it—is Antonio Gramsci's (1891–1937). A founder of the Italian Communist Party in 1921, imprisoned by the Fascists in 1926—Mussolini said, "We must prevent this brain from functioning for twenty years"—he was tortured and refused medical attention until he died. From prison Gramsci wrote the thirty-three *Prison Notebooks* and *Prison Letters* that, smuggled out of jail by a friend, still have a large international audience. The notes left on his grave by visitors in 2003 express impassioned gratitude for his courageous voice on behalf of Italy's poor.

The play of light and shadows, and the memory of the great spirits buried here make this a revelatory destination, even for travelers whose itinerary doesn't usually include cemeteries. Oscar Wilde called it "the holiest place in Rome," it deeply moved George Eliot, and Henry James buried Daisy Miller here.

Before Shelley died, only a year after Keats, he wrote of this place, "It might make one in love with death to think that one should be buried in so sweet a place." His heart is buried here, in a grave against the rear wall opposite the entrance, inscribed COR CORDIUM or "Heart of Hearts." He wrote his elegiac poem "Adonais" in memory of his friend Keats.

> Go thou to Rome, at once the Paradise,
> The grave, the city and the wilderness;
> And where its wrecks like shattered mountains rise,
> And flowering weeds and fragrant copses dress
> The bones of Desolation's nakedness
> Pass, till the spirit of the spot shall lead
> Thy footsteps to a slope of green access
> Where, like an infant's smile, over the dead
> A light of laughing flowers along the grass is spread.

(Open Tues–Sun 9–5, but some Sundays closes at 2.) Bus 23 and 27 to Porta San Paolo, and Metro linea B to Piramide. Contributions for the care of the cemetery's cat population go the AISPA—Anglo-Italian Society for the Protection of Animals—136 Baker St., London W1U 6DU, England, Attn: Cats of the Protestant Cemetery, Rome. Off Via Marmorata, there are excellent places to eat in Testaccio, uncrowded with tourists. Volpetti is the best known, the Formaggiomania at number 47—www.volpetti.com; www.fooditaly.com—a favorite of poet Mark Strand when he was a writer at the American Academy. A few doors away, **Barberini's** *Snack Bar and Gelateria, number 41–43, is a friendly local spot, as is* **Da Bucatino**—*Taverna Testaccio—in Via Luca della Robbia 84–86 [open Tues–Sun 12:30–3:30, 6:30–11:30 P.M., tel 06 574 6886]. In summer, the midday Sunday meal is quiet and cool at* **Trattoria lo Scopettaro,** *to your right as you cross Ponte Sublico into Testaccio, on Lungotevere Testaccio 7 [tel 06 575 7912], open every day for lunch and dinner. The morning food and clothing market [Mon–Sat] in* **Piazza di Testaccio** *is one of the best in Rome.)*

On the other side of the city from Keats's grave is the terracotta house where he died of tuberculosis, now the **Keats-Shelley Memorial,** Piazza di Spagna 26 (open Mon–Fri, 9–1, 3–6, Sat 11–2, 3–6). He arrived in Rome in November, 1820, having been advised by his doctor to spend the winter, weird advice given the damp chill that can make

Roman streets less than comforting at that time of year. By February, Keats was gone. His small room overlooking the Spanish Steps is preserved in this small museum, which is filled with collections of Keats's poetry (and Shelley and Byron), Keats's death mask, his sketch of a Grecian urn, locks of his hair. It's a moving place, true to the spirit of the poet who loved until death "the beauty that must die."

MURIEL SPARK

1918–

After a youth in Edinburgh, where she was born of Italian-Jewish parents, and some years in Rhodesia (now Zimbabwe) and London, Muriel Spark settled in Rome, considering it "a good place to work." Her conversion to Roman Catholicism in 1954 has colored her twenty-three novels (including The Prime of Miss Jean Brodie, *her masterpiece) with theological themes; she brings a moral scrutiny to human character. Her delineations of evil are corrosive, of goodness slant and funny. Her heroines often choose spiritual integrity and an essential solitude over the urgencies of the flesh. Hailed in the London press as "Britain's greatest living novelist," Mrs. Spark is an "enchantress" to her American admirer, John Updike. The following sketch of her Rome comes across in the brisk voice that makes her novels so bracing. Without a wasted phrase or syllable, she makes her city live, and then dismisses us. (Dismissing Rome in 1979, she moved to a hillside rectory in Tuscany.)*

❧

MY ROME

I settled in Rome long ago in 1967 because I found myself returning there again and again, staying longer and longer. I think what attracted me most was the immediate touch of antiquity on everyday life. If you live in central Rome you have only to walk down the street and you come to a fountain by Bernini in which children are playing or a Michelangelo embassy or some fine fifteenth-century building with today's washing hanging out.

The names Bramante, Raphael and Borromini become like those of friends. One comes into the territory of the Republican ages, the Caesars, the emperors or the medieval popes at any turn in the road, at any bus stop. Here is the Rome of Garibaldi's troops, of Keats and Shelley, of Arthur Hugh Clough (whose narrative poem *Amours de Voyage* contains one of the funniest descriptions of the English in Rome during the troubles of 1848); Byron's Rome, Henry James's Rome and Mussolini's big fat dream Rome with grandiose popular centers and concepts.

The first apartment I occupied was in the Piazza di Tor Sanguigna, not far from the Tiber on the corner of Via dei Coronari, an ancient street of antique furniture shops. I was at that time dazzled by the adjacent Piazza Navona (as indeed I still am), and I greatly desired a permanent home in the piazza. I did find a flat there, with a picturesque view of Bernini's marvelous Four Rivers fountain, but devoid of everything else, including water. The bathroom and the kitchen, explained the landlord, and the plumbing, electricity and other trivialities, were to be laid on by the lucky tenant who succeeded in obtaining from him a contract limited to one year's residence. The rent alone was high, and I knew right away that the project was impossible, but I still enjoy the memory, as I did the experience, of standing in that dark, vaulted, cavelike apartment while the landlord explained in a mixture of Italian, French and English those terms which I discerned, by careful deciphering, were exorbitant.

I fairly egged him on, as far as my powers in Italian permitted, so keen was I to see with my novelist's curiosity how far he would go. The tenant had to be an American, he said. I was a Scot, I informed him, and I doubted that he would find an American to pour capital into his property with a tenure of only one year. He replied that the apartment was in a famous fifteenth-century building in which many famous lords had lived, which was true enough. So he went on, while I looked out the window, watching the Baroque fountain playing in the fine October light of Rome. The theatrical figure representing the Nile, his great hand held up as if to ward off some falling masonry, seemed apt to my situation. "Speak to me," Michelangelo is said to have challenged his Roman statue of Moses; and indeed, the sculptures of Rome do speak.

At that time I made lifelong friends among the expatriate community of Rome, mostly British and American, almost all of them anxious to put me on the right track as a newcomer. Eugene Walter, a writer and actor, enormous in girth of physique and heart, held the nearest thing to a salon; he was an unofficial reception committee and all roads led to him. With Eugene I did my first round of the sights and heard all the thousand legends he kept in his head attaching to various monuments, and in his favorite restaurants and trattorie I learned the mysteries of what best to order where. I was still living in the Tor Sanguigna, and that first year I began to learn Italian and wrote a novel with a Roman background.

The memories I retain of that first year have imprinted themselves on all subsequent experience. I recall summer evenings at Galeassi's restaurant in the Piazza Santa Maria in Trastevere, where the golden frieze of the twelfth-century church gleamed in its floodlight. On the opposite side of the square is a former cardinal's palace. "Every night at midnight," said Eugene in one of his apocryphal moments, "a hand comes out of that door and pulls in the first living thing that passes."

I moved to an apartment full of history in the Palazzo Taverna, and I radiated out from there. The palazzo was at the top of the Via dei Coronari, overlooking Castel Sant'Angelo. The main room was enormous, a Renaissance Cardinal Orsini's library, and the upper walls and the ceilings were painted with classical scenes and Orsini emblems. I didn't try to furnish it, but made a sitting room in a remote corner while the rest of the room, with its polished Roman tiles, was for going for walks. (It would have made a good skating rink.) In one of the corridors a Roman pillar had been let into the wall.

By this time I was getting used to permanent residence in historic Rome—part of the excitement of visiting one's friends was to see what portion of history their living space occupied. The Palazzo Taverna, with its fountain in the great courtyard, its arches and small courtyards, was fun to live in, and my echoing cardinal's room was to many of my friends one of the wonders of the world. My cats used to love to sit on a rug while we whizzed them round the vast floor. After dinner everyone in the palazzo would go down to the courtyard to take the air with the neighbors. One of the fascinations of Old Rome is that there are no exclusive neighborhoods. Rich and poor live on top of each other.

The wives of ambassadors to Rome are hard put to seat their guests according to protocol; there are several different hierarchies. In the first place, Italy is a republic, but the Vatican cardinals and ambassadors top the cake. Then there is the Old Aristocracy, whose ancestors were Popes; they stood, up to the early 1970s, very much on ceremony if they deigned to go outside their palace walls at all. The New Aristocracy comprise the hurly-burly of princes and counts who have sprung up since the time of Napoleon—Bourbon descendants fall somewhere among this category, but I know neither where nor who does know. And ex-monarchs usually find their way to Rome, which is another headache for the embassies. (Fortunately these were not my problems, for whenever I throw a party, high and low as it may include, I make it a buffet.)

Nowadays there are fewer ex-royals. But I remember once having stopped by the office of Jim Bell, then in charge of the Rome bureau of an American news magazine, who often played golf with exiled Constantine of Greece. Before we left for lunch a secretary put her head round the door.

"The king wants to speak to you," she said.

"The king of what?" Jim Bell wanted to know.

I always go to the Rome Opera in the winter. Each year on the night the opera opens there is a great embracing and greeting of fellow ticketholders and *"Bentornato"* ("Welcome back") all round. One never sees these people anywhere else; they are one's opera friends.

On one special evening, when Montserrat Caballé was singing in a Bellini opera, the rain started coming through the roof. Now, a well-known Roman of that time was the late Mario Praz, a critic and scholar of English literature (he wrote *The Romantic Agony*). He was said to have the Evil Eye and was known as the Malocchio. This nickname wasn't attributed with any repugnance, but rather as an affectionately recorded and realistic fact (for such people are regarded as carriers rather than operators of the Evil Eye). Naturally, everyone noticed when Mario Praz was present at a party, and waited for the disaster. There was usually a stolen car at the end of the evening, or someone called away because his uncle had died. Well, when I saw the rain coming in the roof at the Opera, and heard the commotion behind me, I looked round instinctively for Mario Praz. Sure enough, there was our dear Malocchio sitting under the afflicted spot. He died recently and was mourned on a national scale. (The Italians put their artists and people of letters on a higher level than anywhere else I have known.) Before his house could be unsealed for his heirs, robbers got in and looted his lifetime collection of museum pieces and memorabilia.

In the summer I always try to see the open-air performance of *Aïda* at the Baths of Caracalla. These mighty ruins are extremely well adapted to the mammoth spectacle with its superabundance of camels and cavalry, its luxurious scenery and massed troops. The ancient Romans, for whom the Baths were built as a social and cultural center, would have loved it. But I think it is a great blessing to us that the Baths have fallen into ruin, nature's magnificent sculptures that they are. The originals must have been of decidedly totalitarian dimensions. Against a late afternoon light all Rome looks sublime, and especially the ruins of Caracalla. They are floodlit at night; the environs used to be a favorite night walk,* but nobody takes lonely walks in Rome any more. The footpaths are rife. Even the girls of the night, with their picturesque roadside bonfires, have deserted the vicinity of the Baths, and the nightingales sing to the ghosts.

My stay at the Palazzo Taverna came to an end after three years, when the landlady wanted the flat "for her daughter." My next flat looked out on the Tiber at the front, and at the back on the rooftops and winding alleys of ancient Trastevere. Here again I had one big room surrounded by a few small rooms. The best thing about it was the view of the river at night with a moving bracelet of traffic on either side of the Tiber and over the bridges; and if I

---

*In Fellini's *The Nights of Cabiria*.

was working very late at night I loved to go for a walk in my big room and look out at the three floodlit monuments of my view: the clocktower of Santa Maria in Trastevere; up on the Gianicolo the Fontana Paola; and behind it the church of San Pietro in Montorio. Eventually my landlady wanted this apartment, too, "for her daughter."

Tired of landladies' daughters, I acquired for my own the apartment I live in now, a small but very exciting place just emerging from slumdom. It is in a little street between Piazza Farnese, where Michelangelo added a floor to what is now the French Embassy, and the great Campo dei Fiori, the colorful flower and fruit market. This is deep in the Rome of the Renaissance. My apartment dates from the fourteenth century at the back and the fifteenth at the front. It belonged to an inn called La Vacca owned by La Vanozza, mistress of Pope Alexander Borgia and mother of Cesare Borgia. Her coat of arms, those of her husband and those of the Pope, all three joined, are set in the outside wall near my windows. When the workmen were getting this apartment ready for me they tore down some paper that covered the ceilings to reveal beautiful woodwork. A window was found in a wall leading to the main part of La Vanozza's property. Embedded in the old tiles of the floor they found the remains of a speaking tube that communicated with the street door. Whether or not this was used by La Vanozza's fifteenth-century call girls, I will never know.

Wherever I live I am in the writer's condition: Work is pleasure and pleasure is work. I find Rome a good place to work. The ordinary Roman is nearly always a "character," which is to say there are no ordinary Romans and therefore life among them, although it may be exasperating at times, is never boring. The extraordinary, Byzantine bureaucracy of Italian living and the usual bothers of life are always present, but if I can get, say, a glimpse of the Pantheon— even passing in a taxi on my way to fulfill some banal commission— I find the journey worthwhile. At night, if I go to dine near the Pantheon, I love to walk around with friends in the great, solid portico for a while. It is sheer harmony; the bulk is practically airborne.

For The Literary Traveler

The pleasure of reading Muriel Spark on Rome intensifies as you roam around her first neighborhood, northwest of Piazza Navona, along **Via dei Coronari** (closed to cars). It takes you to one of her early residences—**Palazzo Taverna on Monte Giordano.** In the small streets and piazzas leading off Coronari, there is architecture, atmosphere, medieval and Renaissance, there's a view of Castel Sant'Angelo and a streak of the Tiber, there are antique shops. To borrow Henry James's exclamation: *Stupendissimo!* Bear left at the end of Coronari, then left again into Via di Monte Giordano, named after the artificial hill which Dante mentions in the *Inferno,* XXVIII, 12, and on which Spark's **Palazzo Taverna** stands. In the shadowy mossy courtyard, a lovely flowing seventeenth-century fountain waves ribbons of sunlight. Continuing from the Taverna, bear left into a medieval street that descends a bit from Monte Giordano; you pass small artisans' shops, serious workplaces where children assist their parents (for instance, "Kouki" in Via di Monte Giordano 64). Before you wind back into Via dei Coronari, the "Antica Taverna" of Paolo and Michele (Via Monte Giordano 12; tel 06 688 01053) draws you in because you don't want to leave this neighborhood. An exquisite prospect for looking over where you've just explored is from the rooftop restaurant of the vine-covered **Hotel Raphael,** two minutes from Via dei Coronari, with Picasso ceramics in the lobby. (Largo Febo 2, near Piazza Navona. Tel 06 682 831; www.raphaelhotel.com.) The view from the luxurious Raphael takes in the dome of the nearby church of **Santa Maria della Pace,** and the Bramante cloisters, harmonious, sublime.

Of course Mrs. Spark decided to stay for good.

In the nearby home of her opera* friend, Mario Praz (1896–1982), now the **Museo Mario Praz** (Via Zanardelli, north of Piazza Navona, toward Ponte Umberto on the Tiber, on the right, top floor, 9–1, on the hour, 2:30–6:30 on the half hour, closed Mon A.M.), a fascinating tour presents another rich and original imagination. Italy's greatest and most prolific modern essayist, the author of *The Romantic Agony* and many

---

*Open-air opera at the Baths of Caracalla has recently returned to Rome, after a long absence. See page 211.

works of art history, who taught English literature at the University of Rome from 1932 to 1966, Mario Praz collected an incredible variety of furniture and books on his travels, and designed some wonderful spaces to hold them. The house, like his autobiography, *The House of Life* (1964), is a revelation.

A treat for Spark afficionados is a trip out of Rome to **Lake Nemi** in the Alban Hills (access preferably by private car or by Carrani Group Coach Tours, Via Orlando 95; tel 06 474 2501), with a copy of her novel *The Takeover* for company. The setting is Nemi, a circle of sapphire glinting deep on the floor of a dark valley—*Specchio di Diana* (the Mirror of Diana)—the surrounding groves the haunt of the goddess Diana who was worshipped here; those rites inspired Sir James Frazer's study of comparative religion, *The Golden Bough*. From the coach you look down on the lake from a high and winding Via del Laghi. But you can hike down there, and around the pretty town of Nemi. Byron knew this place, and Spark weaves his poem about it into the priceless satiric characterizations of the novel:

> Lo, Nemi! navell'd in the woody hills
> So far, that the uprooting wind which tears
> The oak from his foundation, and which spills
> The ocean o'er its boundary, and bears
> Its foam against the skies, reluctant spares
> The oval mirror of thy glassy lake;
> And calm as cherish'd hate, its surface wears
> A deep cold settled aspect nought can shake,
> All coil'd into itself and round, as sleeps the snake.

" *'It's a perfect description,' said Nancy Cowan, the English tutor. 'Can you imagine what Byron meant by "calm as cherished hate"?—It's mysterious, isn't it?' "*

And the divine Spark is off, to imagine the ways and means of "cherish'd hate . . . all coil'd into itself . . ."

*(There's a wonderful view of Lake Nemi, Diana's looking-glass, from **La Trattoria della Sora Maria,** tel 06 936 8020.)*

ALICE STEINBACH

1936–

Pulitzer Prize–winning journalist Alice Steinbach took a year off to see Europe on her own. Without Reservations: The Travels of an Independent Woman *is the book she wrote along the way, in Paris, London, Oxford, Venice, and Milan. The story of her time in Rome, which follows here, unfolds a pilgrim's psychological progress. "Rome and I are not lovers," she says at the beginning. "We are not even friends." By the time she leaves, her tone has changed. Hers has been a voyage of discovery. Having felt Rome's sinister side, she comes, paradoxically, into a richer love of life.*

❧

From WITHOUT RESERVATIONS

SPANISH STEPS

Dear Alice,

    I have remained a stranger in Rome. Which is why I send you this happy reminder of a city I love: Venice. Rome and I are not lovers. We are not even friends. I can only hope that Camus was right when he wrote that "what gives value to travel is fear." I suppose it's possible that a little dash of fear gives value to more than just travel. For one thing, it can teach us to be brave.

Love,
Alice

Three days after arriving in Rome I had my *first* real brush with danger. Until then I'd encountered only the routine mini-scares faced by most tourists. Yes, there was the evening in Paris when I was window-shopping along a quiet street near St. Sulpice and a burly man approached me, demanding I give him money. He took off, however, when several people emerged from the door of a nearby café. And there was that Sunday in London when two menacing young men circled me while I waited to change trains in an out-of-the-way Underground station. But then the train came and I jumped on, leaving them behind.

The incident in Rome was different. For one thing, I already had negative feelings about the city. Although I knew it to be a premature and unfair judgment, Rome struck me as frenetic and indifferent, a place where everyone seemed unfriendly, hassled, and in a hurry. Where was that warm, laid-back attitude that prevailed in the other Italian cities I'd visited? Not here.

Here, I seldom walked along a street without someone bumping into me or rudely pushing their way ahead of me. Here, I walked in a tense, alert state, always on the lookout for the noisy, polluting motorbikes whose drivers seemed to extract pleasure from terrorizing pedestrians.

Noisy, polluted, indifferent, crowded: this was my impression of Rome.

I knew it was a superficial one; I knew that if I dived deeper into the real city beneath the tourist attractions, my view of Rome would change. But I had no desire to ingratiate myself with the city, as I had done in the past with Paris or Milan or Venice. I had made a feeble attempt the day before, crossing over the Tiber River to visit the old Trastevere district where, despite rampant gentrification, the authentic Rome was said to reside still. And it was true.

In Trastevere I wandered through a maze of narrow streets and alleys, walking occasionally beneath a canopy of wash hung out between buildings to dry. Although I'd been told to look out for purse-snatchers in Trastevere, I was quite at ease walking by myself through the area. This was a real neighborhood, one where mothers walked with children to and from the market and shopkeepers stood at their doors calling out to passers-by. At times I had an eerie feeling that somehow I'd wandered onto the set of a Sophia Loren movie.

Of course, it had its beauty spots, too. I was particularly drawn to the lovely Piazza di Santa Maria in Trastevere, which I wandered into quite by chance. With its elegant raised fountain and charming sidewalk cafes, the square was an oasis of pleasant neighborhood bustle—minus the motor scooters. I had an iced coffee, and then headed across the piazza to the twelfth-century church of Santa Maria in Trastevere. I was unprepared for the majesty of the church's interior: its enormous, glowing nave and gigantic columns were as beautiful as any I'd seen.

Still, as pleasant as my visit to Trastevere was, it was not enough to change my mind about Rome. I remained a stranger, wandering through a city as indifferent to me as I was to it.

It didn't matter that deep down I recognized my disenchantment with Rome for what it was: an attempt to deny that I was homesick. It was much easier to blame Rome than to deal with my longing for the comfort of routine. I yearned to have lunch with my friends at the paper; to dig in my garden and feel the damp earth between my fingers; to hear the sound of neighbors calling in their dogs late at night; to shop at the neighborhood market, where everybody knows my name; and to lie in bed, waiting for the soft thud that signals the arrival of my cat.

To counteract such feelings, I devised a plan. During my short stay in Rome—a week's stopover, really, before working my way north to Tuscany and the Veneto—I would seek out all things familiar. Meaning: I ate at English tearooms, visited John Keats's house at the bottom of the Spanish Steps, went to lectures given in English at a nearby school, and saw the original English-speaking version of *Roman Holiday* with Audrey Hepburn and Gregory Peck. One day I even had a Big Mac and french fries at McDonald's, something I never did at home.

As silly as it was, *le plan d'Angleterre*—as I came to call it—

actually worked. My homesickness or anxiety or whatever it was began to dissipate and my curiosity returned. At last Rome beckoned. And I responded. So I set out to do what I always do in a strange city: walk and walk and walk. I even responded to the Romans, chatting with the clerks in bookshops and with espresso-drinkers in the stand-up coffee bars.

My flirtation with Rome, however, proved to be a brief one. It ended abruptly two days later on a busy, fashionable street near my hotel on the Via Sistina.

After spending the morning and early afternoon visiting art galleries on the Via Margutta, I decided to walk over to a coffee bar I liked: the Antico Caffè Greco. Something of an institution in Rome, the 200-year-old cafe was a hangout for writers and artists, as well as a rest stop for wealthy shoppers on the Via Condotti. I'd discovered the cafe on my first day in Rome and liked it instantly. It was a great place to sit and observe the Italian scene. Soon I was going there almost every day; sometimes for a quick espresso at the stand-up bar, sometimes to linger over a cappuccino.

Standing next to me at the bar on this particular day was a man I recognized as a cafe regular. He had the look of an artist about him, I thought, studying his scruffy corduroy jacket, uncombed hair, and gaunt face. But then again, for all I knew, he could be an eccentric billionaire, the Howard Hughes of Italy.

I drank my espresso and left, planning to walk directly back to my hotel. To my surprise the streets outside were pleasantly uncrowded. I looked at my watch. It was a little before three. The shops, closed down for the traditional long lunch break, would not reopen for another hour. The perfect time, I decided, to explore this fashionable district; to window-shop and read the menus posted outside restaurants and duck into the occasional bookstore or gallery still open.

It was on the Via Borgognona, near the bottom of the Spanish Steps, that I first sensed someone was following me. I began paying attention to a tall man dressed in a corduroy jacket and pants who,

I noticed, stopped whenever I stopped and started walking again when I did.

Was he following me? I wondered. Or was it just my imagination? But after two blocks of being trailed in this way I was sure his presence was no accident. When he began closing the distance between us I saw it was the man I'd noticed in the cafe. Suddenly I was afraid. Then another man, a stocky fellow in dark pants and a checkered shirt, approached me from the opposite direction.

I knew then I had not imagined myself to be in danger; I *was* in danger. I'm going to be mugged, I thought, my heart pounding; or worse. I tightened my grip on my handbag, braced myself, and looked around for help—a person or an open door or even a motor scooter that I could stop. I saw nothing and no one. I cursed myself for not being more vigilant. At that moment the tall man brushed up against me, grabbing my arm. Without hesitating I broke into a run and started screaming for help.

The two men ran after me. I continued making as much noise as I could, overturning some trash cans along the way, hoping the noise of the rolling metal, plus my screaming, would alert someone. It did. By the time I reached the corner of the main street, doors had opened and several people appeared on the street, yelling at the two men to stop. It worked. The men chasing me immediately took off in the opposite direction.

After watching them disappear I sank to the curb. I sat shaking, the adrenaline still pumping through me, my head and ears pounding. I hadn't yet allowed myself to fully acknowledge the fear I felt. That would come later. Mainly I was embarrassed. What must the small crowd gathered round me think of this crazy woman who'd run screaming up the street?

But that seemed not to be what they were thinking about at all. What was on their minds was my well-being. I was touched by their concern and kindness as they helped me compose myself, asking over and over again if I was all right.

Si, si, grazie, I am all right, I said. I kept repeating it—*Si, Si, grazie. I am all right*—until the crowd dispersed.

But I wasn't all right. Something had happened to me, something that left me feeling vulnerable in a way I'd not experienced for a long time. It was as though a tiny hairline crack had suddenly appeared in the self-sufficient image I had constructed over the years.

Not since my mother's death ten years earlier had I felt so painfully aware of how little control I had when it came to the grand scheme of my life.

Things happen, I thought, and we respond. That's what it all comes down to. To believe anything else, as far as I could tell, was simply an illusion.

Over the next few days I found myself unable to stop thinking about the incident on the Via Borgognona. First came the self-recriminations, and the attempt to deal with feelings of guilt that somehow I was responsible for what happened. My thoughts raced: *I should have taken another street. I shouldn't have been wandering around alone. I should have been more alert. I should have carried pepper spray or Mace. I shouldn't have looked at the man in the cafe.* Intellectually, I knew none of these things applied, knew that I hadn't done anything wrong or anything I hadn't done safely a hundred times in the past. Still, a voice kept saying: *My fault. My fault. My fault.*

Worse, however, was the loss of confidence that settled over me. I was overcome with a heavy inert feeling, one that prevented me from entering into life with any sense of trust. I tried putting into action the theorem I'd attributed to Albert back in Oxford— M=EA (Mishap equals Excellent Adventure)—but to no avail. I simply hadn't the energy or desire necessary to make such a plan work.

Now when I was out on the streets, I was so busy looking for danger that I barely saw the city. At night I slept with the bathroom light on, comforted by its dull glow through the half-closed door. Sleep, however, did not refresh me. I awoke fatigued. It was trauma fatigue, I decided one morning after waking to a memory of the chronic tiredness I'd felt years earlier after serious back surgery.

It was time, I decided, to get out of Rome.

Intellectually I knew Rome wasn't the problem; that I was the problem. Still, when I changed my train tickets to Florence for an earlier departure, I breathed a sigh of relief. From Florence I planned to take the bus to Siena, a town I remembered as quiet and serene, one bereft of motor scooters and dangerous situations.

In the two days left before my departure, I spent my time taking bus tours organized for tourist groups. That way I was never alone. In the evening I followed the routine of eating dinner at a fancy hotel near mine and then returning to my room to sit outside on an adjoining veranda.

The veranda had come as a pleasant surprise in an otherwise disappointing choice of hotel. I'd discovered the outdoor balcony only a few days earlier, after opening a door hidden behind a curtain in my room. Like my room, it was in need of sprucing up— dead leaves lay scattered on the stone floor and the metal chairs were rusted—but I liked it anyway. It had a nice view of the Via Sistina and I found if I leaned over the stone balustrade and looked to the right, I could catch a glimpse of the Spanish Steps. Given my mood, the veranda was exactly what I needed: a retreat where I could sit and think. Or, more often, sit and *not* think.

In the evenings I'd sit there drinking wine and smoking an occasional cigarette, a habit I'd retrieved after the attempted mugging. I'd wait until the light faded and the lamps came on over the Spanish Steps before walking up the hill to have dinner at the usual place. Afterward I would return and, wrapped in a blanket, sit outside looking at the stars.

On my last night in Rome the rains came, turning my veranda into a shallow swimming pool. Reluctantly, I abandoned my usual routine. Instead I propped myself up in bed and turned to my old friend Freya,* hoping to find comfort and, perhaps, advice in her books, her observations. As usual, she did not disappoint.

"The unexpectedness of life, waiting round every corner, catches even wise women unawares," she wrote. "To avoid corners altogether is, after all, to refuse to live."

---

*Freya Stark, travel writer who also travelled solo and wrote many books about her adventures.

Reading this, I let out a small shriek of recognition. It was as though someone in charge had said to me: not guilty. Permission granted to continue on with your life as usual.

It would take some time, I knew, to regain my confidence about approaching life's corners. But, as Freya pointed out, avoiding them would be the same as saying "no" to life. And I wasn't about to do that.

I had been asleep for only an hour or two when a loud, booming sound awakened me. For one wild moment I thought a bomb had exploded. I sat upright, still groggy. Then I heard it again. *Boom!* It was even louder than the first one. Suddenly a great burst of light lit up my room. I ran to the veranda door and looked outside. Rain was pelting the empty streets below and forks of lightning illuminated the dark sky like arteries exposed on an X-ray. Thunder rolled across the city in great waves.

I looked at the clock. It was 3:00 A.M. I was already packed and ready to leave for Florence later that morning. If I went back to bed right away, I thought, I could catch maybe another three hours of sleep.

But I already knew I wasn't going to do that. Instead I put on my Reeboks, threw a raincoat over my pajamas, and left the hotel. It was as impulsive an act as anything I'd ever done. But something in me said: never again will you have the opportunity to stand at the top of the Spanish Steps with Rome lit up and spread out beneath you.

Put that way, I had no choice.

Outside, the streets were empty. The lightning and thunder were now off in the distance, but the rain had not let up. Leisurely, almost playfully, I walked the short distance—a hundred feet or so—from my hotel to the top of the Spanish Steps. There, like a sentinel I stood watch over the sleeping city of Rome.

With the city stretched out beneath me I looked off into the distance, across the Tiber. I watched as silent flashes of lightning, like strobes going on and off, revealed briefly domes and towers and church spires set against the sky. For the first time I felt the ancient majesty of Rome. Caught up in the strange beauty of the storm, I imagined all the Romes buried beneath this one. It was like being back in Pompeii. Watching, my thoughts excavated the city back through the centuries, back to a time when all roads led to Rome.

As I stood at the top of the Spanish Steps—a temporary traveler passing through Rome, and through life, in *anno Domini* 1993—an intense feeling of awe and respect came over me. Rome had endured. And when I was gone from Rome, and from life, she would still endure. It was then that I bowed with respect, like a younger member of the tribe, to the wisdom and tradition possessed by this honorable elder.

When I returned to the hotel I was no longer sleepy. The rain had stopped so I stepped out onto the veranda. Again, I wondered why I'd acted so impulsively. Was it because I needed to feel in control again? Perhaps. Perhaps not. For some reason the question no longer interested me.

I stood looking down over the streets near the hotel. Directly below on the Via Sistina a few people were venturing out: early risers, dog-walkers, people coming home from jobs that ended as day began. The street lamps were still on, but dawn was moving up quickly into the sky, turning it into a pale pink dome.

I ran back into the room and got my camera. Then, leaning out as far as I could over the veranda wall, I faced the Spanish Steps and gently squeezed the shutter release. It was my first photograph of Rome. And my last.

Whatever I wanted to remember of the city, I decided, would be there, in that single picture of Rome after the storm.

FOR THE LITERARY TRAVELER

The Spanish Steps—*Scalinata della Trinità dei Monti*—136 in all, built in the 1720s, take their name from the Spanish Embassy located in the Piazza di Spagna, to the left of Bernini's boat fountain, the *Barcaccia*, if you're looking down from the top where the church of Trinità dei Monti dominates the hill. Edith Wharton remembers playing on the Steps as a four-year-old. In Steinbach's account, there's nothing nostalgic or romantic about this neighborhood, the one most visited by foreign travelers; in the eighteenth century it was called *il ghetto de l'Inglesi,* the English ghetto. Hers is a cautionary tale. A woman traveler on her own in Rome should keep her eyes open and watch her step. It's fine to walk out alone, take in a concert at night, meet for a late dinner. But know where the taxi stand is before the concert starts or the trattoria closes.

Mostly, the neighborhood of Steinbach's rude awakening provides diverse relief from the inevitable tensions of traveling solo (or in company).

At the top of the Steps is the five-star Hotel Hassler (Piazza Trinità dei Monti 6, tel 06 678 2651), Audrey Hepburn's home while filming *Roman Holiday.* **Hassler's Roof Restaurant** serves an elaborate Sunday brunch, with a stunning view of the city, and, on weekdays, of the rivers of shoppers and shopping bags flooding the streets around the Piazza di Spagna: Via Frattina (where the impoverished Joyce lived, bank-clerking by day, beginning *Ulysses* after hours); Via Clementina; Via Condotti, where the Caffè Greco attracts tourists like Steinbach and the occasional predator. A few streets to the north, in Via della Croce 81, at the end of a cobblestoned courtyard, there's modest dining at **Otello alla Concordia,** with its delightful cornucopia fountain in the center of the main dining room (tel 06 67 91 178; closed Sun). In *Italian Days,* Barbara Grizzuti Harrison, another independent traveler who didn't deny Rome's dark side, sees this trattoria's decor as an emblem of Italy's generosity of spirit.

The northern end of Piazza di Spagna, an oasis of palm trees, flower stalls, and bright-colored houses—a scene Dufy might have liked—leads into **Via del Babuino** ("street of the baboon"). Babuino's antique shops are a delight, as is browsing in this neighborhood's bookshops, **The Lion** in Via dei Greci 33/36, off the Corso, and **The English Bookshop** in Via di Ripetta 247/49. The Anglican church in Babuino, All Saints, hosts Verdi and Puccini operas, starting at 9 P.M. (Tickets at the church the afternoon of the performance.) *TRASTEVERE,* however, "a real neighborhood," in Steinbach's words, is her favorite Rome, *molto simpatico, molto bella.* Likewise Colette, who wrote about it during World War I.

Solo women opera-goers take note: exiting the church / opera house, the taxi stands are to your right in Piazza di Spagna and to the left, at the end of Babuino in Piazza del Popolo.

WILLIAM MURRAY

1926–

William Murray spent his first eight years in Rome, the child of a Roman mother, then moved to America to escape Mussolini. After the Second World War, he returned to the city of his birth to live and work for many years. As the author of "Letters from Italy" for The New Yorker *and many books, including* The Last Italian *and* Italy: The Fatal Gift, *his many years in Rome distinguish his* City of the Soul, *excerpted here. An elegant and brief guide (a volume in the Crown Journeys series), it does much more than provide information. Murray tells stories as he walks us through the city. At the end, we wish for a much longer trek.*

☙

From City of the Soul

Directly beyond the Pantheon and to the left of it is the Piazza della Minerva, with its charming church named Santa Maria over* Minerva. It was erected over the ruins of a temple built by Pompey the Great and dedicated to Minerva, the goddess of wisdom. In the center of the square stands one of the city's most entertaining small monuments, the statue of an elephant supporting on its back an Egyptian obelisk, one of three found among the ruins in the area. The epigraph at the base of the monument, dictated by Pope Urban VIII, declares that the selection of the elephant, "the strongest of the animals," was designed to impart an impression of solid thinking in a sound mind. Gian Lorenzo Bernini, who designed the monument, apparently had no such in-

---

*Sopra, in Italian.

tent in mind. Invited to tour France by King Louis XIV in 1665, he found himself so famous that everywhere he went he was besieged by ogling crowds of admirers. Exasperated by so much attention, the artist was heard to say, "What is this? Have I become some sort of rare beast, an elephant?" Back in Rome, he designed his monument to reflect his French travails, choosing the statue sculpted by Ercole Ferrata as its dominant feature. The Romans, with their gift for irreverence and irony, soon began referring to it as "Minerva's flea."

The unprepossessing little church, with its unique exterior, was built in 1280 and contains a number of extraordinary treasures, including the tombs of several celebrated Roman families and monuments to various important popes and cardinals. The body of Saint Catherine of Siena, renowned for her mystical visions and revelations, and influential in persuading Pope Gregory XI to leave Avignon and return to Rome in 1377, is buried under the main altar. In the Carafa Chapel are Fra Filippo Lippi's extraordinary frescoes, including his *Assumption of the Virgin,* which occupies an entire wall. Also in a corner of this chapel is the tomb of Pope Paul IV, the fearsome pontiff who was responsible for enclosing the Jews in the ghetto and launching the Inquisition on the Roman populace. He was so unpopular that when he died in 1559, a Roman mob laid siege to the Dominican monastery next to the church and tried to burn it down. The Dominicans had carried out the pope's orders, which they apparently took permanently to heart, because it was there, four generations later, that Galileo was brought to trial for his heretical views concerning the planets revolving around the sun and was forced to abjure them. It is not for nothing that the Romans have acquired a reputation for disliking the clergy.

The church's most famous treasure is Michelangelo's statue *Christ Carrying the Cross,* sculpted between 1514 and 1521. So many worshipers bent to kiss the statue's foot that a sandal was added later in order to keep it from being worn away by so many fervent lips. The Romans may not like their popes, but they revere their artists. They also appreciate inspired advice. There used to be an inscription somewhere in the church that I was never able to locate but

which read, "In order not to be killed by Rome's foul air, it is necessary to purge oneself every week, avoid bad smells, not tire oneself much, not suffer either hunger or cold, to renounce all faults,
love, and to drink hot liquids."

Perhaps no other church in Rome is so revered by the citizens as
this one. When Anna Magnani, Italy's most celebrated stage and
movie actress, died on September 26, 1973, it seemed entirely appropriate that her funeral service be held here, in the heart of the
old city she had come to symbolize and where she had passed most
of her life. The enormous, grief-stricken crowd that came to say
good-bye to her spilled out of the church and filled the square to
overflowing. And when her coffin was raised up to be carried out,
the people applauded, as if to thank her for what she had come to
represent for them—the vital spirit of their city.

FOR THE LITERARY TRAVELER

Murray reflects on Rome's religious history in the setting of the **Minerva,** the beautiful Dominican church modelled on Santa Maria Novella
in Florence. The paradoxes are as striking as the interior decoration.

In the **Carafa Chapel,** the frescoes of Fra Filippo Lippi (1489) depict
a gorgeous Assumption of the Virgin into heaven where she is ringed by
a band of dancing musical angels. Sibyls adorn the vault. Looking at it
straight (bring coins to operate the light box), you see a painted rhap-
sody of sensual and spiritual delight. The French notion of *jouissance*
comes to mind. But turning to the left you see the tomb and monument
commemorating the man for whom the exquisite chapel is named, Gian
Carafa, Pope Paul IV, whose ugly legacy Murray recounts and Elsa
Morante fictionalizes (see page 276–92).

To the left of the high altar, Michelangelo's sculpture **Christ Carrying
the Cross** (1514–1521) expresses the grace and strength of a naked
Christ. But in later years, some vigilante of the anti-Renaissance, repeating the cover-up of "The Last Judgment," added a bronze drapery.

In this church where Rome said good-bye to Anna Magnani, the
remains of the Dominican Saint Catherine of Siena (1347–1380) lie beneath the high altar. She spent her life caring for the poor, the sick, the

imprisoned. Her intense prayer life inspired her to scold a lax clergy and a few runaway popes about their failures as Christian pastors. And yet her ascetic practices were variations on the theme of self-destruction. Some say she starved herself to death, others that she died after several strokes which were caused by her self-induced emaciation. (The room from the house where she died, nearby in Via Santa Chiara 14, was moved to the sacristy of the Minerva and is opened on request.)

The history of Sopra Minerva and the attached Dominican monastery (the setting of Galileo's heresy trial) are the background against which Murray discusses the anticlericalism of Romans. Though officially Roman Catholic, the city's church attendance is as low as 15 percent in some areas. It doesn't seem to matter that the pope lives smack in the middle of the city, forbidding artificial birth control; Italians have had one of the world's lowest fertility rates for twenty-five years. In 1981, voters approved abortion by a margin of two to one.

(*A few minutes away, on the Corso Vittorio Emanuele, facing Largo Argentina,* **Il Delfino** *sells good take-out food; across the street* **Frulatti di Frutta** *makes a terrific frulatto di frutta—an Italian smoothie. Next store,* **Feltrinelli's** *bookstore is well-stocked and air-conditioned, and upstairs in the English language section, there are chairs you can occupy all the sweltering afternoon.*)

ANDRÉ ACIMAN

1951–

André Aciman's prize-winning memoir Out of Egypt *tells the story of his early years in Alexandria before he left to live in Italy, France, and now New York, where he teaches at the CUNY Graduate Center. In his essay "Shadow Cities," included in* Letters of Transit: Reflections on Exile, Identity, Language, and Loss *(1999), he wanders his new place, the Upper West Side of Manhattan. It is not his home. "An exile reads change the way he reads time, memory, self, love, fear, beauty: in the key of loss." Stopping in tiny Straus Park and noting the fountain, he reclaims "the memory of water": Rome comes back to him, and himself in Rome as an impoverished young man; he remembers the Fountain of the Four Rivers in Piazza Navona (see pages 145–50). His love of the city of his youth is aroused, inspiring "Roman Hours," the memoir that follows here, which became the first entry in* The Best American Travel Writing 2002.

❧

ROMAN HOURS

Today, again, I stared at the small knife on my desk. I had purchased it months ago on the Campo de' Fiori, just before buying bread rolls and heading down the Via della Corda to find a quiet spot on the Piazza Farnese, where I sat on a stone ledge and made prosciutto and Bel Paese sandwiches. On the way to the Palazzo Farnese, I found a street fountain and rinsed a bunch of muscatel grapes I had bought from a *fruttivendolo*. I was leaning forward to cleanse the new knife as well, and to douse my face while I was at it, when it occurred to me that this, of all my days in Rome, was perhaps the one I would like most to remember, and that on this cheap knife—which I had originally planned to discard as soon as I was finished using it but had now decided to take back with me—was inscribed something of the warm, intimate feeling that settles around noon on typically clear Roman summer days. It came rushing to me in the form of a word—one word only, but the best possible word because it captured the weather, the city, and the mood on this most temperate day in June and, hence, of the year: serenity. Italians use the word *sereno* to describe the weather, the sky, the sea, a person. It means tranquil, clear, fair, calm.

And this is how I like to feel in Rome, and how the city feels when its languid ocher walls beam in the midday sun. When over-brimming old fountains dare you to dunk your hands in and splash your face and rest awhile before resuming your walk through yet narrower twisting lanes along the Campo Marzio in the *centro storico* (historic center) of Rome.

This warren of old alleys goes back many centuries, and here, sinister brawls, vendettas, and killings were as common in the Renaissance as the artists, con artists, and other swaggerers who populated these streets. Today, these lanes with tilting buildings that have learned to lean on each other like Siamese twins exude a smell of slate, clay, and old dank limestone; wood glue and resin drift from artisans' shops, attesting to the timeless presence of workshops in the area. Otherwise, the streets are dead past midday. Except for bells, an occasional hammer, the sound of a lathe, or an electric saw that is no sooner heard than it's instantly silenced, the only sound you'll hear on the Vicolo del Polverone or the Piazza Quercia is the occasional clatter of plates ringing from many homes, suggesting that lunch is about to be served in all of Italy.

A few more steps into the Largo della Moretta, and suddenly you begin to make out the cool scent of roasted coffee emanating from hidden sanctuaries along the way. These havens—like tiny pilgrimage stations, or like the numerous churches to which men on the run, from Cellini to *Tosca*'s Angelotti, rushed to seek asylum—each have their old legend. Caffè Rosati, Caffè Canova, Caffè Greco, Caffè Sant'Eustachio, Antico Caffè della Pace—small oases where blinding light and dark interiors go well together, the way hot coffee and lemon ice go well together, the way only Mediterraneans seek the shade and wait out the sun they love so much.

There is a magic to these summer hours that is as timeless as the tiny rituals we invent around them each day. Here are mine. Strolling in the dry heat and suddenly rediscovering the little-known Vicolo Montevecchio, where a huge off-white *ombrellone* suddenly sprouts, spelling food and wine. Wasting yet another bottle of sparkling water by washing a hand unavoidably made sticky with food purchased on the fly. Baring both feet by the Turtle Fountain in the Piazza Mattei, the empty square basking in the ocher glory of its adjoining buildings, and when no one's looking, letting them soak awhile in a pool of water so peaceful and translucent that not even the quietest beach on the quietest day could rival it.

Getting lost—the welcome sense that you are still unable to find your way in this maze of side streets—is something one never wishes to unlearn, because it means one's visit here is still very young. The rule is quite simple: Scorn maps. They never show all of Renaissance Rome anyway; they merely stand between you and the city. Stray instead. Enforced errancy and mild disconcertment are the best guide. Rome must swim before your eyes. You'll drift and wander and suddenly land, without knowing how, at the Piazza Navona, or the Campo de' Fiori, Sant'Andrea della Valle, the Pantheon, the Piazza di Spagna, or the Piazza del Popolo, with its stunning *tricorno* fanning out in three directions: the Via del Babuino, the Via del Corso, and the Via di Ripetta. "Could this be the Trevi Fountain?" you wonder, half fascinated by your internal compass, which knew all along where you were headed and which, in retrospect, gives you a sort of proprietary claim on the piazza, the way a prince may think he alone is entitled to marry a particular debutante simply because he was the first to spot her at court. How we discover beauty is not incidental to it; it prefigures it. The accident that brings us to the things we worship says as much about them as it does about us. What I want is not just to see the Turtle Fountain but to stumble upon the Turtle Fountain inadvertently.

This protean city is all about drifting and straying, and the shortest distance between two points is never a straight line but a figure eight. Just as Rome is not about one path, or about one past, but an accumulation of pasts: You encounter Gogol, Ovid, Piranesi, Ingres, Caesar, and Goethe on one walk; on another, Caravaggio and Casanova, Freud and Fellini, Montaigne and Mussolini, James and Joyce; and on yet another, Wagner, Michelangelo, Rossini, Keats, and Tasso. And you'll realize one more thing that nobody tells you: Despite all these names, masonries, and landmarks, despite untold layers of stucco and plaster and paint slapped over the centuries on everything you see here, despite the fact that so many figures from one past keep surfacing in another, or that so many buildings are grafted onto generations of older buildings, what ultimately matters here are the incidentals, the small elusive pleasures of the senses—water, coffee, citrus, food, sunlight, voices, the touch of warm marble, glances stolen on the sly, and faces, the most beautiful in the world.

And this, without question, is the most beautiful city on earth, just as it is the most serene. Not only is the weather and everything around us serene, but we ourselves become serene. Serenity is the feeling of being one with the world, of having nothing to wish for, of lacking for nothing. Of being, as almost never happens elsewhere, entirely in the present. This, after all, is the most pagan city in the world; it is consumed by the present. The greatest sites and monuments, Rome tells us, mean nothing unless they stimulate and accommodate the body; unless, that is, we can eat, drink, and lounge among them. Beauty always gives pleasure, but in Rome, beauty is born of pleasure.

Twice a day, we come back to the Antico Caffè della Pace, off the Piazza Navona. The *caffè* is a few steps away from the Hotel Raphaël (a luxurious place whose roof garden offers an unimpeded view of the Campo Marzio). At the *caffè,* dashing would-be artists, models, drifters, and high-end wannabes sip coffee, read the paper, or congregate, which they do in greater numbers as the day wears on. I like to come here very early in the morning, when the scent of parched earth lingers upon the city, announcing warm weather and blinding glare toward noon. I like to be the first to sit down here, before the Romans have left their homes, because if I hate feeling that those who live here or were born after I'd left Rome, years ago, have come to know my city better than I ever will, then being here before they're ready to face their own streets gives me some consolation. While I retain the privileged status of a tourist who doesn't have to go to work, I can easily pretend—an illusion sanctioned by jet lag—that I've never left Rome at all but just happened to wake up very early in the morning.

By evening, the jittery *caffè* crowd spills over into the street. Nearly everyone holds a *telefonino* in their hand, because they expect it to ring at any moment but also because it's part of the dress code, a descendant of the privileged dagger that conferred instant status at the unavoidable street brawl. One of these twenty- to thirty-year-olds sits at a table, staring attentively into his *telefonino* as though inspecting his features in a pocket mirror. Watching the flower of Rome, I see how easy it is to reconcile its cult of the *figura* with the beauty that abounds on a Baroque square such as the Piazza Navona. There will always remain something disturbingly enticing about this shady clientele. This, after all, is the universe of Cellini and Caravaggio. They lived, ate, brawled, loved, plotted, and dueled scarcely a few blocks away. Yet from some unknown cranny in their debauched and squalid lives, they gave the world the best it is ever likely to see. Here, as well, lived the ruthless Borgia pope Alexander VI, whose children Lucrezia Borgia and Cesare Borgia are notorious to history. A few steps away, and a hundred years later, Giordano Bruno was brought to the Campo de' Fiori, stripped naked, and burned at the stake. Scarcely a few months earlier, an event had taken place that shook Rome as probably nothing had since the martyring of the early Christians: the brutal decapitation of the beautiful young Beatrice Cenci by order of the pope himself.

We may never become Roman, and yet it takes no more than a few hours for the spell to kick in. We become different. Our gaze starts to linger; we're less fussy over space; voices become more interesting; smiles are over-the-counter affairs. We begin to see beauty everywhere. We find it at Le Bateleur, a charming rundown antiques and curios shop on the Via di San Simone, off the Via dei Coronari, where we find stunning French watercolors. Or at Ai Monasteri, which sells products made in Italian monasteries and where I found a delicious spiced grappa, the best Amaro, and the sweetest honey I've ever known. Or at the Ferramenta alla Chiesa Nuova, seemingly a hardware store but actually a nob, door handle, and ancient keys gallery where people walk in bearing precious antique door hinges they despair of ever finding a match for, only to have the owner produce a look-alike on the spot.

The city is beautiful in such unpredictable ways. The dirty ocher walls (fast disappearing under new coats that restore their original yellow, peach, pink, lilac) are beautiful. And why not? Ocher is the closest stone will ever come to flesh; it is the color of clay, and from clay God made flesh. The figs we're about to eat under the sun are beautiful. The worn-out pavement along the Via dei Cappellari is, however humble and streaked with dirt, beautiful. The clarinetist who wends his way toward the sunless Vicolo delle Grotte, wailing a Bellini aria, plays beautifully. The Church of Santa Barbara, overlooking Largo dei Librari, couldn't offer a more accurate slice of a Roman *tableau vivant,* complete with ice-cream vendor, sleeping dog, Harley-Davidson, canvas *ombrelloni,* and men chatting in gallant fashion outside a small haberdashery where someone is playing a mandolin rendition of "Core 'ngrato," a Neapolitan song, while a lady wearing a series of Felliniesque white voiles cuts across my field of vision. This sixty-year-old aristocratic eccentric is, it takes me a second to realize, speeding on a mountain bike, barefoot, with an air of unflappable *sprezzatura.*

What wouldn't I give never to lose Rome. I worry, on leaving, that like a cowered Cinderella returning to her stepmother's service, I'll slip back into my day-to-day life far sooner than I thought possible. It's not just the beauty that I'll miss. I'll miss, too, the way this city gets under my skin and, for a while, makes me its own, or the way I take pleasure for granted. It's a feeling I wear with greater confidence every day. I know it is a borrowed feeling—it's Rome's, not mine. I know it will go dead as soon as I leave the Roman light behind.

This worry doesn't intrude on anything; it simply hovers, like a needless safety warning to someone who's been granted immortality for a week. It was there when I purchased the ham, the rolls, the knife. Or when I saw the Caravaggios in San Luigi dei Francesi; or went to see Raphael's sibyls in Santa Maria della Pace but found the door closed, and was just as pleased to admire its rounded colonnade instead. Could any of these timeless things really disappear from my life? And where do they go when I'm not there to stare at them? What happens to life when we're not there to live it?

I first arrived in Rome as a refugee in 1965. Mourning my life in Alexandria, and determined never to like Rome, I eventually surrendered to the city, and for three magical years the Campo Marzio was the place I came closest to ever loving. I grew to love Italian and Dante, and here, as nowhere else on earth, I even chose the exact building where I'd make my home someday.

Years ago, just where the Campo is split by the ostentatious nineteenth-century thoroughfare, the Corso Vittorio Emanuele II, I would start on one of two favorite walks. As soon as the school bus had crossed the river from Vatican City, I'd ask the driver to drop me at Largo Tassoni—rather than bring me all the way to Stazione Termini, from where I'd have to take public transportation for another forty minutes before reaching our shabby apartment in a working-class neighborhood past Alberone. From Largo Tassoni, either I would head south to the Via Giulia and then the Campo de' Fiori, ambling for about two hours before finally going home, or I'd head north.

I liked nothing better than to lose my way in a labyrinth of tiny, shady, furtive, ocher-hued *vicoli,* which I hoped would one day, by dint of being strayed in, finally debouch into an enchanted little square where I'd encounter some still higher order of beauty. What I wished above all things was to amble freely about the streets of the Campo Marzio and to find whatever I wished to find there freely, whether it was the true image of this city, or something in me, or a likeness of myself in the things and people I saw, or a new home to replace the one I'd lost as a refugee.

Roaming about these streets past dark had more to do with me and my secret wishes than it did with the city. It allowed me to re-cast my fantasies each time, because this is also how we try to find ourselves—by hits and misses and mistaken turns. Dowsing around the Campo Marzio like a prospector was simply my way of belonging to this area and of claiming it by virtue of passing over it many, many times, the way dogs do when they mark their corners. In the aimlessness of my afternoon walks, I was charting a Rome of my own devising, a Rome I wanted to make sure did exist, because the one awaiting me at home was not the Rome I wanted. On the twilit lanes of a Renaissance Rome that stood between me and an-cient Rome just as it stood between me and the modern world, I could pretend that any minute now, and without knowing how, I would rise out of one circle of time and, walking down a little lane lined by the mansions of the Campo Marzio, look through win-dows I had gotten to know quite well, ring a buzzer downstairs, and through the intercom hear someone's voice tell me that I was, once again, late for supper.

Then one afternoon, a miracle occurred. During a walk past the Pi-azza Campitelli, I spotted a sign on a door: AFFITASI ("to let"). Un-able to resist, I walked into the building and spoke to the *portinaia*, saying that my family might be interested in renting the apartment. When told the price, I maintained a straight face. That evening, I immediately announced to my mother that we had to move and would she please drop everything the following afternoon and meet me after school to visit a new apartment. She did not have to worry about not speaking Italian; I would do all the talking. When she reminded me that we were poor now and relied on the kind-ness of relatives, I concocted an argument to persuade her that since the amount we paid a mean uncle each month for our cur-rent hole in the wall was so absurdly bloated, why not find a better place altogether? To this day I do not know why my mother de-cided to play along. We agreed that if we couldn't persuade the *portinaia* to lower her price, my mother would make a face to sug-gest subdued disapproval.

I would never have believed that so rundown a facade on the Campo Marzio could house so sumptuous and majestic an apartment. As we entered the empty, high-ceilinged flat, our cautious, timid footsteps began to produce such loutish echoes on the squeaking parquet floor that I wished to squelch each one, as though they were escaped insects we had brought with us from Alberone that would give away our imposture. I looked around, looked at Mother. It must have dawned on both of us that we didn't even have enough money to buy a kitchen table for this place, let alone four chairs to go around it. And yet, as I peeked at the old rooms, this, I already knew, was the Rome I loved: thoroughly lavish and baroque, like a heroic opera by George Frideric Handel. The *portinaia*'s daughter was following me with her eyes. I tried to look calm, and glanced at the ceiling as though inspecting it expertly, effortlessly. I slipped into another room. The bedrooms were too large. And there were four of them. I instantly picked mine. I looked out the window and spotted the familiar street. I opened the French windows and stepped out onto a balcony, its tiles bathed in the fading light of the setting sun. I leaned against the banister. *To live here.*

The people in the building across the street were watching television. Someone was walking a dog on the cobbled side street. Two large glass streetlights hanging from both walls of an adjoining corner house had started to cast a pale orange glow upon its walls. I imagined my mother sending me to buy milk downstairs, my dream scooter I'd park in the courtyard.

My mother had come well-dressed that day, probably to impress the *portinaia*. But her tailor-made suit, which had been touched up recently, seemed dated, and she looked older, nervous. She played the part terribly, pretending there was something bothering her that she couldn't quite put her finger on, and finally assuming the disappointed air we had rehearsed together when it became clear that she and the *portinaia* could not agree on the rent.

"*Anche a me dispiace, Signore*—I too am sorry," said the *portinaia*'s daughter. What I took with me that day was not just the regret in her dark, darting eyes as she escorted us downstairs, but the profound sorrow with which, as if for good measure, she had thrown in an unexpected bonus that stayed with me the rest of my life: *"Signore."* I had just turned fifteen.

I have often wondered what became of that apartment. After our visit, I never dared pass it again and crafted elaborate detours to avoid running into the *portinaia* or her daughter. Years later, back from the States with long hair and a beard, I made my next visit. What surprised me most was not that the Campo Marzio was riddled with high-end boutiques, but that someone had taken down the AFFITASI sign and never put it up again. The apartment had not waited.

And yet the building I never lived in is the only place I revisit each time I come back to Rome, just as the Rome that haunts me still is the one I fabricated on my afternoon walks. Today, the building is no longer drab ocher but peach pink. It too has gone to the other side, and, like the girl with the blackamoor eyes, is most likely trying to stay young, the expert touch of a beautician's hand filling in those spots that have always humanized Roman stone and made the passage of time here the painless, tiny miracle that it is. At fifteen, I visited the life I wished to lead and the home I was going to make my own someday. Now, I was visiting the life I had dreamed of living.

Fortunately, the present, like the noonday sun here, always intrudes upon the past. Only seconds after I come to a stop before the building, a budding indifference takes hold of me and I am hastening to start on one of those much-awaited long walks I already know won't end before sundown. I am thinking of ocher and water and fresh figs and the good, simple foods I'll have for lunch. I am thinking of my large seventh-story balcony at the Hotel de Russie, looking over the twin domes of Santa Maria di Montesanto and Santa Maria dei Miracoli, off the Piazza del Popolo. This is what I've always wished to do in Rome. Not visit anything, not even remember anything, but just sit, and from my perch, with the Pincio behind, scope the entire city lying before me under the serene, spellbinding light of a Roman afternoon.

I am to go out tonight with old friends to a restaurant called

Vecchia Roma on the Piazza Campitelli. On our way, I know we'll walk past my secret corner in the Campo Marzio—I always make sure we take that route—where I'll throw a last, furtive look up at this apartment by the evening light. An unreal spell always descends upon Rome at night, and the large *lampadari* on these empty, inter-connecting streets beam with the light of small altars and icons in dark churches. You can hear your own footsteps, even though your feet don't seem to touch the ground but almost hover above the gleaming slate pavements, covering distances that make the span of years seem trivial. Along the way, as the streets grow progressively darker and emptier and spookier, I'll let everyone walk ahead of me, be alone awhile. I like to imagine the ghost of Leopardi, of Henri Beyle (known to the world as Stendhal), of Beatrice Cenci, of Anna Magnani, rising by the deserted corner, each one always willing to stop and greet me, like characters in Dante who have wandered up to the surface and are eager to mingle before ebbing back into the night. It is the Frenchman I'm closest to. He alone understands why these streets and the apartment up above are so important to me; he understands that coming back to places adds an annual ring and is the most accurate way of measuring time. He too kept coming back here. He smiles and adds that he's doing so still, reminding me that just because one's gone doesn't mean one loves this city any less, or that one stops fussing with time here once time stops everywhere else. This, after all, is the Eternal City. One never leaves. One can, if one wishes, choose one's ghost spot now. I know where mine is.

FOR THE LITERARY TRAVELER

"This protean city is all about drifting and straying," Aciman says, re-membering his three years wandering the streets of what he considers "the most beautiful city on earth." His passions take in the whole city, but some are more specific than others.

The piazza and church of **Santa Maria della Pace,** just to the west of Piazza Navona. Aciman's *caffè* of choice, the **Antico Caffè della Pace,** a hangout for Romans and foreign celebrities, faces the church.

(Via della Pace 3,4,5,7; tel 06 6861216; 9 A.M.–2:30 A.M., Tues–Sat; 5 P.M.–2:30 A.M., Mon; closed Sun). He loves the Sibyls by Raphael inside the church, but the Sibyls are *in restauro* in 2004, and the church is only open Mon–Sat, 10–1. The magnificent Cloisters are the work of Bramante, arguably his finest achievement in Rome. Sometimes used for art exhibits, the Cloisters, from their second level, allow a close-up view of the church's dome and campanile.

Across the Corso Vittorio Emanuele II, Aciman remembers his awed wandering through the streets around **Campo de' Fiori**—Via del Pellegrino, Via dei Cappellari ("Street of the Hatmakers"), Via Montoro, Via Monserrato, which over the years don't seem to change. The Campo, as the site of Giordano Bruno's execution, recalls Rome's ruthlessness. Yet the daily market scene, the mounds of vegetables, fruit, and flowers, the gaggle of artichoke women preparing the *carciofi alla romana* (David Downie presents the scene—with recipes—in *Cooking the Roman Way*), these works and days on the Campo underscore the undaunted vitality of Rome, the horrors of history notwithstanding.

(*A short stroll from the Campo,* **Hosteria dei Pesce,** *Via di Monserrato 32; tel 06 686 5617, serves incredibly fresh seafood; in the other direction, closer to the Corso—behind the church of Sant'Andrea della Valle—Fazi's* **Trattoria del Pallaro,** *[Largo del Pallaro 15, tel 06 68801488], serves delicious Roman "comfort food" at lunch and dinner. On the Campo, the* **Forno Campo de' Fiori** *bakery, Piazza Campo de' Fiori 22, 7:30–2:30, Mon–Sat, has a fantastic take-out panini menu, though Aciman enjoys making his own.*)

Walking south from the Campo, crossing Via Arenula, and continuing straight on through the medieval Jewish Quarter, which antedates the construction of the Ghetto, you'll come—with luck—into the rectangular **Piazza Campitelli,** where the impoverished young Aciman played out his fantasy of renting a palazzo. The spell cast by this elegant space on a sensitive young man's imagination is entirely believable. To this day Campitelli leaves you yearning: to stay *here.* Or at least in this city. As Aciman puts it, "We begin to see beauty everywhere." Rainaldi's church of Santa Maria in Campitelli (1662–1667) is welcoming, its painting of the "Birth of St. John the Baptist" by Baciccia toward the front, on the left, an example of the sensuality of Italian Catholicism, especially in afternoon sunlight, the warm flesh tones and swirling curvy exaltation of childbirth bearing little relation to the images of torture and death agonies revered in other Catholic cultures. At Christmas, this church, built in honor of Mary as Mother of Good Health—she is said to have saved Italians from the plague—plays "White Christmas" in its *presipio* (Nativity scene). At the far end of the piazza, behind the fountain, is the **Sala Baldini,** a concert hall and music academy built as an extension of the church. You may listen to rehearsals, attend concerts, the shadows of the Capitoline Hill and the Theater of Marcellus at your back. (Tickets at the door, or reserved at tel 06 8713 1590; for a schedule of concerts, visit www.tempietto.it.)

At the piazza's opposite end, the restaurant **Vecchia Roma,** Piazza Campitelli 18, with its frescoed rooms and alfresco dining in summer, is a delightful place to end up after an outdoor evening concert just down the hill at the **Theater of Marcellus.** (Reservations required; tel 06 6864604; closed Wed.)

Leaving the piazza—along Via Caetani, Via de' Funari, Via Michelangelo—you'll pass the huge Palazzo Mattei comprising five Renaissance and Baroque palaces. On the second floor of one of them—the stairways are just before the large courtyard—is the **Centro Italiano di Studi Americani** in which the library and reading room are open to visitors. The hours change with the seasons. A few steps away in **Piazza Mattei** is the Turtle Fountain, or **Fontana delle Tartarughe.** If you come upon it at night, "inadvertently," like Aciman, you will never lose this astonishing "memory of water" under moonlight.

No longer a poor boy, when Aciman visits Rome now, he stays in the **Hotel de Russie,** with views of the domes of Piazza del Popolo, where Picasso and Cocteau once leaned off their terraces to pick oranges from the hotel gardens built into the side of the Pincian Hill (Via del Babuino 9; tel 06 328881; www.rfhotels.com).

ROMANS ON ROME
Since World War II

VIA NOMENTANA ❧ PIAZZA IN PISCINULA, TRASTEVERE
THE JEWISH GHETTO ❧ SAN LORENZO ❧ TIBURTINO
TESTACCIO ❧ FOSSE ARDEATINA ❧ PIAZZA DEL POPOLO
THE TREVI FOUNTAIN ❧ VIA VENETO

❧

Natalia Ginzburg ❧ Elsa Morante ❧ Federico Fellini

. . . *the great film of Roberto Rossellini . . . Roma ciftà a perta
[Rome: open city, 1945] . . . was not just a movie, it was
convincing evidence that the Italian spirit—the country's vital
creativity—was once more ablaze. Soon . . . there was further
testimony . . . in contemporary Italian literature, brilliantly
proving that Fascism had been unable to keep great writers from
writing . . . [or stop] that thrilling postwar explosion of Italian
genius.*

—WILLIAM WEAVER

NATALIA GINZBURG

1916–1991

In Italy Natalia Ginzburg is recognized as one of the most powerful writers of the post–World War II era and one of Italy's most famous women writers. Her international audience is growing, thanks to the continuing translations that are making her novels, essays, and plays more available. Some titles available in English include The Road to the City; *the novellas* Valentino, Sagittarius, Family, *and* Borghesia; All Our Yesterdays; The Little Virtues *(the title essay, a masterpiece);* Voices in the Evening; *the autobiographical* Family Sayings; The Manzoni Family; *the plays* The Advertisement *and* I Married You for the Fun of It; *and* A Place to Live, *from which the following essay is taken. Ginzburg's voice is unmistakable. The severity of her insights into the spiritual poverty created by a culture of money make you flinch. But her honesty and humanity make her nod to the pleasures of everyday life more credible.*

Born Natalia Levi in Palermo, raised in Turin, an anti-fascist fugitive with three small children during World War II (her husband, Leone Ginzburg, died as a prisoner of the Nazis in Rome's Regina Coeli prison), and a long resident of Rome, Ginzburg was a member of the Italian Parliament for the Left from 1983 until her death.

❧

SUCH IS ROME

Though it seems to do its utmost to be as ugly as possible, I still find Rome, the city I live in, very beautiful. Besides finding it so beautiful, I love it dearly and wouldn't leave it for anything in the world. Nevertheless, it has become quite difficult both to love it and to live in it, since these days it is a jungle of automobiles. If ever there was a city made for walking, it's this one; the cars seem to have invaded it by stealth, like an attack of blight. I cannot understand who wanted them, since everyone curses them. They overrun the city like a river at flood tide, they appear to have erupted from the bowels of the earth, and every so often they fill the city with a long, exasperated, mocking shriek that sounds at once like a jeer and a cry for help.

The cities we choose to make our own, as adults, are a composite of the image we had of them in childhood, before we ever saw them; the image they presented when we saw them for the first time; the yearning we've felt when far away; and finally, our indifference or anger as we walk through them after long years of residence. The feelings they inspire in us after so many years are no different from the feelings inspired by people, when a prolonged and daily habit of living together has streaked our love with intolerance and anger. At some point we become aware that the intolerance and anger, grown over the love like lichen, have not worn it down but rather made it stronger, deeper, and inextinguishable. Then we try to call up distant images of these people or these places at our first encounter, when we didn't yet know whether it was to be a minor, fleeting encounter or something essential and enduring.

We often tend to compare the cities we chose as adults with those where we spent our childhood. Often we congratulate ourselves for having pulled up our early roots and set down new roots and habits elsewhere. And, strange to say, having grown old now, we maintain this peculiar pride in having sunk roots and habits far from our childhood landscapes. Why we should feel such pride is a mystery, since one doesn't deserve any special credit, in the scheme of things, for having left one's city of origin. And yet, till our dying day, the inexplicable banner of our pride flutters over the cities we chose as adults.

In the past, when I had spent brief periods in Rome or when I recalled it longingly from far away, I used to enumerate the reasons why I loved it. I thought that I loved its strange air of seeming small while it was enormous. At night in Rome, one had the feeling of ambling down village lanes. What made it resemble a village might have been the cats or the silence or the rich peace of certain vast, deserted piazzas, or the uncanny, pervasive sense of an invisible countryside, wooded and boundless, quite close by. How on earth the country could seem so close by, in those stony surroundings, that we could feel, amid the darkness, the rustling expanse of fields and trees, I cannot say. We could sit down on a staircase, gaze at the cats, the grass, the moon, the fountains and the ruins, and enjoy a strange and solemn pastoral silence. We could think it was summer when in fact it was winter. I found the seasons in this city often jumbled, which felt extraordinary to one who grew up in Turin. I was used to Turin's interminable freezing winters, when fog and darkness would hold the city clamped and stiff in a stern, impenetrable slumber. It seemed Rome could never sink so totally into winter, for beyond the cold one could always be surprised by an unlikely whiff of indolence, of summer vacations. It seemed a place where something unpredictable was always happening. When it rained and the entire city was like one enormous puddle, there might appear in the midst of the rain, from I don't know where, a sudden warmth and glimmer of spring. A sky heavy with swollen yellow clouds might suddenly be lit by a fiery twilight color. All these reasons were why I thought I loved it. Still, it is true that during my first few years in Rome I pined with homesickness for Turin and its endless winters. Even as I walked through Rome or leaned against its balustrades thinking how warm and mild the stone here always felt, I had a wrenching nostalgia for Turin and specifically for one street in Turin, and that was Via Nizza. Why I yearned for Via Nizza I don't know. It was a street in my old neighborhood, but not the street where I grew up. And yet I would have given anything at all to be on Via Nizza, walking among its very tall buildings sealed with ice, breathing in its fog, its winter and melancholy.

Indeed I think my early love for Rome was mingled with that nostalgia for Turin, my native city, from which, at that time, the war kept me. Our feelings for cities, like our feelings for people, are always rather confused, with all sorts of things mixed in. What is clear is that we don't love cities, or love people, for any reasons that can be enumerated. In the Rome of today I don't see the slightest trace of the reasons for which I once claimed to love it. It's no longer possible to look at the sky here, or to be aware of the seasons. It's not even possible to exchange an affectionate word or glance with the city anymore. Cars overrun its sidewalks. It is stricken by cars as by some malignant disease. Nothing, nowadays, feels as distant and remote as the countryside. The cats and the ruins remain, but it never occurs to anyone to look at them—you'd have to seek them out behind the cars. And at night Rome definitely doesn't feel like a village. But it doesn't feel like a great, restless city either, not by night or by day; the fact is that it doesn't feel like anything. It's as if it no longer knows what to be. The cars do thin out at night, but the silence in the streets now is never tranquil and profound. It is a silence without peace, an expectant silence, prostrate with exhaustion. It is a silence still vibrating with the echo of that lacerating, querulous shriek, the shriek of cars tied up in traffic, and the whole city waits for that shriek to start all over again very soon, with its harrowing, mocking appeal for help. Around the edges of the city, houses keep springing up that bear no resemblance to it nor to each other, all of them dreadful but each one dreadful in its own individual way, houses that appear leprous and decrepit from the moment they are built. They don't know what to be either—city houses or country houses—yet they seem to seek a connection with the city's center. The only connection they manage to achieve, though, is that they too writhe in the stranglehold of the cars. Years ago, an outcropping of new houses had already sprouted up on the edges, a tangled, deformed, fragile vegetation, but the city, in its supreme and oblivious indifference, seemed able to shelter and sustain every species of deformity. Now its indifference, apparently doomed to last forever, has given rise to a vague weariness, a hidden bafflement and sadness, in a city which was never weary or baffled or sad. It is the sadness of having lost its essential nature and being unable to assume another.

This is the Rome of today, which I no longer like, which no one seems to like, and yet we all love it, for the truth is that cities, like people, are loved for no reason at all or for a tangle of reasons, different for everyone. In Rome during the war, I lived in hiding in a convent on Via Nomentana, sharing a room with an old Jewish woman from Vienna whom I made friends with. She was very kind, and when I went out she would mind my infant daughter. I had a small electric stove, and now and then this little old lady would ask if she could use it. Although I had told her many times that she could use it whenever she liked, still she would announce every time she was about to use it. On cold afternoons, she would get up from the bed and say, "My dear Signora, I make myself the tea." One might well ask how in the world this little old woman in exile, whom I haven't seen since and who must be long dead, enters into my feelings for the city. But for me, Via Nomentana and the dark corridor of the convent and its high windows grazed by trees are inseparable from the memory of that very tiny old woman sitting on the bed in a brown shawl, and I think I began to love Rome while seeking some kind of maternal protection in that little old woman, who in turn wanted my protection along with my stove. So that now, when I go down Via Nomentana, buried in cars and unrecognizable, I remember how beloved that street is to me; I recover the keys to my affection by murmuring those long-lost words, "My dear Signora, I make myself the tea."

December, 1970

FOR THE LITERARY TRAVELER

Visitors will have no trouble connecting with Ginzburg's lament for a Rome ruined by traffic. Is there anyone who hasn't stood petrified on a Roman street corner, loath to step off the curb, visualizing the wheelchair life threatened by every revved-up fleet of Vespas and taxis? Since 1970, when Ginzburg wrote "Such Is Rome," things have improved a bit. Piazzas that had turned into parking lots now ban parking completely. Some streets have become pedestrian walkways. Still. As you stroll into the Piazza del Quirinale . . . *Guarda, signora! Ferma!* Ginzburg's concern, of course, is not endangered tourists. It's that car travel destroys the human connection with places.

Ginzburg hid from the Nazis in a convent on the comfortable **Via Nomentana,** which, from 1925, was the address of Mussolini at the Villa Torlonia. A further irony is that the villa's grounds cover the site of Rome's Jewish catacombs, the entrance just below the villa's stables. Since the war, Torlonia's grounds have been transformed into a public park, the site of concerts in summer (open 7:30 A.M.–dusk). But the Jewish catacombs remain closed, their contents—gold glassware, fragments of sarcophagi—removed to the Vatican museums.

When the Allies liberated Rome from the German occupation in June 1944, the American army entered the city along Via Nomentana, through Porta Pia. The convent where Ginzburg hid with her child and the old Viennese woman remains anonymous, like the many convents and churches in Rome that sheltered Jews during the occupation. In *Benevolence and Betrayal: Five Italian Jewish Families Under Fascism* (1991), Alexander Stille names a few specific locations of this underground resistance movement, including the ancient tiny church of San Benedetto, across from the Jewish Ghetto—on the other side of Tiber Island and the Ponte Quattro Capi, once called the Bridge of the Jews—in Trastevere's Piazza in Piscinula (number 40). Ring the bell of the convent next door for admission. Another irony: behind this stately piazza, through the low arches, Catholic households on the winding streets and alleys of ancient Jewish Trastevere—Via del Salumi, Via del Genovese, Via Anicia (the setting of novelist Dacia Maraini's macabre crime novel, *Voices*)—hid the hunted Jews, the Jews who had lived here long before the word "Christian" was ever heard in Catholicism's capital city. Partly because of this network of shelters throughout Italy, she had the highest Jewish survival rate in Nazi-occupied Europe. Just behind San Benedetto's, in Vicolo dell'Atleta 13–14, stands a synagogue (now a restaurant—Spirito Di Vino), founded in the eleventh century. On the central column of the arches of the facade, Hebrew characters are still visible. The proprietors will show you the ancient cellars, if you ask.

ELSA MORANTE

1912–1985

Else Morante was born poor and from childhood knew the neighborhoods of the working poor—San Lorenzo, Tiburtino, Testaccio, the Ghetto—that are as vivid as human characters in History: A Novel *(1974), excerpted here. In the words of her friend and translator, William Weaver, "Any reader of* History *will realize that she knew her native city stone by stone." The author of the prize-winning novels* House of Liars *(Natalia Ginzburg, an editor at Einaudi, pushed for its acceptance),* Arthur's Island, *and* Aracoeli, *Morante's masterpiece is the antiwar epic,* History. *"One of the few novels in any language that renders the full horror of Hitler's war, the war that never gets into the books," wrote Alfred Kazin. "An enormous canvas," [by] "a storyteller who spellbinds," said Stephen Spender. Morante shows what the war was like in Rome for the starving masses. (The "sub-proletariat" is Pier Paolo Pasolini's word.) Throughout the novel, Morante's "eye is on the sparrow," in the words of Barbara Grizzuti Harrison's introduction to the new Steerforth edition, "the playthings of war . . . a species that gives no news of itself . . . we love them because she so greatly does." A plaque inscribed in Morante's memory in Testaccio, where she lived as a child (Via Amerigo Vespucci 41, to your right off Via Marmorata, as you head toward Porta San Paolo), captures her politics, morality, and religion in a few words:* Solo Chi Ama Conosce. *"Only those who love understand." In Ricorda Della Scrittrice, Elsa Morante.*

Morante was married to the novelist Alberto Moravia. As known anti-fascists, and in danger during the German occupation, they spent nine months hiding out in the mountains south of Rome until the Liberation by the Allies on the night of June 4, 1944.

From History: A Novel

The protagonists of History *are Ida Mancuso, a half-Jewish single mother and poor schoolteacher, and her small bastard son, Useppe. (She's also the mother of Nino, a teenage son by her husband, who has died.) Useppe was born after a German soldier on his way to North Africa raped Ida. The survival of this child in war-torn, occupied Rome becomes her passion. At the beginning of the novel, she lives in San Lorenzo, commutes to her school in the Testaccio, and, after school, shops in the Jewish Ghetto. She's terrified that her mixed racial identity—her mother was a Jew—will be discovered; yet she feels drawn to the Ghetto.*

. . . *19* . . .

After reporting to the registry, Ida had resumed her former life. She lived just like an Aryan among other Aryans, no one seemed to doubt her total Aryan-ness, and on the rare occasions when she had to show her documents (for example, at the Bursar's office), though her heart was pounding in her breast, her mother's maiden name went completely unnoticed. Her racial secret seemed buried, once and for all, in the files of the Registry; but she, knowing it lay recorded in those mysterious tombs, was still afraid some news of it might filter to the outside, branding her—but especially Nino!—with the mark of the outcast and the impure. Moreover, particularly at school, where she, a clandestine half-Jew, enjoyed the rights and functions due *Aryans,* she felt guilty, a usurper, a counterfeiter.

Also on the rounds of her daily shopping, she had the feeling she was begging, like an orphaned stray puppy, in other people's territory. Then one day, she who, before the racial laws, had never encountered another Jew except Nora, began to follow an incongruous trail of her own, preferring the confines of the Roman

Ghetto, the stands and shops of some little Jews who, at that time, were still allowed to continue their humble trade as before.

At first her shyness led her to trade only with certain old people, with half-spent eyes and sealed lips. But chance gradually brought her some less taciturn acquaintances, usually some neighborhood woman, who, encouraged perhaps by Ida's Semitic eyes, would chat with her in passing. . . .

Not distant from her school, the Ghetto was a small, ancient quarter, segregated—until the last century—by high walls and gates that were locked in the evening, and subject in those days to fevers, because of the vapors and muck of the nearby Tiber, which did not then have embankments. Since the old quarter had been made more hygienic and its walls torn down, its population had done nothing but multiply; and now, in those same few narrow streets and those two little squares, thousands of people contrived somehow to live. There were many hundreds of infants and youngsters, mostly with mops of curls and lively eyes; and at the beginning of the war, before the famine began, numerous cats still roamed around, resident among the ruins of the ancient Theater of Marcellus, a stone's throw away. The inhabitants, for the most part, were peddlers or rag-men, the only trades allowed the Jews in past centuries, though soon, in the course of the war, these would also be forbidden by the new Fascist laws. A few of these little merchants had, at most, a room or two on the street, to use as a shop or a storehouse. And these, more or less, were all the resources of the small village, where the racial decrees of 1938, still in force, had not been able to affect their lot much.

In certain families of the quarter, the news of those decrees had hardly been noticed, as if they were things concerning the few rich Jewish ladies and gentlemen who lived scattered through the bourgeois residential districts of the city. And as for the various threats, which circulated darkly, the information Ida gathered about them there was incomplete and confused, like prison grapevine news. In general, among her acquaintances in the little shops, there reigned an ingenuous and trusting incredulity. If she, as an Aryan, gave some faint little hint of knowledge, those poor busy little women, for the most part, responded with an evasive heedlessness or else a reticent resignation. So much of the news was invented for propaganda. And besides, in Italy, certain things could never happen. They trusted in the important friendships (or also in the Fascist merits) of the heads of the Community or of the Rabbi; in Mussolini's benevolence towards the Jews; and even in the protection of the Pope (whereas Popes, in reality, over the centuries, had been among their worst enemies). If some one of them seemed more skeptical, they didn't want to believe him . . . But, to tell the truth, in their position, they had no other defense.

Among them, now and then, there was an aged spinster by the name of Vilma, whom they treated, in those parts, like an imbecile. The muscles of her body and of her face were always restless, while her gaze, on the contrary, was ecstatic, too luminous.

She had been orphaned very young, and, unable to do anything else, she adapted herself to heavy jobs, like a laborer. She ran around all day long tirelessly, in Trastevere and in Campo dei Fiori, where she also begged for leftovers, not for herself, but for the cats in the Theater of Marcellus. Perhaps the only holiday in her life was when, towards evening, she would sit there on a ruin, in the midst of the cats, scattering half-rotten fishheads and bloodstained offal on the ground for them. Then her always feverish face would become calm and radiant, as in Paradise. (However, with the progress of the war, these blissful encounters of hers were to become only a memory.)

For some time, Vilma brought back to the Ghetto from her daily laboring rounds strange, unheard-of information, which the other women rejected as fantasies of her brain. And in fact, her imagination was always toiling, like a convict, in Vilma's head; however, later, certain *fantasies* of hers were to prove far less fantastic than the truth.

She insisted that the person who kept her so informed was a *Nun* (she went to work in a convent, among other places . . .); or else a *Signora* who, in secret, listened to some forbidden radio broadcasts, but Vilma was not to say the lady's name. In any case, she tried hard to convince them her information was genuine; and every day she would repeat the news, through the quarter, in a hoarse, urgent voice, as if she were pleading. But realizing that no one listened to her or believed her, she would burst into an anguished laughter like whooping cough. The only one, perhaps, who did listen to her, with terrible seriousness, was Iduzza,* because in her eyes Vilma, in her appearance and her behavior, resembled a kind of prophetess.

At present, in her messages, as obsessive as they were futile, she harped constantly on the warning to *save the children at least,* declaring she had learned confidentially from the *Nun* that in the imminent future's history a new slaughter was written, worse than Herod's. As soon as the Germans occupied a country, the first thing they did was herd all the Jews, without exception, in to one place, and from there, drag them off, beyond the borders, nobody knew where, in "the night and in the fog." Most collapsed or died on the journey. And all of them, the dead and the living, were thrown on top of one another into huge pits, which their companions or relatives were forced to dig in their presence. The only ones allowed to survive were the stronger adults, sentenced to work like slaves for the war. And the children were all slaughtered, from first to last, and thrown into the common ditches along the road. . . .

(*In October 1943, when the Jews of the Ghetto are taken captive, Ida and Useppe, who've been bombed out of their home in San Lorenzo, are living with other refugees in a shelter in Pietralata, one of the slums on the outskirts of Rome created by the Fascist demolitions in the city center. (Pietralata—and Primavalle, Tiburtino, Quarticciolo— appear in Pier Paolo Pasolini's stories of Rome's shantytowns, and in his movie* Mamma Roma [1962]*.*)

---

*Ida.

. . . *1943* . . .

O ne Sunday, Caruli's brother Tore, returning from some of his dealings in the city, pointed out to Ida in the newspaper, *Il Messaggero,* the news that schools would reopen on November 8th. Among all The Thousand,* Tore was the least illiterate, and he liked to display his culture by commenting on items in the papers, especially the sports page. That Sunday, among his other com- ments, he remarked that in the *Messaggero* there was no trace of a piece of news that was, however, circulating inside Rome, and that had even been broadcast, they said, by Radio Bari: yesterday, Sat- urday (October 16th), the Germans had rounded up all the Jews of Rome at dawn, house by house, and loaded them into trucks for an unknown destination. The Ghetto had been totally stripped of all its Jewish flesh, and only its skeleton was left; but also in the other sections and neighborhoods, all of Rome's Jews—individuals and families—had been rooted out by some SS who had come on pur- pose, a special company, supplied with an exact list. They had taken them all: not only the young and the healthy, but also the old, the seriously ill, even pregnant women, even babes in arms. It was said they were all being taken off to be burned alive in big ovens; but this, according to Tore, was maybe an exaggeration.

At that moment, the gramophone was playing a dance tune, and the kids were all jumping around: so the comments on this news were lost in the uproar. And in the course of that same Sunday, the Jews' story was actually forgotten among The Thousand, in the flow of news that arrived every day by direct or oblique routes, collected in the city or brought by acquaintances of listeners to Radio Bari or Radio London. After their journey, however brief, these items usually reached the big room distorted, or expanded, or confused. And Ida had learned to protect herself by ignoring them all, treating them like folk tales; but not this last piece of news, no, because she had been expecting it for some time, even without ad-

---

*The refugees in the shelter.

mitting it to herself. From the moment she heard it, fear never stopped thrashing her, like a spiked scourge, until every hair on her head ached at the root. She didn't dare ask Tore for further clarification, impossible at any rate; nor did she know to whom to turn, to find out if halfbreeds were also written down in the list of the *guilty* (this was the very term she used in her thoughts). And in bed, with the darkness, her terror increased. When curfew struck, she heard Carlo Vivaldi return—in that period he wandered around the city more than ever—and she was almost tempted to get up and ask him. But she heard him cough; and she thought she could sense, in that cough, something terrible and rejecting. It's true that some (also Nino?) murmured that he might be a Jew; but others (given, to tell the truth, scant credence) also insinuated that he was perhaps a Nazi-Fascist spy. She suspected that, merely hearing her utter the word *Jews,* he, like the others, would immediately see her secret written all over her face, and tomorrow might report her to the Gestapo.

She had gone to bed with her clothes on, and she had left Useppe dressed, too; and she hadn't even taken her sleeping pill, so that the Germans, if they came for her in the night, wouldn't catch her unprepared. She held tight to Useppe, having decided that, the moment she heard the soldiers' unmistakable tread outside and their knocking on the door, she would try to escape through the fields, dropping from the roof with her baby in her arms; and if pursued, she would run and run all the way to the marsh, to drown herself there, along with him. The terrors brooded over for years, erupting in the immediate fear of this night, grew in her to a raving fantasy, without release. She thought of going out into the streets at random, with the sleeping Useppe in her arms, heedless of the curfew, since night-wanderers, when terrestrial horror reaches a certain degree, become invisible . . . Or else of running towards the mountains of the Castelli, hunting for the Madman, to plead with him to hide Useppe and herself in the partisans' lair . . . But most of all she was soothed by the thought of going off with Useppe into the Ghetto, to sleep in one of the empty apartments. Again, as in the past, her contradictory fears finally followed a mysterious comet, that invited her in the direction of the Jews: promising her, there in the distance, a maternal stable, warm with animals' breath, and with their big eyes, not judging, but only pitying. Even these poor Jews from all of Rome, loaded into trucks by the Germans, tonight hailed her like Blessed Spirits who, unknown to themselves and even to the Germans, were going off, through a splendid deceit, towards an Oriental realm where all are children, without consciousness or memory . . .

"Do not look at my black skin,
for the sun darkened me,
my beloved is white and ruddy,
his curls are golden.
There, my beloved's voice knocks:
open to me, my dear, my dove.
I rose to open but I could not find him,
I sought him and could not find him.
The watchmen searching the city found me:
have you seen my soul's beloved?
I have not tended my own vineyard
and he took me into the house
and his banners of love were over me!
I sought him in the streets and squares and did not find him
I called him and had no answer.
Before the day ends and the night,
return my stag, my beloved kid.
Oh if you were my brother
who sucked my mother's breasts!
then on meeting you, I could kiss you
and no one would scorn me.
In his body I rested
and he savored me with his lips and his teeth,
come, my brother, let us see if the vine has blossomed.
I beseech you, should you find my beloved
tell him I am sick with love . . . "

Where had she learned these verses? In school perhaps, as a little girl? She had never recalled knowing them, and now, in her confused wakefulness, it seemed to her that her own voice, as a child, was reciting them in a languid tone, affected and tragic.

Around four she dozed off. The usual dream returned to her, the one that had visited her often, with some variants, since the previous summer: about her father, sheltering her under his cloak. This time, in the cloak's shelter, she wasn't alone. Useppe was there too, all naked (even smaller than in real life), and Alfio her husband, also naked and stout. And she herself was naked, but it didn't embarrass her, for all her being old as she was now, and decrepit. The streets of Cosenza became confused with those of Naples, and of Rome, and of who knows what other metropolises, as usual in dreams. It was pouring rain, but her father had a large, broad-brimmed hat on his head, and Useppe amused himself by kicking his feet in the puddles.

In the dream it was pouring, but instead, when she woke, the morning was sunny. Ida got up hastily, knowing that on this Monday morning she had planned to buy Useppe a pair of new shoes (with the points of her clothing-ration card), since the homemade bound sandals had become unserviceable, especially as winter was approaching. She and Useppe were quickly ready, having slept in their clothes. At first, there had flashed into Ida's brain the bizarre notion of going, for her purchase, to a certain little cobbler in the Ghetto . . . But she had second thoughts in time, remembering the Ghetto had been emptied; only its skeleton remained, as Salvatore had said. And then she decided on a shoeshop in the Tiburtino quarter (which she had already patronized when she lived in that area) where she counted on still finding remainders of the very smallest sizes and, among them, some pre-war shoes of real leather, which she had had her eye on since last spring. And she decided to take this opportunity also to drop by Remo's tavern (in her eyes he had become a Gray Eminence, thanks to the Madman's hints) with the thought of receiving, perhaps, some information from him about the guilt, or innocence, of halfbreeds . . .

After a fairly long stretch on foot, they had to wait more than half an hour for the bus to the Tiburtino. To make up for this bad luck, they were fortunate in the purchase of the shoes, being able to discover, after much searching (the shoes noted by Ida had unfortunately been sold just a few days before), a real pair of little boots, covering the ankles, the like of which Useppe had never owned. They actually seemed of real leather, the soles were of crepe; and to his mother's satisfaction (since in making such exceptional expenses for his wardrobe, she was worried about his *growth*), they were almost two sizes too large for Useppe. But he was especially attracted by the laces, which were a handsome carmine color, in contrast with the pale brown of the footgear. In fact, the shopkeeper explained, these were *two-tone boots*.

Useppe wanted to wear them immediately: and this was an advantage, because, as soon as they were outside the shoeshop, near the station, the disastrous traces of the air raids appeared around them; but he was too intent on his new feet, and paid no attention.

Meaning to go to the tavern, Ida chose some little side-streets, avoiding, as a doubly frightening sight, the Via Tiburtina, with the long wall of the Verano cemetery. She was beginning to feel tired after her almost sleepless night; and as she turned towards the familiar places of San Lorenzo, she stupidly began walking faster, at the blind stimulus that drives mares and donkeys towards the manger. But a resistance from Useppe's little hand, imprisoned in hers, restrained her. And in a sudden reawakening she lost the courage to continue on that route which for her had once been the way home. Then, giving up the visit to Remo, she turned back.

In reality, she no longer knew where to go. Her night-suspicion that she was wanted by the Germans was growing to a paranoid certainty in her weakened mind, blocking off like a colossus the return roads to the big room in Pietralata. Nevertheless, she followed Useppe's little footsteps, which went again towards the bus stop, convinced and spellbound even if somewhat unsteady in the oversized and still stiff boots. At Piazzale delle Crociate a middle-aged woman passed them, running like a lunatic in their same direction. Ida recognized her: she was a Jew from the Ghetto, the wife of a certain Settimio Di Segni, who ran a little store, buying and selling second-hand goods, behind Sant'Angelo in Pescheria. On various occasions in recent years, Ida had gone to his place to offer some household object for sale, or some piece of personal property; and sometimes she had happened to deal with his wife, running the shop in his place. On some days, in their minuscule storeroom, she had met a few of their numerous children and grandchildren, all of whom lived with them in a couple of rooms over the shop.

"Signora! Signora Di Segni!"

Ida called, walking faster after her, with a voice of almost exultant surprise. And when the other woman didn't seem to hear her, she immediately took Useppe in her arms and ran after her, clinging to that alien encounter like an earthling lost in the deserts of the moon who has run into a close relation. But the woman didn't turn or listen; and when Ida was beside her, the woman barely glanced at her, with the grim and hostile eyes of a lunatic rejecting all relationship with normal people.

"Signora! . . . Don't you recognize me? I . . . " Ida insisted. But the woman was paying no attention to her; indeed, she seemed not to see or hear Ida, though, at the same time, she had started walking faster, to shake her off, suspiciously. She was sweating (she was rather fat), and her bobbed yellow-gray hair was sticking to her forehead. Her left hand, with the "patriotic" steel wedding ring, clutched a wretched little change-purse. She had nothing else with her.

Ida ran along beside her, jolting the baby, in a kind of gasping panic: "Signora," she said suddenly, getting as close to her as she could and speaking in a very low voice, as if to an intimate confidante: "I'm Jewish, too."

But Signora Di Segni didn't seem to understand her, nor did she listen to her. At that point, shaken by some sudden alarm, the woman moved away from there, bursting into an animal dash across the square towards the railroad station opposite.

After the bombings, the station had been promptly reopened; but its low rectangular façade, of a yellowish color, was still scorched and blackened by the smoke from the explosions. Since it was a secondary station, there was never much of a crowd, especially on Monday; but today the movement seemed even less than usual. In these times of war, and especially since the German occupation, troops were often loaded or unloaded there. But there were no soldiers in sight today, and only a few civilians moved around, without haste. On that late morning of a Monday, the building had an abandoned and temporary look.

But Useppe gazed at it as if it were a monument, perhaps also in a vague reminiscence of the days he had gone there with Ninnuzzu* to enjoy the spectacle of the trains. And he remained quiet, looking all around with curious eyes, momentarily forgetting his private, personal impatience: he was in a big hurry, in fact, to go back to Pietralata, instead of bouncing around here in his mother's arms; he couldn't wait to carry, finally, to Ulì and to all of them today's big news: the boots!

And Ida, meanwhile, had almost forgotten he was in her arms, since she was bent solely on not losing sight of Signora Di Segni's isolated form, which drew her along like a will-o'-the-wisp. Ida saw her head towards the passengers' entrance, then come back again, in her great and furious untouchable's solitude, expecting no help from anyone. Not running any more, but stumbling in haste on her old summer shoes with enormous orthopedic soles, she was now moving along this side of the station's façade, then she turned left towards the freight yard, towards the service entrance. Ida crossed the square and took the same direction.

The gate was open: there was no one on guard outside; and no one shouted at her even from the police sentrybox, just inside the gate. Perhaps ten paces from the entrance, she began to hear, at some distance, a horrible humming sound, but for the moment she couldn't understand precisely where it was coming from. That station area, at present, seemed deserted and idle. There was no movement of trains, or traffic of freight; and the only people visible were beyond the boundary of the yard, distant, within the precincts

---

*Nino, his older half-brother.

of the main station; two or three ordinary employees, apparently calm.

Towards the oblique road leading to the tracks, the sound's volume increased. It was not, as Ida had already persuaded herself, the cry of animals packed into cattle-cars, which could sometimes be heard echoing in this area. It was a sound of voices, of a human mass coming, it seemed, from the end of the ramps, and Ida followed that signal, though no assembled crowd was visible among the shunting tracks, which crisscrossed the gravel around her. In her progress, which seemed to go on for miles, and sweaty like a march through the desert (in reality it was perhaps thirty steps), she encountered only a solitary engine-driver, eating from a piece of wrapping paper, beside a spent locomotive, and he said nothing to her. Perhaps the few watchmen had also gone to eat. It must have been just past noon.

The invisible voices were approaching and growing louder, even though they sounded somehow inaccessible, as if they came from an isolated and contaminated place. The sound suggested certain dins of kindergartens, hospitals, prisons: however, all jumbled together, like shards thrown into the same machine. At the end of the ramp, on a straight, dead track, a train was standing which, to Ida, seemed of endless length. The voices came from inside it.

There were perhaps twenty cattle-cars, some wide-open and empty, other closed with long iron bars over the outside doors. Following the standard design of such rolling-stock, the cars had no windows, except a tiny grilled opening up high. At each of those grilles, two hands could be seen clinging, or a pair of staring eyes. At that moment, nobody was guarding the train.

Signora Di Segni was there, running back and forth on the open platform, her legs without stockings, short and thin, of an unhealthy whiteness, and her mid-season dust-coat flying behind her shapeless body. She was running clumsily the whole length of the row of cars, shouting in an almost obscene voice:

"Settimio! Settimio! . . . Graziella! . . . Manuele! . . . Settimio! . . . Settimio! Esterina! . . . Manuele! . . . Angelino! . . ."

From inside the train, some unknown voice reached her, shouting at her to go away: otherwise *they* would take her, too, when they came back in a little while: "No-o-o! I won't go!" she railed, in reply, threatening and enraged, hammering her fists against the cars, "my family's in there! Call them! Di Segni! The Di Segni family!" . . . "Settimiooo!!!" she burst out suddenly, running, her arms out towards one of the cars and clinging to the bar on the door, in an impossible attempt to force it. Behind the grille, up above, a little head had appeared, an old man's. His eyeglasses could be seen glistening over his emaciated nose, against the darkness behind; and his tiny hands clutched the bars.

"Settimio!! The others?! Are they there with you?"

"Go away, Celeste," her husband said to her. "Go away, I tell you: right now. *They*'ll be back any minute . . ." Ida recognized his slow, sententious voice. It was the same that, on other occasions, in his cubbyhole full of old junk, had said to her, for example, with sage and pondered judgment, "This, Signora, isn't even worth the cost of mending . . ." or else, "I can give you six lire for the whole lot . . ." but today it sounded toneless, alien, as if from an atrocious paradise beyond all access.

The interior of the cars, scorched by the lingering summer sun, continued to reecho with that incessant sound. In its disorder, babies' cries overlapped with quarrels, ritual chanting, meaningless mumbles, senile voices calling for mothers; others that conversed, aside, almost ceremonious, and others that were even giggling. And at times, over all this, sterile, blood-curdling screams rose; or others, of a bestial physicality, exclaiming elementary words like "water!" "air!" From one of the last cars, dominating all the other voices, a young woman would burst out, at intervals, with convulsive, piercing shrieks, typical of labor pains.

And Ida recognized this confused chorus. No less than the Signora's indecent screams and old Di Segni's sententious tones, all this wretched human sound from the cars caught her in a heart-rending sweetness, because of a constant memory that didn't return to her from known time, but from some other channel: from the same place as her father's little Calabrian songs that had lulled her, or the anonymous poem of the previous night, or the little kisses that whispered *carina, carina* to her. It was a place of repose that drew her down, into the promiscuous den of a single, endless family.

"I've been running all over the place the whole morning . . ."

Leaning towards that bespectacled face at the grille, Signora Di Segni had started chatting hastily, in a kind of feverish gossip, but also in the familiar and almost ordinary manner of a wife who is accounting for her day to her husband. She told how that morning around ten, as planned, she had returned from an expedition to Fara Cabina with two flasks of olive oil she had managed to find. And arriving, she had discovered the neighborhood deserted, doors barred, nobody in the houses, nobody in the street. Nobody. She had inquired, she had asked here, there, the Aryan café keeper, the Aryan news-vendor. And questions everywhere. Even the Temple deserted. ". . . and I ran this way and that way, to this one and that one . . . They're at the Military Academy . . . at the Termini station . . . at Tiburtino . . ."

"Go away, Celeste."

"No, I won't go away. I'm just as Jewish as you! I want to get into this train too!"

"*Reschut,* Celeste, in the name of God, get out, before *they* come back."

"Nooo! No! Settimio! Where are the others? Manuele? Graziella? The baby? . . . Why can't I see them? Why don't they show their faces?" Suddenly, like a madwoman, she burst out screaming again: "Angelinooo! Esterinaaa! Manuele!! Graziella!!"

A certain shifting could be heard inside the car. Having climbed somehow to the grille, a head with a mop of hair, two little black eyes, could be seen behind the old man . . .

"Esterinnaaa! Esterinaaa! Graziella!! Open up! Isn't anybody in charge around here? I'm a Jew! A Jew! I have to go with them! Open up! Fascists! FASCISTS!! Open the door!" She shouted *Fascists,* not as an accusation or as an insult, but as a natural form of address, as one might say *Ladies and Gentlemen of the Jury* or *Officers,* to appeal to Order and Authority in the situation. And she insisted doggedly in her impossible attempt to force the bars.

"Go away, Signora! Don't stay here! It's best for you! Go away quick!" From the central offices of the Station, beyond the yard, some men (porters or clerks) were gesticulating to her from a distance, with agitated urging. But they didn't approach the train. They seemed, indeed, to avoid it, like a funeral or infected chamber.

No one had yet shown any interest in the presence of Ida, who had remained a bit behind, at the end of the ramp; and she, too, had almost forgotten about herself. She felt invaded by an extreme weakness; and although the heat wasn't excessive there in the open, on the platform she was covered with sweat as if she had a fever of 104 degrees. However, she abandoned herself to this weakness of her body as if to the last sweetness possible, as she became confused in this throng, mingling with the sweat of the others.

She heard bells ringing; and there flashed through her head the warning that she had to hurry to conclude her daily round of shopping; perhaps the stores were already closing. Then she heard some deep and cadenced blows, echoing somewhere near her; and she thought at first they were the puffs of the engine starting, and imagined that the train was preparing for its departure. She promptly realized, however, that those blows had been with her for the whole time she had been on the platform, even if she hadn't paid any attention to them before; and that they were resounding very close to her, right against her body. In fact, it was Useppe's heart beating that way.

The child was quiet, huddled into her arms, his left side against her breast; but he held his head turned to look at the train. In reality, he hadn't moved from that position since the first moment. And as she peered around to examine him, she saw him still staring at the train, his face motionless, his mouth half-open, his eyes wide in an indescribable gaze of horror.

"Useppe . . ." she called him, in a low voice.

Useppe turned, at her summons; the same stare, however, remained in his eyes, which, even as they encountered hers, asked her no question. There was, in the endless horror of his gaze, also a fear, or rather a dazed stupor; but it was a stupor that demanded no explanation.

"We're going, Useppe! We're going away."

At the moment she turned to hasten off from there, among the persistent shouts behind her a man's voice could be distinguished, calling: "Signora, wait! Listen! Signora!" She turned: those calls were addressed to her, all right. From one of the little grilles that allowed her to glimpse a poor bald head with intense eyes that seemed ill, a hand stretched out to throw her a piece of paper.

As she bent to pick it up, Ida realized that there, scattered on the ground along the cars (from which a foul smell was already emanating), there were other similar crumpled notes among the rubbish and garbage; but she didn't have the strength to stay and collect any. And as she ran away, she stuffed that little scrawled piece of paper into her pocket without looking at it, while the stranger behind the grille continued shouting thanks after her, and indistinct instructions.

In all, no more than ten minutes had passed since her entrance to the yards. This time, the Italian policemen on guard at the gate came briskly towards her. "What are you doing here? Get out! Hurry! Get out of here!" they ordered her, with an angry urgency, which seemed intended simultaneously to scold her and to safeguard her from a danger.

As she was going out of the gate with Useppe in her arms, a brownish truck arrived from the street, leaving a confused sound behind it as it passed, like a subdued echo of that other chorus from the train. Its load, however, locked inside, was invisible. Its only visible occupants were, in the cab, two young soldiers in SS uniform. Their appearance was normal, calm, like that of the usual Municipal truckdrivers who loaded up their meat supplies at this freight-yard stop. Their faces, clean, a healthy pink, were ordinary and stolid.

Ida completely forgot she had to finish her shopping, feeling only the haste to reach the bus stop. Driven by the exclusive desire to be back behind her sackcloth curtain, she had dismissed her weariness and preferred not to put the child on the ground again. Feeling him in her arms, near and tight, consoled her, as if she had a shelter and a protection; but for the whole distance she lacked the courage to look him in the eyes.

There were many people waiting at the bus stop; and inside the overcrowded vehicle it wasn't easy to maintain one's balance, standing. Unable to reach the straps because of her short stature, Ida, as usual in these instances, performed ballerina exercises to remain on her feet in the crush, to spare Useppe too many shoves and jolts. She noticed his little head was swaying, and she carefully settled it against her shoulder. Useppe had fallen asleep. . . .

The next morning, merry as usual, he had forgotten the events of the previous day and night; nor did Ida mention them to him again (to him or anyone else). In the pocket of her housedress she had the message thrown to her at the station by the Jew in the train; and she examined it, aside, in the daylight. It was a piece of lined copy-book paper, sweat-stained and crumpled. On it, in pencil, there was written in a shaky hand, large and laborious:

> *If you see Efrati Pacificho tell him we're all in good health Irma Regina Romolo and everyboddy going to Germany hole family allright the bill pay Lazarino another hundred and twenty lire debt becau*

That was all. There was no signature, no address (omitted through caution or lack of time? Or perhaps simple ignorance?). *Efrati* was one of the most common family names in the Ghetto: where, for that matter, according to what people said, nobody was left any more. . . .

FOR THE LITERARY TRAVELER

Like the seedy North Dublin of James Joyce, Morante's Rome is not your usual tourist country. The places dramatized in *History* that you can still find have a more shadowed identity than the popular sites and walking routes.

The **Ghetto** that Morante's Ida knew both before and after the roundup—the *Judenaktion*—of October 16, 1943, still exists as the distinctive center of Jewish life; many of Rome's fifteen thousand Jews still live or work in the neighborhood. The one main street, **Via Portico d'Ottavia,** the heart of the district and named for the ancient portico built by the emperor Augustus for his sister Octavia, divides the old and the new sections. On one side, a few of the remaining medieval buildings rise over stepped dark alleys: **Via Reginella,** leading up to the Turtle Fountain in Piazza Mattei; and the zigzaggy **Via Ambrogio,** where Ida walks; on the other side, between the main street and the Tiber, are the turn-of-the-century buildings erected after the unification of Italy and the emancipation of the Jews in 1870. The monumental **Great Synagogue,** the symbol of the Jews' emancipation, its square dome an imposing presence above the Tiber, houses a Jewish Museum of history and art (Mon–Thurs 9–2:30; Fri 9–1; Sun 9–12). (The oldest synagogue in the western world is at Ostia Antica in the vicinity of Porta Marina.)

You can roam through the piazzas of the Ghetto, Costaguti, Giudea, Cinque Scole (its one synagogue housed five congregations), shop for judaica and kosher food in groceries, pizzerias and bakeries—the wonderful **Il Forno del Ghetto,** Via Portico d'Ottavia 2, is run by three generations of Jewish women—read the inscriptions on the handsome Casa di Lorenzo Manilo (at number 1), shop for housewares in Limentani's across from the busy restaurant Da Giggeto's, and visit the well-stocked Menorah bookstore. Off Piazza Cinque Scole and up a mound—on your left the tiny church of San Tommaso, built over the ruins of the Circus of Flaminius, on your right the rear walls of Palazzo Cenci—you're entering the sinister world of *la famiglia Cenci* (see page 183). Excellent traditional Jewish Roman food is served behind San Tommaso, in the Ghetto's best restaurant, **Piperno** (tel 06 688 06629; Via Monte de Cencia; 12:30–3 P.M.; 8–11 P.M. Tues–Sat; Sun 12:30–3 P.M.; reserve in advance). Edda Servi Machlin's *The Classic Cuisine of the Italian Jews* is a guide to the extensive menu, Piperno's *carciofi alla giudia,* fried artichokes Jewish-style are incomparable.

The Ghetto is undergoing gentrification now, once dank hovels have been gutted and restored as boutiques and art galleries, the gaiety of the *passeggiata* can be heard evenings along the crowded main street.

Merchants welcome shoppers from New York. *"I have nephew in Bronx! The Concourse?"*

But Morante's novel is in the key of sorrow, and this neighborhood where the half-Jewish Ida scrounges and eavesdrops, all through the Occupation fearing for the life of her baby and herself, reminds us of a tragic and cruel history: October 16, 1943, was no stray bullet. The location of the Roman Jews, along with their degraded status, had been fixed and well known since 1555.

Confined here in that year by the Carafa Pope Paul IV, bigot and inquisitor, the Jews were forced to wear orange caps and special clothing with yellow patches, to work only as rag-pickers and money lenders, to observe a curfew. Eight gates were erected to lock them inside at night. Historians surmise that in the hysteria of the Counter-Reformation, Paul IV, and then his successors, sought safety for their Church in segregation, fearing that contact between Jews and Catholics might corrupt the purity of the Catholic faith. After unification in 1870, the Ghetto was opened, but many Jews stayed, having no place else to go.

Every year now on October 16, Roman Jews and Christians process with candles from the Campidoglio to the square in front of the ancient Portico of Octavia where Vespasian once celebrated his son Titus's destruction of Judea with a pageant. In the church that's built inside the portico, **Sant'Angelo in Pescheria,** Jews were once forced to listen to Christian sermons, their ears inspected to see that they hadn't stuffed them with cotton; next to it, inside the Theater of Marcellus, Jews were held on that October Saturday until more trucks arrived to take them to the freight cars Ida observed in the Tiburtina train station. This square was renamed, on the sixtieth anniversary of the roundup, its new title inscribed on a plaque affixed to the small medieval Casa dei Vallati: *Largo I6 Ottobre 1943 Deportazione Degli Ebrei Di Roma.*

In the end, 2,091 Roman Jews died in concentration camps, along with 6,000 other Italian Jews, a quarter of the Jewish population of Italy. Behind the Synagogue, facing the Ghetto, the facade of the church of **St. George of the Divine Pity,** painted with a crucifixcion scene, still bears an old inscription in Latin and Hebrew, reproaching the Jews: "All day long I have stretched out my hands to a rebellious people who walk in an evil way, following their own thoughts, to a people who continually provoke me to wrath."

The deportation happened a few days after the roundup, and closer to Ida's home, near the workers' district of **San Lorenzo.** (The beginning of *History* describes a prelude to the Nazi-fascist violence of 1943: A column of the Italian Fascists' March on Rome, October 30, 1922, entered the city by the San Lorenzo gate; when the "Red" rebels of the neighborhood resisted, the black shirts killed them "on the spot.")

The **Tiburtina Railway Station** is beyond San Lorenzo and Piazzale Crociate, out where Via Tiburtina bears right, in the vicinity of the **Pietralata** slum and the shelter where Ida's taken refuge. With Useppe in her arms, Ida sees the freight cars packed with human beings, and pockets the note for Efrati Pacificho. "Of the one thousand fifty-six passengers on the Rome-Auschwitz train from the Tiburtina Station," Morante writes, "the survivors were fifteen." Alexander Stille's *Benevolence and Betrayal: Five Italian Jewish Families Under Fascism* (1991) is an excellent companion to the sections in *History* about the deportation of the Jews, as is Roberto Rossellini's movie *Rome, Open City,* which captures the resistance to the Nazi occupation, heroic in the face of the torture chambers in Via Tasso.

From Porta San Lorenzo, Via Tiburtina cuts through a grim working-class enclave, which takes its name from the ancient and beautiful **Basilica of San Lorenzo Fuori le Mure.** The church, and much of San Lorenzo's housing, was badly damaged during the war. Hundreds of civilians were killed. The Allied bombing on July 19, 1943, was intended to destroy the Tiburtina Railway Station but hit San Lorenzo instead. To the right of the basilica is the entrance to the vast **Verano Cemetery,** Rome's largest, with its operatic funeral monuments, and where the anti-Fascist "Red" rebels of October 30, 1922, were buried. On the far side of Verano is the section reserved for Jews (7:30–5 daily). On the other side of Via Tiburtina, the buildings of the *Città Universitaria* exemplify the fascist architecture of 1935. An impoverished, gritty neighborhood in Morante's novel, San Lorenzo is now a bohemian and student quarter. (Bus 492 from Termini takes you to Piazzale Verano; bus 71 from the city center to Piazza San Lorenzo.) The seedy Castro Pretorio section, between Porta San Lorenzo and Porta Pia, where Ida gives private lessons after school; Via Porta Labicana; and Piazza Sanniti are still the neighborhoods of Rome's workers, students, and intellectuals.

In the "1944" section of the novel, as the occupation continues, Rome is starving. Ida, existing on a diet of grass and insects, moves with Useppe to **Testaccio,** not an outlying quarter, but, like San Lorenzo, inhabited during the war by destitute workers. (Walk from Trastevere over Ponte Sublicio or from the Aventine along Viale Aventino toward Porta San Paolo.) They live in two rooms in **Via Bodoni,** from which "you could see the square of **Santa Maria Liberatrice.** In this square stood a church decorated with some mosaics that Ida . . . considered beautiful, because in the light they glowed with gold." Her building, like many of the housing blocks in Testaccio, was vast, "with two courtyards and numerous entries. Ida's was Stairway Number Six; and in her courtyard a palm tree grew." Other landmarks of Morante's Testaccio are **Via Marmorata** and **Piazza dell'Emporio;** in **Gianicolense** in southern Trastevere where she teaches school and steals eggs to feed Useppe.

Like the Ghetto, Testaccio is now in a slow process of gentrification. Its all-night clubs and bars are crowded hangouts. If you wander around, however, past the parks and the courtyards of the low-cost housing put up at the end of the nineteenth century to house workers for the new capital city, it's not hard to imagine a poor single mother here, with no one to turn to for help. In Piazza Testaccio, just down from Piazza Santa Maria Liberatrice—the church is usually closed—children play and scrawny dogs and beggars check out the dumpsters. There's no trace of designer clothing in the parks, or the latest electronic toy. Along Via Marmorata on a hot summer day, gypsies take shelter from the sun under trees, beside drizzly water fountains, their squalor a reminder of Morante's—and Pasolini's—people, still despised, and forgotten.

Also in the "1944" section of the novel, Morante mentions the atrocity of Ardeatina. In retaliation for a partisan attack on a truckload of SS police in Via Rasella, the Germans, on March 24, 1944, massacred 335 innocent Italians in the Ardeatine Caves—originally a sandstone quarry—and then blew up the caves to hide the corpses. After the German withdrawal, the caves were opened, the bodies identified and buried; a large Cross and Star of David above the caves and a sculpture of martyrs mark the site. A twenty-minute ride (bus 218 from the Lateran) will take you out to the **Fosse Ardeatina** in Via Ardeatina between the Catacombs of Domitilia and San Callisto, not far from the Jewish Catacombs. The Mausoleum is the most moving World War II memorial in Europe, according to Eleanor Clark. In 1996, German SS commander Erich Priebke, who admitted to shooting two of the victims, was tried and convicted. (Open 8:15–5:45, Mon–Sat; 8:45–5:15 Sun; tel 06 513 6742.)

In **Via Tasso** (near the Piazza of St. John Lateran and parallel with Via Mercelana), the former command center of the SS and Gestapo, where the Nazis tortured and imprisoned partisans and Jews—forcing Morante and Moravia into hiding—has been turned into the Museum of the Liberation of Rome.

Morante's Ida Mancuso hardly noticed the entrance of the Allies into Rome and the Germans' withdrawal the Sunday night of June 4. It took a long time before there was food in Testaccio, or in any of the city's poor neighborhoods.

FEDERICO FELLINI

1920–1993

Born of a Roman mother in Rimini, Fellini moved to Rome after high school in 1938, starting out in the film industry as a writer of screenplays. During the German occupation, he was captured by the Germans but played a trick on his captors and escaped from their truck in Via del Babuino. In 1943 he married Guilietta Masina. Working with Roberto Rossellini, the director of Rome, Open City, *accompanying him as he shot his films Fellini said he "discovered Italy." His own first film—*Variety Lights*—in 1950, established him as Italy's most original filmmaker, a reputation that never lost momentum. His most famous films include* I Vitelloni *(1953);* La Strada *(1954), for which he won his first of four Oscars;* The Nights of Cabiria *(1957);* La Dolce Vita *(1960), a view of Roman high life on the Via Veneto shot without a script, its theme of souls damned to meaninglessness inspired by Dante's* Inferno; 8½ *(1963), regarded as his masterpiece;* Juliet of the Spirits *(1965);* Satyricon *(1969), a portrait of the decadence of pre-Christian Rome;* Roma *(1972); and* Amarcord *(1973). Fellini has called Rome "the feminine city"; in all his movies she is protagonist, antagonist, "the place of the universal imagination," in the words of Borges. Many of the following conversations between Fellini and the journalist Costanzo Costantini took place on the set of the legendary Cinecittà Studios where Fellini made nearly all his movies in Stage Five, the largest sound stage in Europe.*

From CONVERSATIONS WITH FELLINI

COSTANZO COSTANTINI: *How did Rome strike you when you were eighteen or nineteen?*

FEDERICO FELLINI: One of the things I found most striking was the monumental rudeness that I encountered everywhere. A gigantic rudeness and a gigantic vulgarity. This vulgarity is part of the character of Rome, that magnificent vulgarity to which the Latin authors have left testimony—Plautus, Martial, Juvenal. It is the vulgarity of Petronius's *Satyricon*. It is a kind of liberation, a victory over the fear of bad taste, over propriety. For anyone who observes the city with the aim of expressing it creatively, the vulgarity is an enrichment, an aspect of the fascination that Rome inspires. But Rome seemed to me immediately a familiar, welcoming and friendly city—perhaps because my mother was a Roman. . . .

COSTANZO COSTANTINI: *What in particular do you now remember about* La Dolce Vita?

FEDERICO FELLINI: For me the film is identified more with Anita Ekberg than with the Via Veneto. . . .

COSTANZO COSTANTINI: *Ekberg immersed herself in the Trevi Fountain without difficulty?*

FEDERICO FELLINI: Ekberg came from the North, she was young and as proud of her good health as a lioness. She was no trouble at all. She remained immersed in the basin for ages, motionless, impassive, as if the water didn't cover her nor the cold affect her, even though it was March and the nights made one shiver. For Mastroianni it was a rather different story. He had to get undressed, put on a frogman's suit and get dressed again. To combat the cold he polished off a bottle of vodka, and when we shot the scene he was completely pissed.

COSTANZO COSTANTINI: *How long did you take to shoot that scene?*

FEDERICO FELLINI: It took eight or nine nights. Some of the owners of the surrounding houses would rent out their balconies and windows to the curious. At the end of each take the crowd would cheer. A show within a show. Every time I look at the picture of Ekberg in the Trevi Fountain, I have the sensation of reliving those magic moments, those sleepless nights, surrounded by the meowing of cats and the crowd that gathered from every corner of the city. . . .

Anita Ekberg's Version

It is amusing to hear Anita Ekberg's account of her performance in *La Dolce Vita* and of the sequence where she plunges herself into the Trevi Fountain:

Ever since I was a little girl I dreamed that one day I would go to Rome. I went there for the first time in 1955, to act in *War and Peace,* directed by King Vidor. I stayed at the Hotel de la Ville, near Trinità dei Monti. At that time there wasn't the chaos that there is now and from the hotel to Cinecittà took only five minutes. I drove a Mercedes 300SL convertible with the top always down, even when it rained, my hair blowing in the wind. Probably Fellini noticed me passing in the street or at Cinecittà.

When we were shooting, each day Fellini would write some lines and then ask me, "What do you think of them? If you don't like them we'll change them." We came to the scene in the Trevi Fountain. That scene had already happened in reality, before Fellini thought it up. One night I was having photos taken by the film's photographer Luigi. I was barefoot and I cut my foot. I went in search of a fountain to bathe my bleeding foot and, all unawares, found myself in the Piazza di Trevi. It was summer. I was wearing a white-and-pink cotton dress with the upper part like a man's shirt. I lifted the skirt up and immersed myself in the basin, saying to Luigi, "You can't imagine how

cool this water is; you should come in, too." "Just stay like that,"
he said and started taking photos. They sold like hotcakes. But
the difference was that I took the plunge in August, whereas
Fellini made me do it in March. . . .

COSTANZO COSTANTINI: *Are you not aware that Rome has become
more and more neurotic, chaotic and jammed up?*

FEDERICO FELLINI: I tried to depict these aspects of Rome in
other films, but I was accused of not liking the city. The neurotic
attack, as long as it is not too serious, can be compared to a kind of
providence, as Jung teaches. It obliges us to make contact with remote and unknown parts of ourselves. For an artist the pathologi-
cal aspect of neurosis reveals itself as a kind of hidden treasure. In
another way, Rome is always for me what I make of it, indeed,
what I remake of my earlier creation, like the reflections in a mirror. On the other hand, Rome is a myth, and myths are perpetuated because they represent the unconscious, like a subterranean
journey, a submarine exploration, a descent into hell in search of
the monsters that lie at the heart of man. Poets, writers, painters in
expressing themselves through their mediums are doing nothing
other than recounting their adventures on this journey, the torment of this exploration.

COSTANZO COSTANTINI: *But collective neurosis, the kind one experiences in Rome, produces effects altogether different from those of individual
neurosis, of the kind suffered by artists.*

FEDERICO FELLINI: Rome is a lot less neurotic than other big
cities, just because it possesses something of the African, the prehistoric, the atemporal. It has an ancient wisdom, which somehow
saves it from the ills that are killing the great modern metropolises
or the postmodern megalopolises. I'm not a Roman, but my
mother was, as I've said. She was a Barbiani, a Roman family which
goes back seven generations. She helped me to understand the
mentality, the psychology, the way of life of the Romans. The first

words, the first phrases, the first idioms in the Roman dialect, I heard from her mouth. I could recount an endless string of anecdotes about the calm, the phlegmatic character, the sleepy immobility of Rome and its people. . . .

COSTANZO COSTANTINI: *Foreign observers say that Rome has become a "dead city."*

FEDERICO FELLINI: Death cannot but be present in a city with one of the most spectacular architectural heritages in the world. It is present not just in the ruins, but also in the severity of the baroque palazzi, in the façades of the churches, in the city's religious rituals. It is present, as I've already said, in the heart of Roman life.

COSTANZO COSTANTINI: *The same foreign commentators say that Rome is culturally dead.*

FEDERICO FELLINI: Rome does not need to make culture. It *is* culture. Prehistoric, classical, Etruscan, Renaissance, Baroque, modern. Every corner of the city is a chapter in an imaginary universal history of culture. Culture in Rome is not an academic concept. It's not even a museum culture, even though the city is one enormous museum. It is a human culture, just because it is free of every form of cultural faddishness, or neurotic trendiness. . . .

COSTANZO COSTANTINI: *Have you ever thought of going to live in another city?*

FEDERICO FELLINI: There are so many things in Rome that I don't like: the traffic, the Gogolesque bureaucratic quagmire, the endless expanse of car roofs, the violence. I live in Via Margutta and sooner or later, to get back into my house, I shall have to walk over the hoods of cars or the roofs of the palazzi. But Rome is still endlessly fascinating. For me it is the ideal city, if not quite the heavenly Jerusalem. Where could you recapture the light of Rome? A flash of sunlight through a flotilla of shifting clouds glancing between two cinquecento palazzi is enough for the city to appear renewed in all its charm. And the Roman climate; so sweet, so airy, so cooling? "We're waiting for the westerly breeze," men and women say, standing stock-still with an enigmatic air in the streets or the piazzas like a picture by Delvaux, Magritte or Balthus. Rome is a therapeutic city, good for the health of body and spirit. It's a friendly city. It's like the court in Kafka's *Trial:* it welcomes you when you come and forgets you when you go.

FOR THE LITERARY TRAVELER

Rome is Fellini's muse, her paradoxes his obsession. The beauty, the ugliness, he knew and showed off every inch of her.

His own neighborhood was **Piazza del Popolo,** the people's square, a background character in many movies. A magnificent space, the old entrance to Rome from the north, to this day it exhibits on a grand scale the multiple personalities of Fellini's eternal feminine: the sacred architecture and art of its three churches, the main one, Santa Maria del Popolo built over the spot haunted at night by apparitions of Nero's ghost; a sprawling fountain pouring itself forth beneath the overhanging Pincio; an ancient obelisk, dated 1300 B.C. brought from Greece; the Roman glitterati, foreign shoppers; high-spirited *ragazzi; polizia* standing guard against anarchists, determined that the newly cleaned stone in the piazza stays free of graffiti. Now that traffic has been banned, it's risk free to sit in the center and watch the flow of people as they crisscross north to south, east to west, *telefoninos* at every ear. *Ciao, Mama! Come stai?*

Fellini lived around the corner in **Via Margutta** 110—a charming, tucked-away artists' street, once home to Rembrandt, Picasso, Simone de Beauvoir, and Marcello Mastroianni. Fellini is said to have stopped at **Bar Canova** first thing every morning (Piazza del Popolo 16/17; 8–1 A.M. Sun–Thurs; 8–2 A.M. Fri and Sat); Joe Wolff's *Café Life Rome* quotes the proprietors' affectionate memories of their most famous customer. In the Fellini Room, photographs of him and his friends, whom you'll recognize if you've seen his movies, hang on the walls.

Across the piazza, **Caffè Rosati** (Piazza del Popolo 4/5; 7:30–

11:30 P.M.) welcomed Fellini and many other writers, actors, directors, politicians, during the heady years of the fifties and sixties when Rome, distinguished by such neorealist and post-neorealist masterpieces as Rossellini's *Rome, Open City,* Vittorio de Sicca's *The Bicycle Thief,* Michelangelo Antonioni's *L'Avventura,* and Pier Paolo Pasolini's *Mamma Roma,* was the new cinematic capital of Europe. The bar's decor is splendid; likewise the *granità di caffè* served outdoors on a slow July afternoon when the shops on the Corso are closed, and the city sleeps behind closed shutters.

Fellini and his fellow artists dined regularly a few doors away at **Dal Bolognese,** still a first-rate restaurant popular with Romans (Piazza del Popolo 1/2; tel 06 361 1426; reservations necessary; closed Mon).

But more than any particular restaurant or cafe, it's the piazza that holds your attention, a vital poetics of Fellini space: his intimate friend, in a very good mood and looking her best. The whole area is called *Il Tridente*—the Trident—the point of convergence of three roads in the vast piazza: Via di Ripetta, nearest the Tiber; in the middle, Via del Corso; and Via del Babuino (paralleling Via Margutta), which leads south to Piazza di Spagna. (At the Di Spagna Metro station you can catch a train out to the **Cinecittà** stop in Via Tuscolana, Fellini's studio now mostly used for the storage of his sets and the filming of television.) Via Sistina, to the right, at the top of the Spanish Steps, where Fellini had an office, leads across Via del Tritone to the Fontana di Trevi, where *La Dolce Vita* turned into a baptism.

Swarming with tourists night and day, the **Trevi Fountain** is still magical. Late at night, when it's by no means deserted, you can imagine the shoots, for nine nights in March, Fellini trying to get it right, Mastroianni nursing his vodka, a freezing Anita Ekberg becoming immortal beneath the niche figures of "Health" and "Abundance" and the giant Tritons. Trevi's water comes from the Acqua Vergine aqueduct, built by Marcus Agrippa in 19 B.C.

A few minutes away, the **Via Veneto** rises and curves between the Piazza Barberini and its multiscreen Cinema Barberini and the far end where it ends under pines at the Porta Pinciana entrance to the Borghese Gardens. The mythic street associated with partying stars and the

idle rich in the fifties and sixties is just that. Mythic. "In my movies,"
Fellini told an interviewer, "the Via Veneto never existed." The setting of
La Dolce Vita, he claimed, was his own invention, an allegorical conve-
nience. Before his movie turned this broad thoroughfare of huge old
trees, sidewalk cafes, and grand hotels into a symbol of decadence, its
personality was suburban, the population on good behavior. Though,
according to some guidebooks, a few centuries back, the neighborhood
was something out of an imagination crossed with Dante, Fellini, and
Pasolini. In the sixteenth century, Pope Julius III (1550–1555) built himself a pleasure palace in the adjoining Borghese. In his Villa Giulia, (now
the beautiful Etruscan Museum), he was entertained by dancers, musi-
cians, and the young men he favored. (In Conversations, Fellini scorns
the legacy of this ancien regime, along with Counter-Reformation puri-
tanism: "the frustrated, infantile, repressed Italian.") Cardinal Scipione,
who created the Borghese Gardens, was another sensualist given to
late-night exploits that Pasolini updates in the fiction he sets in the
Borghese Gardens. During the German occupation, the Nazi command-
ing officers stayed in the Veneto's exclusive hotels. Word that the Germans' withdrawal—and the Liberation by the Allies—was at hand spread
when Kesselring's luggage was seen being carried out of the **Hotel Excelsior** and loaded onto trucks. In postwar Rome, the Excelsior's clientele reflected Rome's new status as "Hollywood on the Tiber." Fellini,
Roberto Rossellini and Ingrid Bergman, Anna Magnani, Mastroianni, they
all enjoyed themselves here, and the sumptuous marble walls and
floors, the extravagance of the furnishings and the rooms play their part
in the movie that gave the hotel's address a worldwide caché (Via
Veneto 125; tel 06 474 5820; 327 rooms).

After Fellini died, the city of Rome affixed a plaque comemmorating
him and the street he mythologized at the intersection of Via Veneto
and Via Ludovisi, to your left as you walk up the Veneto. Fine shopping
is the custom of the affluent Ludovisi quarter, named after the Villa Ludovisi (now gone, its treasures in Palazzo Altemps). Fellini also relaxed in
La Terrazza dell'Eden, Via Ludovisi 49, the incredibly swank and
panoramic rooftop restaurant of the Hotel Eden (tel 06 478 121;
www.hotel-eden.it). He always insisted that "Rome is a myth." In set-

tings like Trevi and the Veneto, it's easy to imagine with him the surreal heights and monstrous depths, and Nero's ghost not resting in peace in Piazza del Popolo.

(*There are some eighty movie theaters in Rome; most foreign films are dubbed into Italian. Check for daily listings in the newspapers; the English section of "Roma C'è"; and the "I Love Rome" Web page: www. alfanet.it/welcomeItaly/roma/default.html. Films in English are shown at the Pasquino, Piazza Sant'Egidio; tel 06 580 3622; and at Alcazar in Via Merry del Val 14; tel 06 588 0099, both in Trastevere; at the Quirinetta, Via Minghetti 4, off Via del Corso; tel 06 679 0012. Outdoor screenings are held in the Parco del Celio near the Colosseum; and in San Lorenzo, at Sotto le Stelle di San Lorenzo, in the gardens of Villa Mercede in Via Tiburtina 113. The multimedia arts center, Palazzo delle Esposizioni in Via Milano 9A, shows international films in the Sala Rossellini. The ubiquitous posters of the* Estate Romana [*"Roman Summer" festival*] *list the details of the many open-air movies shown in summer.*)

FOR FURTHER READING

In addition to the writings mentioned in the text

Bachelard, Gaston. *The Poetics of Space.* 1958.

Cellini, Benvenuto. *An Autobiography.* 1566.

Claridge, Amanda. *Rome: An Oxford Archaeological Guide.* 1998.

"Clement of Rome," in *Early Christian Writings.* 1968.

D'Epiro, Peter, and Pinkowish, Mary Desmond. *Sprezzatura: 50 Ways Italian Genius Shaped the World.* 2001.

De Stael, Germaine. *Corinne, or Italy.* 1807.

Dickens, Charles. *Pictures from Italy.* 1846.

Edel, Leon. *Henry James. A Life.* 1985.

Edwards, Catharine. *Writing Rome.* 1996.

Epstein, Alan. *As the Romans Do.* 2000.

Filippini, Serge. *The Man in Flames: Giordano Bruno.* 1990.

Frei, Matt. *Italy. The Unfinished Revolution.* 1996.

Geller, Ruth Liliana. *Jewish Rome.* 1983.

Grant, Michael. *The World of Rome.* 1960.

Graves, Robert. *I, Claudius.* 1934.

Hibbert, Christopher. *Rome. The Biography of a City.* 1985.

Highet, Gilbert. *Poets in a Landscape.* 1957.

Kenner, Hugh. *The Elsewhere Community.* 2000.

Lawrence, D. H. *Etruscan Places.* 1932.

Lefkowitz, Mary R., and Fant, Maureen B. *Women's Life in Greece and Rome.* 1982.

Macadam, Alta. *Blue Guide. Rome.* 2003.

Maraini, Dacia. *Darkness.* 1999.

McClure, Laura K., ed. *Sexuality and Gender in the Classical World.* 2002.

Moatti, Claude. *In Search of Ancient Rome.* 1989.

Moravia, Alberto. *Boredom.* 1960.

———. *The Woman of Rome.* 1949.

Oberman, Heiko A. *Luther. Man Between God and the Devil.* 1989.

Parenti, Michael. *The Assassination of Julius Caesar: A People's History of Ancient Rome.* 2003.

Partridge, Loren. *The Renaissance in Rome.* 1996.

Pasolini, Pier Paolo. *The Ragazzi.* 1955.

———. *Roman Nights and Other Stories.* 1965.

———. *Stories from the City of God. Sketches and Chronicles of Rome, 1950–1966.*

Plantamura, Carol. *The Opera Lover's Guide to Europe.* 1996.

Pomeroy, Sarah B. *Goddesses, Whores, Wives, and Slaves: Women in Classical Antiquity.* 1975.

Racine, Bruno. *Living in Rome.* 1999.

Richards, Charles. *The New Italians.* 1994.

Rinaldi, Mariangela, and Vicini, Mariangela. *Buon Appetito, Your Holiness. The Secrets of the Papal Table.* 1998.

Russell, Mary Doria. *A Thread of Grace.* A Novel. 2005.

Sciascia, Leonardo. *The Moro Affair.* 1978.

Speller, Elizabeth. *Following Hadrian. A Second-Century Journey Through the Roman Empire.* 2002.

Stendhal. *The Cenci.* In *Three Italian Chronicles.* 1855.

Varriano, John. *A Literary Companion to Rome.* 1991.

Velani, Livia, and Grego, Giovanni. *Rome: Where to Find Michelangelo, Raphael, Caravaggio, Bernini, Borromini.* 2000.

Weaver, William. *Open City: Seven Writers in Postwar Rome.* 1999.

West, David, trans. *The Complete Odes and Epodes of Horace.* 1997.

Williams, John. *Augustus. A Novel.* 1972.

Wineapple, Brenda. *Hawthorne. A Life.* 2003.

Woolsen, Constance Fenimore. "Miss Grief and Other Stories." In *Women Artists, Women Exiles.* Ed. Joan Myers Weimer. 1996.

SOME PLACES TO EAT AND DRINK

Elegant, Plain, and Excellent According to Neighborhood

(*See "For The Literary Traveler" sections for telephone numbers, and other information.*)

THE PALATINE
St. Teodoro. Piazza del Fienili 49-50

THE FORUM AND THE COLOSSEUM
La Piazzetta. Vicolo del Buon Consiglio 23A
Hotel Forum, Rooftop Restaurant. Via Tor Dè Conti 25-30

THE PANTHEON
Sole al Pantheon. Piazza della Rotonda 63
Da Rienzo. Piazza della Rotonda 3
Tazza d'Oro. Via degli Orfani 84
Caffè Sant'Eustachio. Piazza Sant'Eustachio 82
Camilloni Piazza Sant'Eustachio 54
Sant'Eustachio. Piazza dei Capprettari 63

TRASTEVERE
Ferrara. Restaurant & Wine Bar. Via del Moro 1A—
   Piazza Trilussa 41
Caffè di Marzio. Piazza di Santa Maria 14
Galeassi. Piazza Santa Maria 3
Paris Restaurant. Piazza San Calisto 7A
Corsetti's. Piazza San Cosimato 27/29
La Cornucopia. Piazza in Piscinula 18
Spirito di Vino. Via Genovesi 31 A/B—Vicolo dell'Atleta 13
Da Meo Patacca. Piazza Mercanti 30
Da Lucia. Vicolo del Mattonato 2B

THE JANICULUM
Bar Gianicolo. Piazzale Aurelia 5
Antico Arco. Piazzale Aurelia 7
Al Tocco. Via San Pancrazio 1

THE ESQUILINE (*Near Santa Maria Maggiore*)
Agata e Romeo. Via Carlo Alberto 45
I Buoni Amici. Via Aleardo Aleardi 4
Ornelli. Via Merulana 224.

THE VATICAN
Pizzeria Giacomelli. Via Emilia Faà di Bruno 25
Atlante Star Hotel, Rooftop Restaurant. Via Vitelleschi 34
Gelateria Pellacchia. Cola di Rienzo 105
Cacio e Pepe. Via Avezzana 11

PALAZZO FARNESE / VIA GIULIA
Camponeschi. Piazza Farnese 50/50A
Hostaria Giulio. Via della Barchetta 19
Pierluigi. Piazza de Ricci 144
Caffè Farnese. Piazza Farnese 106/107

PALAZZO COLONNA
Abruzzi. Via del Vaccaro 1
Peroni. Via S. Marcello 19
Da Ricci. Pizzeria. Via Genova 32 (off Via Nazionale)

CAMPO DE' FIORI
La Carbonara. Piazza Campo de' Fiori 23
Forno Campo de' Fiori. (Bakery) Piazza Campo de' Fiori 22
Hostaria dei Pesce. Via di Monserrato 32
Hostaria Costanza. Piazza del Paradiso 63–65
Da Pancrazio. Piazza del Biscione 92–94
Trattoria del Pallaro. Largo del Pallaro 15
    (near S. Andrea delle Valle)

PIAZZA NAVONA
Tre Scalini. Piazza Navona 28–30
Antico Caffè Della Pace. Via della Pace 3–5

Hotel Raphael. Rooftop Restaurant. Largo Febo 2
Antica Taverna. Via Monte Giordano 12
Papà Giovanni. Via dei Sediari 4
Le Cave di Sant'Ignazio Da Sabatino. Piazza Sant'Ignazio 169
Bella Napoli. (Pastry) Corso Vittorio Emanuele II, 246
Volpetti. Via della Scrofa 32
Il Convivio. Vicolo dei Soldati 31

PIAZZA DEL POPOLO

Buca di Ripetta. Via di Ripetta 36
Hotel de Russie Restaurant. Via del Babuino 9
Bar Canova. Piazza del Popolo 16/17
Caffè Rosati. Piazza del Popolo 4/5
Dal Bolognese. Piazza del Popolo 1/2

VIA APPIA ANTICA

Cecilia Metella. Via Appia Antica 125
L'Archeologia. Via Appia Antica 139

THE CAPITOLINE

Rooftop Caffè of the Capitoline Museum. Piazza dei Campidoglio
Antico Caffè del Teatro Marcello. Via del Teatro Marcello 42
La Taverna degli Amici a Tormargana. Piazza Margana 36/37
Hostaria del Campidoglio. Via dei Fienili 56

THE SPANISH STEPS

Hotel Hassler, Rooftop Restaurant. Piazza Trinità dei Monti 6
Caffè Greco. Via Condotti 86
Babington's English Tea Rooms. Piazza di Spagna 85
Otello alla Concordia. Via della Croce 81

THE JEWISH GHETTO

Vecchia Roma. Piazza Campitelli 18
Piperno. Via Monte de Cenci 9
Il Forno del Ghetto. (Bakery) Via del Portico d'Ottavia 2

THE VENETO

Hotel Excelsior. Via Veneto 125
La Terrazza dell'Eden. Via Ludovisi 49

La Veranda dell'Hotel Majestic. Via Vittorio Veneto 50

Lotti. Bar, Gelateria, Pasticceria. Via Sardegna 19/21

TESTACCIO

Volpetti. Via Marmorata 47

Barberini. Bar, Gelateria. Via Marmorata 41–43

Da Bucatino. Via Luca della Robbia 84–86

Trattoria lo Scopettaro. Lungotevere, Testaccio 7

Pizzeria Remo. Piazza Santa Maria Liberatrice 44

OUTSIDE ROME

Tivoli:

Hotel Ristorante Adriana. (Next to Hadrian's Villa) Via di Villa
    Adriana 194

Bar/Restaurant. Hadrian's Villa

Antica Trattoria del Falcone. Via del Trevio 34

Frascati:

Cacciari. Via A. Diaz 13

Nemi:

La Trattoria della Sora Maria

CREDITS

ABOUT THE AUTHOR

SUSAN CAHILL, PH.D., is the editor of many highly praised anthologies, including *Desiring Italy, For The Love of Ireland, Wise Women, The QPB Anthology of Writing by Women,* and *Women and Fiction.* Author of the novel *Earth Angels* and co-author with Thomas Cahill of *A Literary Guide to Ireland,* she has taught at Queens College and Fordham University. She lives in New York City and, for part of the year, in Rome.